Natural Resources
and the
Informed Citizen

second edition

Steve Dennis

SAGAMORE
PUBLISHING

©2012 Sagamore Publishing LLC
All rights reserved.

Publishers: Joseph J. Bannon and Peter L. Bannon
Director of Sales and Marketing: M. Douglas Sanders
Director of Development and Production: Susan M. Davis
Director of Technology: Christopher Thompson
Editorial: Amy S. Dagit

ISBN print edition: 978-1-57167-634-4
ISBN ebook: 978-1-57167-635-1
LCCN: 2012931953

Sagamore Publishing LLC
1807 N Federal Dr
Urbana, IL 61801

www.sagamorepub.com

For the Porches
Who keep me going

CONTENTS

Preface...*vii*

Acknowledgments...*xi*

About the Author ....*xii*

1 The Values of Natural Resources..1

2 Demands on Natural Resources...9

3 America's Common Lands: Outdoor Recreation
   as an Example of Excessive Demand for Scarce Resources...........15

4 Evolution of a Land Ethic and Natural
   Resource Management Eras...23

5 Federal Resource Managing Agencies and Authority...................51

6 Civics 1A and the Federal Regulatory Process.............................57

7 Federal Agencies: The National Park Service...............................63

8 Federal Agencies: The U. S. Forest Service..................................77

9 Federal Agencies: The Bureau of Land Management....................89

10 Federal Agencies: The U.S. Fish and Wildlife Service 99

11 Federal Agencies: The Bureau of Reclamation and
    U.S. Army Corps of Engineers 105

12 State Government Involvement in Natural Resources.................115

13 Special Districts, County, and Municipal Involvement
    in Natural Resources..121

14 Citizen Involvement in Natural Resources Issues......................131

15 Activism and the Legal Avenues for Public Involvement...........145

16 Theoretical and Legal Foundations of Public Involvement........155

17 Effective Avenues for Public Participation.................................163

18 Forestland and Timber Management Controversies....................173

19 Wildlife Management and Controversies 191

20 Range Management and Grazing..209

21 Water Management and Controversies.......................................221

22 Mineral Resources, Mining, and Management Issues.................243

23 Profiling an Informed Citizen 257

24 Legacy..265

Appendix A: Selected Internet Sites Useful to the Informed Citizen...267

Glossary...273

Index 299

Preface

Everything on Earth can be considered a natural resource. Air, water, land, and energy combine to create a myriad of resources that we manipulate to meet our needs for survival and a quality existence. Our uses of natural resources connect to an ecological web of causes and effects. What we do creates change.

The Earth has been changing throughout its life. The alterations that we initiate occur in an environment already in a constant state of change. As we learn more about the way the world works, we gain a keener perception of how human-caused change fits into the big picture. We also gain an understanding of how we can improve our lives by working with the Earth, rather than working on it.

What we know, however, is not always reflected by what we do. We know, for example, that there are limits to the bounties of the oceans. Yet we harvest fisheries to the brink of extinction. We know that the internal-combustion engine emits gasses that are incompatible with respiration. Yet we build even more automobiles for the benefit of mobility. Why would intelligent critters like humans make these kinds of choices, before we are clear on their consequences? There is any number of answers to this question, but several factors tend to weigh strong on this paradox. One, we have incomplete information. We aren't exactly sure that a choice will have dire consequences, but we can easily envision the benefits that our action might create. So, not knowing everything, we are willing to take the chance to obtain the benefits. Two, we tend to act in self-interest. The benefit that we can derive is more important to us than the cost it might impose on something or someone else. Consequences are not always immediate, so we postpone them and hope they will go away. Three, there is never complete agreement on what we do. People differ in their points of view, and what will seem like a great idea to one group may be the most boneheaded notion ever contrived according to another. These factors influence the choices we make and the courses of action we pursue. They are part of why there is considerable disagreement about the way we should use natural resources.

Being disagreeable is not an effective means to move toward improving the condition of the world. To survive and to improve the quality of life, choices must be considered, decisions made, and actions taken. Disagreeing parties must compete and compromise. This process isn't always pretty. At its worst, the process becomes war. At its best, the process brings about improved conditions for all.

In this modern era, we try to think through the good and bad of activities that use natural resources. We all have a large stake in the welfare of natural resources; so thinking things through is an important task. We do this thinking and communicate our thoughts to one another so our decision makers will make good choices.

We have a lot to think about. Our interactions with natural resources have many effects. Environmental and ecological effects are coupled to economic changes, social impacts, historical trends, scientific conjecture of the future, and the worldview we define through our philosophical, moral, ethical, and spiritual perspectives. These values are brought to the decision-making table by all of us: the stakeholders and barterers. What we do at that table determines our futures, and the futures of all who will follow.

In the decade since the publication of the first edition of this book, the struggle over the use, conservation, development and preservation of natural resources has continued as strongly as in the past. New or increased emphasis has been placed on the debates over global warming, depletion of fossil fuels, and the long-term sustainability of western lifestyles. Evident in the first decade of the twenty-first century is even greater disagreement, more polarization in the political processes surrounding our relationships with natural resources. This is perhaps indicative of the economic concept of scarcity. As things become scarcer they become more valuable. Human levels of consumption have only increased in the last 10 years, without a commensurate increase in the supplies of natural resources. Thus rising scarcity is magnified by continually rising needs. The values for natural resources grow stronger. The conflicts over their stewardship intensify.

The purpose of this book is to introduce some of the processes through which people make decisions about using natural resources. Every one of us has an equal stake in the decisions that are made; yet we differ greatly in our involvement in the processes. Our involvement ranges from activism to apathy. Understanding the processes makes us better thinkers and participants. We can make better decisions when we move closer to being "informed citizens."

Any book professing to engage the topic of natural resources must admit to the huge spectrum of approaches that can be taken to the subject. To study natural resources, one can pursue chemistry, biology, geology, oceanography, ecology; any conglomeration of "natural," "earth," or "geosciences"; professions from forestry and range conservation to wildlife or parks management; economics, political science, geography, history, or other "social sciences"; or humanities from philosophy to religious studies, from literature to art. One of the beauties of our worldview of natural resources is that we look at them from all of these fascinating perspectives. The study of natural resources is truly an interdisciplinary endeavor.

This book looks at the way we make decisions about natural resources in the United States, so it is mostly a political perspective on the subject. It is unfortunate that politics has achieved a negative connotation in this day and age. The term derives from the Greek polis, for city. City implying people, politics became the art of getting along. Webster's defines politic as "having practical wisdom." Thus it seems that a political perspective may not be such a bad way to look at things after all. To take this view, it is necessary to consider history, and to patch in some economics, law, communications, philosophy, environmental science, and fundamentals of resource management practice as employed by the resource professions. The book does not attempt to cover these areas in depth. It is an introduction, intended to create a foundation of awareness and to motivate the reader to further study and involvement. Think of reading this book as acquiring your sea legs in the early stages of a long voyage.

The book is broken into four major parts: (1) Introduction and historical background, (2) Governmental structure of resource management, (3) Citizen participation in resource management policy; and (4) Resource management practices. In part 1, chapters 1 through 4 set the stage for our dealings with natural resources by looking at how we value them and define our possession of them. Chapter 2 quickly reviews the pressures humans place on resources, assuming the reader will have ample exposure to these immense environmental issues from other sources. Chapter 3 presents the issue of outdoor recreation impact as an example of resource use with which many of us have firsthand experience. Chapter 4 takes a historical look at how America's views of natural resources have evolved over time. In part 2, chapters 5 through 13 provide an overview of how we have structured our governmental institutions to manage natural resources. Chapter 5 introduces the federal resource-managing agencies. In chapter 6, we are reminded of what we learned about the federal government in high school civics class. Chapters 7 to 11 explore the federal resource agencies in greater detail. Chapter 12 presents California's resource agency structure as an example of state authority over natural resources, and chapter 13 describes how special districts and local government play their roles in managing natural resources. Part 3 looks at how citizens become involved in the politics of resource management. Chapters 14 through 17 investigate social movements that have changed our views of natural resources and the mechanisms by which citizens influence resources policy and practice. Part 4 provides an overview of resource management practices and why they can be controversial. Chapters 18 through 22 explain the principal methods of forestry, range, wildlife, water, and minerals management. Additionally, controversial aspects of these resource management practices are described. The final two chapters of the book include a description, or profile, of an "informed citizen," and a brief essay welcoming the informed citizen to the natural resources decision-making table.

For quick reference, the book contains a glossary. Selected terms are printed bold-faced within the text on their first appearance, which denotes that the term is included with a brief description or definition in the alphabetized glossary. Additionally, in Appendix A there is a list of selected Internet sites that can provide access to information on government agencies and citizen organizations involved with natural resources.

I hope this book will stimulate your interest in natural resource and environmental issues. I have attempted to provide an unbiased view of the issues, presenting varied perspectives on those that are discussed. I admit I'm a strong believer in intelligent resource stewardship and acknowledge that the reader may notice this leaning here and there. This book is not intended to win you over to one way of thinking. The book's purpose is to start a foundation from which readers can further pursue their own interests in resources management and the environment, and become involved as informed citizens.

Steve Dennis
February 2, 2012
Chico, California

Acknowledgments

I thank the faculty and students of the Department of Recreation and Parks Management at California State University, Chico, for being the home from which this book took root and matured over the years. I especially thank Dr. David E. Simcox for sharing in the development of the "Resources-Needs Matrix," and for our many years as colleagues. Professors Jon K. Hooper, Ronald W. Hodgson, and James E. Fletcher have always provided substance to thinking about natural resources and the environment, particularly the influence of citizens on resource management policy.

I also thank the many contributors of photographs and pictures, who helped add imagery to this discussion.

About the Author

Steve Dennis is a professor of parks and natural resources management in the Department of Recreation and Parks Management at California State University, Chico. He completed his Ph.D. in Renewable Natural Resources Studies at the University of Arizona in 1987. He has worked for the National Park Service and has managed contract programs and research for the U.S. Forest Service. His scholarly work has concentrated on public involvement in natural resources planning and decision making, as well as the influence of citizens' organizations on natural resources policy. He resides in Chico, California, where his current pursuits have included studying the effects of natural resource management policies on the provision of opportunities for outdoor recreation and tourism in the U.S., Costa Rica, and Italy.

chapter one

The Values of Natural Resources

We all depend on natural resources. We consume, waste, and recycle natural resources constantly. To survive, we require air, water, food, and shelter. To thrive, we require energy and mental satisfaction. The planet on which we journey through time and space has the resources we need to survive. Some are in abundance; some are scarce. Some are what we call renewable natural resources, and some are by nature nonrenewable natural resources. Renewable resources are those that are produced as well as consumed. Nonrenewable natural resources are either expended when consumed, or they are produced so slowly that they become scarce or disappear because production cannot keep pace with consumption. Fresh water is an example of a renewable resource. Coal is an example of a nonrenewable resource. What are the differences in the way these two resources are produced that make one renewable and one nonrenewable? What is the relationship of scarcity to renewability and nonrenewability? Is fresh water scarce even though it is renewable? Is coal scarce because it is nonrenewable?

We are inextricably tied to natural resources. We might live a couple of minutes without air, a few days without water, a few weeks without food, and—depending on terrestrial latitude, elevation, and season—minutes or years without shelter. Beyond basic survival, our economies are tied to the production and consumption of natural resources: the building of houses, growth and dissemination of food, and manufacture of widgets for gadgets. Further, we share an intimacy with resources that affects us as emotional and social beings. Resources can wreak havoc, such as a flood or forest firestorm, or they can delight, such as the view of Yosemite Falls, a quiet lake canoe ride, or shredding powder on a snowboard.

Resources are essential. Resources can be scarce. The management of natural resources is critical to the quality of our lives.

Consider the "Resources-Needs" Matrix...

	Air	Water	Food	Shelter	Energy	Quality of Life
Air	Respiration	Evaporation and precipitation	Refrigeration	Heating and air conditioning	Wind electrical generation	Air quality
Water	Evaporation and precipitation	Potable water management	Irrigation	Waste management	Hydroelectric generation	Water-based recreation
Land	Oxygen production (photosynthesis)	Water distribution systems	Agriculture	Forestry	Fossil fuels power generation	Parks
Energy	Ventilation systems	Desalinization	Cooking	Heating and air conditioning	Solar power generation	Transportation

Figure 1.1. The Resources–Needs Matrix provides examples of how we use, manipulate, and protect earth resources to meet human needs.

Forests and rivers exemplify renewable natural resources.
(David E. Simcox Collection)

The interaction of humans and natural resources is as simple as the way the items in the left column are manipulated to meet the needs across the top of the matrix. Once you start thinking these interactions through, however, the complexity expands in a hurry.

Think of the history of humanity's struggles to obtain natural resources. Hunter-gatherers relied on the uncontrollable supply of wild game and vegetation for food, the seasonal vagaries of climate for water, and the availability of natural structures or materials for shelter. Scarcity of these resources immediately equated with death, so hunter-gatherers learned to tap the abundances of resources: moving along migration routes of important game and occupying areas of plentiful water supplies. Learning of these patterns helped people come to understand the opportunities presented by planned agricultural practices, diversion of waters, and the benefits of a less nomadic existence. The eventuation of civilization required this learned harnessing of natural processes, the hand of the human in manipulating resources to his desires.

But scarcity has always plagued people. The distribution of natural resources has never been even, or consistent. Resources could never be fully harnessed, never fully cooperative with human needs. And then there were those who had, and those who did not. Portable resources such as foodstuffs, stones, shells, and other items that could be pulled, or packed on head or back, became trade goods, allowing for the movement of resources among and between peoples. But those resources that could not be easily moved, such as water, soil, and favorable climate, became the bounty of some, while others fought the battle against scarcity. It is no small wonder that most of history's wars have been for the conquest of lands, trade routes, and power over ownership and distribution of natural resources. The haves protecting the security of their resources base, and the have-nots struggling to obtain resources for themselves. On a scale ranging from a farmer's rights to diverted creek water, to World War II, the struggle for control of natural resources is a fact of our lives. It is the way we handle these struggles that will mark our success as a species.

Mineral resources are considered nonrenewable. (David E. Simcox Collection)

The moral of the story at this point is simply this: We (that's all of us) need to be effective **long-term** stewards of *our* natural resources.

So who owns natural resources? One of the most interesting aspects of natural resources is the concept of their ownership, and the implications that ownership carries for the ways resources are managed. Some resources are what we refer to as common. These are resources that are essentially owned by all of us. The easiest examples of common resources are solar energy, air, and the oceans' waters. Another form of ownership is state owned or managed. These would be resources controlled by governments. Examples of state ownership here in the United States include the National Forests, minerals beneath government-managed lands, and wildlife. The third form of resource ownership is private, including corporate possession. Examples of private ownership include title to property such as a private residence, rights to a water supply, or lands owned and managed for timber by a corporation like Weyerhaeuser.

Ownership does not mean absolute control. Instead it refers to a **bundle of rights.** Owners possess certain rights not enjoyed by non-owners. But owners do not possess all rights to specific resources. Let's look at the three main types of ownership to learn how the bundle-of-rights concept operates.

Property ownership has become a focal point for natural resource issues.
(Steve Dennis)

Common resources are owned by all, but their use can be regulated by governments, blurring the distinction between common and state ownership. Air is a common resource. We all use air to breathe, and we could not survive without it. But what other uses do we make of our air? We use air for combustion in automobiles. In that process we produce toxic materials that are released into the air. Air is thus used as a waste treatment mechanism, and we must regulate the release of pollutants in an attempt to maintain good air quality. We use air as a means of travel for planes and regulate its use for safety and national defense. Water in the oceans is common to all of us, but nations maintain zones of control over fishing rights, dumping of waste, and treaties over the harvest of marine mammals and other species. So even though common resources are shared by all people, they are not completely unregulated. The degree and enforcement of regulations, however, varies widely among countries.

State-owned or -regulated resources are managed to control the problems presented by scarcity. Scarcity really means two things: (a) if unregulated, resources can quickly be exploited to ruin or loss and (b) scarce resources can be highly valuable. Wildlife is a good example of a state-regulated natural resource. Years ago, as uncontrolled hunting and harvest of wildlife increased its scarcity or led to extinctions of certain species, governments stepped in to control the taking of wildlife, and acquired title to lands to manage as wildlife refuges. People still fish and hunt, but the amount of these harvests is controlled in order to maintain sustainable populations. Poaching (illegal harvest) remains a severe threat to wildlife despite governmental controls. Another good example of a state-owned or -managed natural resource is a national park such as the Grand Canyon. The Grand Canyon is scarce, because there aren't many comparable ditches of this magnitude. It is also a surprisingly fragile resource, so the National Park Service regulates what people can do there. But the flow of water through the Grand Canyon is controlled by another federal agency (the Bureau of Reclamation); private companies own most of the permits to float through the canyon on the Colorado; and tourist air charters enjoying the scenery from the air are regulated by the Federal Aviation Administration (FAA). Although complex, state ownership of the Grand Canyon has preserved the resource, preventing damage from mining, further hydroelectric development, and an overabundance of tourist attractions.

Private ownership implies that an individual or corporation has most of the bundle of rights associated with a resource or property. It is important to remember that this does not imply that the private owner possesses all rights. Home ownership provides a good example of private property rights. Certain rights to most private property are regulated by the state. In a California subdivision, I may not be able to operate a boat yard, even though I have room. Under a regulation mechanism called **zoning**, the local government has the power to prevent such a use of my yard, basically for my neighbors' sake. This action underscores the concept that the **welfare of the community** is more important than my individual desire to operate a boat yard. Similarly, I'd like to sit down to a venison dinner from the deer that has enjoyed our vegetable garden this summer. Even though the deer is on our property, I don't own it and can't legally shoot it. Deer run a little unclear on the concept of trespass. Throw in the fact that the true owner of our home is actually a rather faceless mortgage corporation, and you can begin to see the complications of ownership. It is enough for now to say that the struggle between individuals for their rights to private property, and governments for their rights to regulate the use of that property, is one of the major themes of this book. Understanding this struggle and how it operates is a crucial step for a citizen to take in becoming an effective resource steward.

Values are another force shaping our definition of natural resources. We value (or place importance) on natural resources for a wide variety of reasons. These values can be categorized as strategic, commodity, aesthetic, and moral. What makes this fun is that we don't all share the same values. One person's commodity value for trees as timber is likely in conflict with another person's value for trees as an aesthetic resource. The decline in salmon populations in the Pacific Northwest is partially blamed on timber harvest practices, thus there is a conflict in values over forests as commodities, and as part of the mechanism of water quality. Our values for natural resources define the ways we'd like to see them used. Between 50 and 60 years ago, people's value for water and hydroelectric power was such that plans were drawn up to build dams on the Colorado River inside Grand Canyon National Park. People who valued a Grand Canyon bottomed by a river rather than a reservoir fought the dam-building faction and kept dams out of the Grand Canyon. Glen Canyon, however, was dammed in the 1960s, backing Lake Powell for 195 miles up the Colorado, northeast of the Grand Canyon. Glen Canyon was not as well known nor as highly valued as the Grand Canyon. The construction of Glen Canyon Dam was an expression of values for those resources in the 1950s and 1960s. It is perhaps unlikely that the same dam and reservoir would be built today. Values change. The maintenance of ecosystems and the protection of biodiversity are more highly valued today than they were a couple of generations ago. Let's take a closer look at some values for natural resources.

Strategic values include views that certain resources must be managed as part of some strategy to maintain or improve some condition. The strategy could be to maintain control over a resource such as oil. Oil is strategically important, as so much of our commerce and electrical supply is dependent on it. A wildlife refuge is likely strategically valued as a habitat for one or more species.

Commodity values consider resources as goods that can be developed for products. This set of values recognizes the utility of resources as raw materials. A commodity value for a forested area would be to believe that a stand of trees in that forest would be best used as lumber to build houses. A commodity value for a river would be to see its energy as potential for hydroelectric power generation, and its water as irrigation for agriculture.

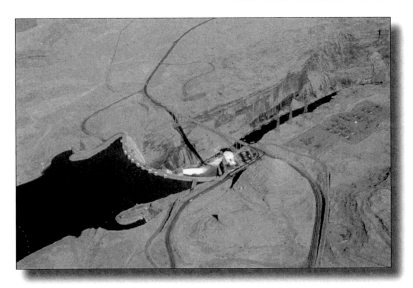

Glen Canyon Dam on the Colorado River created the second largest reservoir in the United States, backing waters 195 miles upriver.
(David E. Simcox Collection)

Aesthetic values see resources for their beauty. It is often aesthetic values that prompt efforts to preserve resources as parks and preserves. An aesthetic value for a forested area would be to prefer its use for hiking, camping, and nature study. An aesthetic value for a river would be to see its best use as a fishing area, as a waterway for canoeing or kayaking, or as a vista suited for scenic contemplation.

Moral values for resources include a broad array of perceptions that resources should be treated ethically and morally. Moral values view resources not only for their utility to humans, but also for their importance as elements of the earth. Moral values can include conflicting points of view. One view might hold that it is wrong to kill animals, while another may hold that the killing of animals is appropriate as part of humans' "dominion" over nature. Moral values include the ethical standard that we must save resources for future generations. An expression of moral values is found in the adage: "We do not inherit the earth from our ancestors; we borrow it from our children."

Values for natural resources are constantly changing, ranging from apathetic to vehement, and always providing conflict. We all see resources as what we want from them, whether that is economic gain, spiritual refreshment, or hope for our grandchildren. When values are strongly held by large numbers of people, the bundle of rights implied by ownership can become more flexible, and negotiation may rearrange ownership rights to more closely match the values of groups other than the owners or managers. Even private property rights can be adjusted, though not without constitutional consequences. This is a really important concept to keep in mind. This is the way our National Parks were set aside. Citizens, through their congressional representatives, changed

Electrical energy is produced using both renewable and nonrenewable resources.
(John Cowan Collection)

the bundles of rights to lands that were declared to be National Parks. Through similar action, our National Parks could be irreversibly changed in the future.

We are all just temporary stewards of our lands, waters, and resources. Ownership comes and goes as lands are purchased, taken by conquest, set aside "for the people," or redefined for special purposes. In peacetime, most resource ownership exchanges take place as purchases and redefinition through litigious, legislative, and regulatory processes. People, citizens, are the players in these processes. We are all affected by the decisions over stewardship of natural resources, and we all have roles to play in this drama throughout our lives.

chapter two

Demands on Natural Resources

The struggle over ownership and management of natural resources stems from resource scarcity. Scarcity is both a natural phenomenon and one caused by ourselves. Useful resources that are scarce are valuable because of that scarcity. Compare the cost of one ounce of pure gold to one ounce of pure drinking water. That's about $1,400 for the gold and a couple of pennies for the water. Gold is a lot harder to find. The earth just doesn't have as much gold as it does water. On the other hand, there are resources on the earth that are or have been considered to be abundant. There is an abundant supply of air and an abundant supply of saltwater. But fresh water is only regionally abundant, and in some parts of the world it has become dangerously scarce at times. Similarly, forests are abundant in some parts of the world, and in other parts, scarce. As freshwater and forests are renewable natural resources, it is possible that they can be replenished as we use them–unless we use them at a rate faster than they can recover. And more and more, the ability of resources to recover is shrinking as we place greater demands on them to meet our needs.

Several factors help to explain why certain resources on this earth get overused and sometimes permanently lost:

- Populution (misspelling intended) and consumption
- Industrialization, automation, and technology
- Urbanization
- Mobility
- Work and leisure time
- Income
- Culture, philosophy, and education

Populution

Populution is considered by many to be the greatest threat to our resource base, and thus the long-term welfare of humanity. In 1999, the earth's population surpassed 6 billion. Increasing monthly by 6 to 7 million, we are on course to pass 7 billion in 2012. That's 7,000 cities of a million people each. That's a lot of eating, drinking, procreating, defecating, and urinating organisms. We're still well outnumbered by ants and termites, but among large mammals, there is a bunch of us. Big numbers are interesting, but the concern among population ecologists lies not in the 7 billion people here, but the rate at which our population is increasing ever upward. As an illustration, check the rate of population change in Figure 2.1.

How many years did it take for the first doubling to occur? The second? The third? Given the continuation of this rate of population increase, in what year would our population reach 12 billion?

Just for fun, let's line everybody in the world up on the equator, shoulder to shoulder. That's about two feet per person. We'll build big rafts across the oceans so nobody sinks in our lineup. That line of people would stretch around the globe more than 100 times!

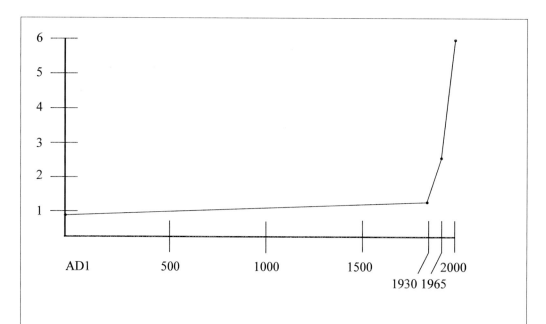

Figure 2.1. Human Population Increase Over the Last 2,000 Years. The classic "J" curve of population dynamics, indicating rapid acceleration of human population growth.

Our natality rate is roughly 360,000 births per day. Our mortality rate is roughly 140,000 deaths per day. That means we add approximately 220,000 people to the earth's population every day. We could check them all in through the Rose Bowl in Pasadena. Fill the stadium twice a day, and welcome to our world!

Ecologists are as much concerned with the rate at which people **consume** resources as they are with our large numbers. Some even say that it isn't large populations that threaten, but rather the levels of resource consumption. Twelve billion people, they claim, could be sustained, but not if everyone gets an SUV and an Exxon-Mobil card.

It is obvious to all of us that people around the globe live very different lifestyles and consume varying amounts of natural resources. When I consider the home, car, appliances, toys, and other assorted stuff I own, it is a compilation of material that probably exceeds what is owned by 90% of the individuals in the world. And I'm just a typical American. Consumption of natural resources is not equitably distributed around the globe in much the same way that resources themselves are not equitably distributed. The Worldwatch Institute (2011) notes the western nations of North America and Europe account for only 12% of the world's population, but represent 60% of the consumption of goods and services worldwide. The 33% of the Earth's population living in South Asia and sub-Saharan Africa consumes only 3.2% of worldwide goods and services. The inequity in this example is obvious.

It is not the purpose of this book to decry despoliation of the earth's resources. Students are bombarded with such information every time an environmental education instructor gets hold of them. This awareness is important, but knowing that forests are disappearing at a rate close to 500 square kilometers per day does little but breed a sense of despair. It is better to learn about why that is happening and then to look toward means of alleviating the problem. What use is made of half of the wood from our disappearing forests? The answer isn't paper or plywood; it is fuel–fuel for cooking and heating. That's because people throughout the world can obtain wood for these purposes easier than electricity or gas. It is a matter of resource distribution, of a scarcity of the resources needed to pipe gas or generate electricity.

Rather than go on about the levels of resource consumption in the world, it might be easiest to simply present an estimate of the solid waste generated by the United States in one day: we throw out 90 million bottles and jars, 46 million cans, 150,000 tons of paper, 30,000 cars, and 25,000 TV sets (Bailey, 1983). Our use of industry and transportation leads us to pump half a million tons of pollutants into the air every day. What we do not know is whether these levels of consumption are **sustainable.** Global warming and climate change are trends feared as a result of our consumption patterns, but scientists disagree on its intensity and significance.

Industrialization, Automation, and Technology

Industrialization, automation, and our ability to bring into use new **technologies** are other factors that enable greater demand on resources. We have built machines that have increased our efficiency in agriculture, engineering, and travel, and we have allowed resource development to improve our ability to use resources and thus increase our numbers. The rate of industrialization and technological innovation is unprecedented in human history. Within the last century, we've witnessed the explosion of the internal-combustion engine, the development of the industrial assembly line, the engineering of vast waterworks for irrigation and hydroelectric generation, and the late-century emergence of what is called an "information revolution." The Athenian culture of ancient Greece was built on a system of slavery that provided an average of 15 slaves per citizen. In the United States today, the working power of the gadgetry used by each citizen is considered to approximate 500 slaves. Just consider the energy and infrastructure you use on a daily basis, from the coffeemaker, to the auto, to the hot shower, and on. Imagine what it would have taken to harness that kind of power in the era before electricity and fossil fuels combustion.

Urbanization

Urbanization is the process by which we inexorably spread our living quarters over the landscape. The major conflict over urbanized use of lands is in the values of many lands for agriculture, forests, aquifer recharge, wildlife habitat, and open space. As our cities and suburbs spread, many of these other land values are lost. There has been a 200-year migration from farmlands to cities in the United States. At the time of the Revolutionary War, 92% of the population lived on farms. Today it is less than 2%. Part of this decline is due to the efficiencies of agricultural machinery. A single farmer today feeds 150 people.

As we have gathered in cities and towns around our industrial and service vocations, our economic viability has enabled us to aspire to "single-family homes" arranged in suburbs filled with roads and fringed with commercial development. Many of us in the United States today live in communities designed for automobile access, allowing us to spread out much farther from the workplace, our schools, and commerce than in pre-auto times. The result is known as **urban sprawl**. The name for the largest of our new living areas is **megalopolis**, some with catchy names such as the eastern seaboard's Bowash for the Boston-to-Washington urbanized area, and Sansan for the stretch from San Diego to San Francisco. The conflict over land for living space versus agriculture is perhaps nowhere more noticeable than in California's Central Valley, where sprawling cities such as Stockton and Sacramento sprout on some of the richest agricultural soils on earth.

Mobility

Mobility, our ability to get ourselves and our things around, is tied directly to industrialization, automation, and technology. But it deserves special mention because of the relationship between resources and where they are ultimately used. Trade has been part of human interaction from prehistoric times. People packed goods from points where they could be extracted or grown to places where they could not, and traded what was plenty for what was scarce. Over time, the loads grew larger and moved to the backs of domesticated animals and the keels of canoes. Wheels and sails smoothed the gravitational effects on cargoes, and carts and shore coasting vessels plied new roads and waterways with larger burdens for exchange. Steam and then gasoline, diesel, and jet engines quickened and overpowered the work of horses and canvas, leading to a transportation revolution that moves people and goods worldwide in a blink of an eye compared to yesteryear. The emigrant trail from St. Joseph, Missouri, to Sacramento was at least a six-month ordeal in the 1850s, and not a lot of cargo made it. Today, a couple of buzz-eyed days on the interstate, and you can cover the same ground, complete with your own wagonload of possessions. Trim your gear to a suitcase or two, and you can watch the pioneer landscape from 35,000 feet and arrive in three hours.

Our mobility allows us to move products in containerized shipping, supertankers, rail freight, and semis. Worldwide trade is of a scale and complexity beyond most people's comprehension. And the location of product assembly may be half a world from the sources of a product's component raw materials. The United States, once the leading steel-producing nation in the world, now imports most of its steel. The need to mine the raw materials of steel has been exported.

Our mobility also allows us to smile our friendly faces in places where a few generations ago people barely knew we existed. No longer is it so unique to go trekking in Nepal or kayaking the river canyons of the southwest. Mobility spawned tourism, and worry over diminishing world resources and uniqueness has spawned ecotourism. The Beach Boys' hit song "I Get Around" rings in our ears while a web of flight paths, highways, sea-lanes, and satellite trajectories envelopes the globe.

Work and Leisure Time

Work and leisure time are factors that primarily affect our use of resources for recreation and leisure. For years, leisure theorists proclaimed that the workweek was growing shorter and that automation and technology would free us from toil to enjoy lives of recreational bliss. Indeed, labor-saving inventions such as the washing machine, the dishwasher, and the frozen dinner were designed to minimize work and give us choices of better ways to spend our time. But rather than bathe in free time, we have increased our time at work. One need only consider the percentage of women in the workforce now, as compared to 40 years ago to understand an obvious trend toward employment. The outcome of this change back toward employment is that people have shorter periods of time available for outdoor recreation. The trip to a distant campground or resort by the lake for a couple of weeks is often no longer an option for many. We are thus increasing our demand for recreational environments close to home, closer to the sprawl that in some cases has permanently expunged aesthetic values from our proximity. Our work habits have led to our need to refocus on our living environments, for we often no longer have as much time to simply load up the family auto and escape for a while.

Income

Income is another factor that enables our increased consumption of resources. All of this producing, transporting, and trading leads to economic increases, reduced product costs, and greater opportunities to acquire. And this, of course, leads to greater need to produce and higher levels of resource use. More striking, however, is the rate at which income varies across countries, regions, and socioeconomic classes. The inequities of income provide the opportunity to exploit the resources of the poor, because their resources and labor can be obtained on the cheap.

Culture, Philosophy, and Education

Culture, philosophy, and education are characteristics that mark nations and assemblages of people. They are characteristics that identify values, morals, and ethics. These are factors that define our links to natural resources beyond mere biological need and into the realm of laws, science, and religion. Our cultural perspectives are defined by our histories and our relationships with our environments. Philosophies ponder and guide our thinking about ourselves and others. Education increases our understandings and prepares each subsequent generation for the task of carrying on. These factors are our guides, our interpreters of things we may not understand. They define our differential values and explain our worldviews. They are the foundations of the debate over how we will manage the resources of the earth now and into the future.

Suggested Readings

Bailey, A. (1983). *A day in the life of the world.* Garden City, NY: Doubleday.

Commoner, B. (1971). *The closing circle: Nature, man, and technology.* New York: Knopf.

Ehrlich, P. (1975). *The population bomb.* Rivercity, MA: Rivercity Press.

Friedman, T. L. (2008). *Hot, flat, and crowded.* New York: Farrar, Straus, and Giroux.

Knudson, D. M. (1980). *Outdoor recreation.* New York: MacMillan.

Reid, T. R. (1998, October). Feeding the planet. *National Geographic, 56-74.*

Wackernagel, M., & Rees, W. E. (1996). *Our ecological footprint: Reducing human impact on earth.* Philadelphia, PA: New Society Publishers.

Weeks, J. R. (2011). *Population: An introduction to concepts and issues,* (11th ed.). Belmont, CA: Wadsworth Publishing.

Worldwatch Institute. (2011). The state of consumption today.Retrieved from http://www.worldwatch.org/node/810

chapter three

America's Common Lands
Outdoor Recreation as an Example of
Excessive Demand for Scarce Resources

The United States is fortunate to have large tracts of land set aside for the common good. Roughly one third of the nation's land mass is managed by the federal government under designations that include national parks, monuments, wildlife refuges, forests, reserves, waterways, seashores, and public domain lands. Fully 80% of these lands are managed under a doctrine of **multiple use**. Under this management designation, lands are managed to produce benefits to society that include **timber**, water, grazing, minerals, **wildlife**, and **outdoor recreation**. The philosophy of multiple use is evolving into a new paradigm referred to as **ecosystems management**. We'll come back to the history of how this landed estate came to be and what it means today. For now, let's take a quick look at outdoor recreation in the United States to provide an example of how competing individual demands for resources lead to conflicts.

When the United States changed from a colonial to an independent democratic nation, the concept of private ownership of land was embraced and protected. Land was immediately the most abundant resource in the country, and vast tracts of it lay to the west, ripe for purchase, conquest, and exploitation. Government regulation was minimal, as the nation grew under a pioneer mentality that saw resources as limitless, and people as free to develop them. During this pioneer era, immigration from Europe populated cities to the bursting point, giving rise to the urbanization of America. Exploitation took its toll on the land, in some places in a period spanning less than a generation. Eventually, the federal government got into the resources game, setting aside the lands that would come to be our national parks, national forests, and other publicly owned resource lands.

Regrowth on a harvested site managed under multiple use. (David E. Simcox Collection)

Outdoor recreation is another product of multiple use management. (Photo by Steve Dennis)

Water management. The water filling the reservoir at Lake Oroville drained from a public land watershed managed for multiple use. (David E. Simcox Collection)

Pronghorn Antelope on public lands managed for multiple use (John Cowan Collection)

Open-pit gold mine in Nevada on public land managed for multiple use. (Photo by Mike Dennis)

Cattle grazing on public lands managed under multiple use. (U.S. Bureau of Land Management)

Residential development changes the character of the landscape. (Courtesy of the Weyerhaeuser Archives)

Integrating human habitat with nature reflects changes in values for wildlife and open space. (David E. Simcox Collection)

Highways and roads are another form of land use on which we depend. (Photo by Steve Dennis)

Agricultural land use is essential to feed our ever-growing population. (Photo by Steve Dennis)

Use of land for industry. (Photo by Steve Dennis)

Shopping malls are an example of commercial or retail use of land. (Photo by Steve Dennis)

Meanwhile, back in the cities, things were getting ugly. In the latter part of the nineteenth century, various reform movements advocated the construction and management of urban parks, shorter workweeks, outdoor living (camps) for citified youth, and in general, improvement in the quality of life for the average working citizen. From this new thinking arose an era of parks development and management. Outdoor recreation flourished as a democratic ideal, and one of America's most popular presidents cut his toothy character from a youth spent outdoors, far from the confines of his privileged home. The camping movement, together with a nostalgia for an all-too-brief pioneering era in our history, helped form in our national character a sense of contact with the outdoors. Our recreation became a part of our culture.

A turn-of-the-century outing was simpler than those at the turn of the millennium.
(Courtesy of Library of Congress)

Today, outdoor recreation has grown beyond the imaginations of the original creators of our national and early urban parks. They could not have foreseen that by the 1990s we would be merrily snowboarding, hang gliding, bungee jumping, and wave running all over the recreational landscape; that at night we would cocoon into pop-up nylon domes and motorized sheet metal boxes with indoor plumbing. But this gadgetry and comfort is a well-established characteristic of our outdoor recreation habit. It is how we come to know ourselves in the great outdoors. It is also part of why our recreation resources are overused, unable to recover from the onslaught of large numbers of fun seekers and their ubiquitous toys.

In 1916, 44 years after the establishment of Yellowstone National Park, the federal government finally got around to creating an agency to manage the

Automotive camping
styles have changed
considerably, as people
have sought higher
levels of comfort.
(Photo by Steve Dennis)

parks and monuments it had set aside since 1872. The National Park Service was organized and given a dual mission to protect the parks and provide for their use. It was the agency's task

> "...to protect the wildlife and natural and historic objects therein, and provide for the enjoyment of same in such manner and by such means as will leave them unimpaired for future generations." (National Park Service Act, 1916)

In 1916, a few thousand people made it to Yellowstone and Yosemite every year. Today the annual visitation at each of these parks is up to 4 million. The largest national park in the east, Great Smoky Mountains, hosts over 9 million people annually. The park planners of yesteryear could foresee neither the quantity of visitors nor the ways they would play. Unlike many other agencies, however, the National Park Service has tried to mold outdoor recreation into what many call "the National Park experience," guided by the phrase *in such manner and by such means*. The lands of many other agencies are left open to provide a "spectrum" of recreational opportunities ranging from solitary wilderness hiking to cavorting on off-road vehicles. Our demand for recreational resources is insatiable.

Demand for places to recreate
outdoors has led to overcrowd-
ing in many areas.
(Courtesy of Yosemite Museum,
National Park Service)

We go to these lands with our skis, water skis, snowboards, wakeboards, personal watercraft, dune buggies, all-terrain vehicles, mountain bikes, RVs, sailboats, drag boats, prams, canoes, bass-trackers, scuba tanks, crampons, pitons, carabiners, GPSs, backpacks, daypacks, fanny packs, lunch sacks, fishing rods, rifles, machine guns, Hummers, sport-utility vehicles, camo-fashions, parasails, water filters, lanterns, stoves, Astroturf, coolers, and beer. Don't forget the beer or the kitchen sink. And with all this fun and stuff, we bring along fistfights, murders, drugs, theft, search-and-rescue operations, litter, more litter, trampling, wildlife harassment, giardia, and water pollution. And this is just from the folks who venture out of their cars. From the "windshield visitors" come smog, traffic jams, and bigger parking lots. We are a nation hooked on **industrial tourism**.

Consider these contradictory and conflicting uses: cross-country skiers vs. snowmobilers; fishers vs. rafters; hikers vs. equestrians; equestrians vs. mountain bikers; mountain bikers vs. hikers; mountain bikers, hikers, and equestrians vs. off-road vehicle drivers; sailors vs. jet-skis; tent campers vs. RV campers; solitude seekers vs. partiers; nudies vs. suities; motors vs. oars; and on and on. And one and all are looking for a good time, the tie that unites.

To manage this menagerie, rangers have become cops, campgrounds have moved to computer reservation services, appointments are made for trailhead departures, entrance and camping fees have climbed, activities have been zoned and banned, and areas have been closed. And we keep finding new ways to encounter the great out-of-doors. Recognize that the mountain bike trend has only been with us a little over two and a half decades and off-road vehicles about five decades. It would be pretty hard to find someone who would answer in the affirmative to the following question: Do you love the wilderness enough to never go there again?

The point of this harangue is that our natural resources available for outdoor recreation are in limited supply. They, too, are scarce, and our values for them vary greatly. Management tries to protect the resource from the very people who come to love it to death, while attempting to keep us from killing one another in search of our own version of nirvana.

Outdoor recreational use sometimes brings conflicts with other resource uses.
(Photo by Steve Dennis)

Our recreational tastes
have brought green land-
scaping to desert areas.
(David E. Simcox Collection)

They use names such as **recreational carrying capacity** and **limits of acceptable change** for methods to (a) provide for enjoyment and (b) protect for future
generations. Their efforts are a metaphor for the use of all natural resources on
the world stage. Their problem is an act in the tragedy of the commons.

What is the Tragedy of the Commons?

Our public lands are commons. They belong to everybody. We have the opportunity to take from them while giving virtually nothing in return. Somebody
else manages them. We use them and go home. We obtain their benefits but do
not absorb the costs. Like many things that are nearly free, we take perhaps
more than we need. Eventually, enough of us have grabbed so much that the
commons begins to deteriorate. But fixing the commons is beyond the capacity
of any individual, so rather than repair, we grasp for the last of the benefits. And
the commons wastes away even faster.

Garrett Hardin (1968) described this ecological conundrum in the late sixties, noting that the population explosion is a **tragedy of the commons**. The
theory is predicated on the fact that humans act in their own self-interest, taking
as many benefits as they can and investing as little as possible in return. The
exploitation of **grazing** lands and forests in the pioneer era of the United States
is a good example of the tragedy at work. The pollution of our air and the un-
sustainable fishing of our oceans exemplify the tragedy of the commons. It is a
powerful force, this collection of individual self-interests.

America's common lands were reorganized under governmental control in
order to stem the exploitation brought about by the free exercise of individual
self-interests. The commons were to be managed to avoid the tragedy await-

ing them. Their management is as controversial today as it was then. Outdoor recreation provides but one small example of the management controversies surrounding our common resources. The way these controversies evolved, and how they're played out, is the direction in which this study will now turn.

Suggested Readings

Abbey, E. (1968). Polemic: Industrial tourism and the national parks. In *Desert solitaire* (pp. 39–59). New York: Simon & Schuster.

Danz, J. (1999, August). Hey (hey!) you (you!) get off of my trail. *Outside,* 86–91.

Hardin, G. (1968). The tragedy of the commons. *Science*, 162, 1243–1248.

Julber, E. (1972, May). Let's open up our wilderness areas. *Reader's Digest*. 125–128.

National Park Service Organic Act of 1916, 16 U.S.C. §1, 2, 3, & 4.

Runte, A. (1997). *National parks: The American experience* (3rd ed.). Lincoln, NE: University of Nebraska Press.

chapter four

Evolution of a Land Ethic and Natural Resource Management Eras

Though history may not be everyone's favorite subject, it is impossible to understand our relationships to natural resources unless we have a background that explains how we got here. The connections with our past are strong. In many cases it is our past—the decisions made by people 100 or more years ago—that rules us today. So let's take a brief look at how our vision for the land has been shaped.

The Road to the Americas

Primitive peoples shared an intimate and immediate relationship with the land. The resources at their disposal were raw, and for the most part, uncontrolled. For most of humans' tenure on earth, our species foraged, gathered, and hunted to survive. If you reconsider the basic earth resources and basic human needs from the matrix in Chapter 1, it is easy to imagine the level at which human survival took place. Nature was the provider, and in many places on earth were useable plants, fruits, fish and shellfish, birds, reptiles, insects, and mammals that could be picked, gathered, snared, netted, speared, and pummeled to obtain food. When resources grew scarce, humans would migrate to seasonal or permanent locales where their needs could be more easily met. Human settlement occurred in those areas where nature provided water, food resources, and materials for shelter.

But nature could also be a destroyer. The same waters that offered sustenance and travel corridors could flood, or they could disappear in drought. Plants that provided food and shelter could erupt in fire. The hunter could also become prey to creatures with greater speed, agility, and appetite. The conditions for primitive peoples were, to rearrange a popular phrase, as follows: "Life was short, and then you died."

It is no small wonder that humans have measured their progress against a yardstick that ticks off the subjugation of nature. From the development of the earliest tools built by dexterous, opposable-thumbed hands to the revolutionary concept that a planted and cared-for seed could grow into food, people made progress at manipulating nature to enhance their opportunities for survival. Through this progression grew the early worldviews, the values that defined different peoples' relationships with the land. These ranged from fear to hatred to respect and to love. Generally, we loved the nature that provided, and we respected its moods. But the nature that destroyed was hated and feared. The nature that destroyed was best avoided. So humans developed agriculture and irrigation, and began to bend the part of nature they loved so they could have more of it the way they wanted it.

Agricultural talent made it easier for more people to survive at one time, and the human species grew in numbers. Agriculture reduced nomadic living, and people settled longer in resource-rich areas. The need to get along with one another and to protect those we knew from those we didn't became apparent. These gatherings of people with needs formed the fundamental value for civilization. And after a million-plus years of clannish existence, people linked families into the communities of civilized living.

Civilization provided ever more fruitful ground for the exchange of ideas and the accomplishment of cooperative work. As people learned more from one another and retained knowledge that made some aspects of nature more predictable, they also banded together to accomplish things they were unable to do in smaller groups. Early civilizations developed trail and road systems, dug irrigation and waterworks, and built cities with temples to their gods.

The early deities of Egypt, Greece, and Rome were thoroughly connected to the natural world. The gods were what explained the capriciousness of nature, called upon to benevolently grace civilization with mild temperatures, steady supplies of water, and protection from harm. And when nature turned sour, the moodiness of gods was explained in human terms, as nature erupted in gods' emotions such as wrath, jealousy, and greed. Lesser gods inhabited the woods and wild places, assuming bestial qualities such as Pan, the Greeks' half-goat, half-human lord of the forests. The word *panic* derives from the screaming flight of travelers running from the woods, having heard strange noises and presuming an imminent encounter with Pan. Satyrs and centaurs, those half-goat and half-horse creatures dedicated to wine, dancing, and lust, were known to populate the forests, awaiting innocent and civilized humans as their prey.

Civilization marked separation from the wilds, an all-too-near presence that threatened the civilized with a return to chaos, the fearful struggle to survive. Wildness, untamed nature, was viewed as dangerous and foreboding. In the first century B.C., the Roman poet Lucretius wrote that it was a "defect" that so much of the earth "is greedily possessed by mountains and the forests of wild beasts." These wildlands were places to be avoided, or as skills and labor allowed, to be beaten and transformed into people-friendly pastoral landscapes.

The proliferation of civilization could only occur through the transformation of wildlands, and civilization was valued as good, while wilderness rated below bad.

The dominant religious and philosophical movement of the era of early civilizations that marked the development of European "Western" thinking is what is referred to as the Judeo-Christian tradition. This worldview also marked the wilds as a defect of nature, a place to turn the hands of man in the holy struggle for dominion. The term *wilderness* appears more than 200 times in the Old Testament, together with hundreds of similar references to desert and waste. Wilderness was a "howling waste" in which Moses led the Israelites for 40 years on Sinai. Wilderness was the symbol of God's anger, while springs, brooks, and cultivated lands were the signs of His deliverance. Wilderness did, however, serve as a sort of testing ground. It was one place where piety grew and revelations occurred. To survive a turn in the wilderness was to be chosen, and closer to God.

When Rome eventually fizzled into the archaeological record, a thousand years of what we call the "Middle Ages" followed before a few people awoke to smell the coffee and ushered in the Renaissance. During the Middle Ages, European Christianity flourished in a feudally languishing form of civilization. Church and state were virtually one and the same. Education was restricted to the clergy, and a peasantry was kept in slave-like serfdom, providing the workforce that sustained the lives of cities and towns. It was in the church's best interests to maintain the fear of wilderness. Such fear cured wanderlust and maintained respect for the trappings of God-respecting living and civilization. Wilderness thus retained its primeval characterization: a scary place inhabited by ogres, wood sprites, fairies, dragons, werewolves, and trolls. So people continued to live in near-mortal fear of the wilds, a loathing that served to breed a general disrespect for its qualities. And the conversion of wilds to pastoral landscapes gave God-respected purpose to humans' endeavors.

There is another reason that nature appreciation was not in the cards for medieval peoples. The church taught that man's real reward came on ascendancy to heaven. If one were to toil, obey the rules, and pay homage to the church, then when he keeled over by 40, he could spend a blissful eternity behind the pearly gates. People's toil often involved beating back nature's incursions into their agrarian setting, pitting man against nature as good versus evil. Nature appreciation did not buy one a ticket to heaven.

Deep-rooted attitudes toward untamed landscapes were very slow to change. But slowly, the series of individuals and events that helped shape our present view stepped briefly onto history's stage. Early among this group was St. Francis of Assisi, the thirteenth-century cleric who believed that birds, wolves, and other wild animals had souls. This rather blasphemous concept viewed humans as part of, rather than above, nature. It flew in the face of the Bible's teaching in Genesis that man was above nature and should exercise dominion over it. The church had much at stake in the dominance position, but

St. Francis' small group of followers received the blessing of the Pope in 1209, eventually becoming the Franciscan Order.

The Renaissance is often characterized as a light that came on to illuminate the Dark Ages. It was a period when discoveries were made through scientific inquiry, when some of the basic tenets of human thinking were challenged and forever changed. The man-centered-universe concept did not survive Copernicus, Galileo, and Tycho Brahe, who discovered that Earth and the other planets revolved around the sun. Science and discovery provided impetus for change, and the church assimilated new forms of understanding. Gutenberg's invention of the moveable-type printing press provided the opportunity to remove recordkeeping and writing from the domination of monastic scribes– the first slab of concrete on the information superhighway. The exchange of knowledge and information grew, and Europeans began to long for a greater awareness of their surrounding world.

Improved shipbuilding skills, the embryonic science of cartography, and a capitalist vision for trade gave rise to the classic age of exploration that marks indelibly the Renaissance. Europe's burgeoning population (after the bubonic plague passed through) hungered for spices and other trade goods that were not native to the continent. Land routes to Marco Polo's far east were blocked by "infidel" Moslems who had been able to survive the crusades of previous centuries and had little interest in relinquishing their domination of Asian trade. Turning to the sea, captains of the early sea coasting caravels were able to fix their north–south positions of latitude by relying on the varying angles of the sun. But moving east–west and determining longitude depended on a crude guesstimate based on hourglasses and the casting and retrieval of a measured line played out continuously behind the ship. Fortunately, most early exploratory forays required southerly directions as seafarers sought routes east around a sizable African continent. These ventures led to the discovery of the Canary Islands and the Azores, which eventually became the launch pads for cross-Atlantic shots to the New World. Southerly exploration led to the discovery of easterly trade winds that would favor a voyage west to Asia, setting a collision course for what would become known as the Americas.

Thus it was that by 1492, Europeans had developed an ethnocentric Christian ideology, a state of technological advancement beyond that of the rest of the world, and an aptitude and appetite for trade and domination. They were in many ways virtually the opposite of the several million Native Americans they were about to meet, subjugate, and destroy. The first boat people who landed, nearly starving, on the shores of the western hemisphere returned with few riches, except for the knowledge that there was a world to the west. And it was a world apparently unlike anything previously discovered. The race was on, and the next century was filled with voyages to claim new lands for the nations of Europe. Trade was tied to conquest, and exploitation required the labor of slaves. The foundations of Christian ideology, when stretched and abused, provided a rational and convenient mechanism for both needs. To have dominion meant that a Christian nation could proclaim to own the land on which its emissaries set foot. Necessary slave labor could be rationalized as the saving of heathens, whose toil would bring them closer to God. And in abbreviating their lives, it surely did.

The conquest and subjugation of the New World gave rise to a colonial period that still marks the world today. The degree to which a few conquistadors could dominate whole regions was unique to the western hemisphere. A.W. Crosby (1986) explains several factors that worked to assist Europeans in their colonization of the Americas. First, it is noted that European diseases ravaged native populations that had no resistance to the likes of smallpox, cholera, and influenza. Disease moved faster than humans, and whole regions were depopulated before the victors even arrived. Second, the intentional and unintentional introduction of European species of plants and animals altered the ecology of the New World, changing the resource base on which natives had subsisted for thousands of years. Third, Europeans practiced war on the staples of natives, purposely destroying crops on which natives survived. Finally, direct warfare and political oppression succeeded where other measures failed. Gunpowder, metal blades, and armor proved more effective than stone-age implements. Deposed chiefs and kings were easily replaced by beings possessing superior powers. The colonial period tumbled to a thriving start.

The Landing of Columbus, by Edward Hicks, c. 1837.

(Gift of Edgar William and Bernice Chrysler Garbisch. Photograph© Board of Trustees, National Gallery of Art, Washington)

The Era of Abundance: Colonial Period

The Spanish seaborne empire ruled the New World for the first century after Columbus brought back news of his discovery. From the tip of South America to St. Augustine, Florida, and the American southwest, Spaniards wandered in search of gold and silver, enslaving whole populations to do their bidding. The other major presence in the western hemisphere was Portugal, claiming territory that would eventually be known as Brazil. England was somewhat late entering the game, needing first to claim victory over the Spanish Armada before heading west across the Atlantic at latitudes more northerly than the Spanish colonies. France and Holland, too, joined in the colonization rush, claiming territory to be known as Louisiana and New Amsterdam (New York).

The first English colonials in North America nearly failed. Raised amid the pastoral landscapes of northern Europe, they were ill prepared to make use of the natural abundance they encountered. The English settlement on Roanoke Island (1587) disappeared in less than three years, the fate of its hundred-plus colonists still a mystery. Settlements at Jamestown (1607) and Plymouth (1620) would have starved completely had the settlers not learned how to obtain and prepare native foods from the locals. The forests they encountered were considered uninhabitable and required immediate conversion to cropland. Slash-and-burn agriculture cleared areas to establish farms, and the omnipresent wood became the staple construction material and fuel. The forests viewed from atop promontories on the east coast seemed endless. They were endlessly inhabited by Indians (misnamed by early explorers, who thought they'd found an extension of Asia) who could be friend or foe, depending on how they were received and treated by whites. Unhappy encounters with Indians who were not overly pleased at being pushed off their lands led to reprisals and the growing specter of a cultural clash gone sour. The Indians of the forest became the enemy, to be feared and loathed much like the forest creatures that raised Europeans' paranoia back in the old country. Here, too, God-fearing Christians needed to beat back the wilderness to survive. The pastoralization of the Americas depended on the deliberate reduction of the wilds.

We don't often consider the length of America's colonial period. In the Caribbean, Central, and South America, colonies became established in the early 1500s and gained independence only in the nineteenth or twentieth century, following some 350 years of colonial rule. The United States formed its constitution 180 years after the Jamestown colony was established in what eventually became Virginia. This period is marked by the inexorable growth of settlement: the establishment of trade crops such as tobacco for cancer; trees for shipbuilding; and the occasional forays into the land west in search of beaver pelts and other trade goods supplied by Native Americans.

Little or no effort to spare the wilds was made. The few **conservation** measures that were enacted received scant attention, such as the Tree Stamp Act, which reserved certain trees marked for use in building the ships of

England. Indeed, such acts were eventually counted among the abuses of the Crown against the colonists. New Worlders were not entirely pleased to share their bounty with an overseas absentee landlord. The establishment of Boston Common in 1634 marks an early vision of the need for sharing resources. Essentially a preauto parking lot, the Common was used as pasturage for the animals owned by the wealthier people of Boston. In time, its use expanded to more human purposes, and today the Common is often counted as America's first park.

Westward expansion during the colonial era was limited to the fringes of the colonies that were marked by mountain ranges such as the Adirondacks, Alleghenies, and Appalachians. Two decades after the United States had concluded its revolution at Yorktown, Thomas Jefferson started negotiating a deal with France that would double the nation's size and spark a westward expansion that would settle the rest of the continental United States in less than another century.

Era of Exploitation: Westward Expansion

The **Louisiana Purchase** added 530 million acres to America's public domain. At a cost of less than a nickel per acre, it is seen as one of the best real estate deals ever consummated—securing the Great Plains west of the Mississippi, ensuring United States domination of the Mississippi's trade routes, and legalizing the inevitable expansion to the West. It also marked the beginning of a pioneering era quite exploitative in nature, and at a time when settlement and resource policies of a government in Washington, D.C., did not fit the landscapes and peoples of the west. The European craze for felt hats led trappers far west to explore uncharted territory in search of an ever-dwindling supply of beaver pelts. Discoveries of fertile soils brought farmers. Grasslands beckoned to massive herds of cattle. And the dream of fast riches brought gold and silver seekers west by the thousands. **Manifest Destiny** described America's self-proclaimed right to expand west to the Pacific, and a nation of free and independent people would not be deterred from their quest in pursuit of life, liberty, and happiness.

Thomas Jefferson was a regular guy. Settling the nation's open spaces with square plots of land agreed with Jefferson's egalitarian sensibilities. He headed a committee in the Continental Congress that dealt with the question of settling lands that lay between the Mississippi and the original eastern seaboard colonies. Jefferson wrote the first draft of what became the Ordinance of May 20, 1785, through which **alodial** (freehold) land ownership was organized for **disposal** (sale or trade) from the government to private hands. Democratic principles of equality formed the basis for a regular and structured accounting of lands that came to be known as the **Cadastral Survey System.** Land was to be surveyed in square townships six miles on each side and consisting of 36 square miles. Each square mile was labeled a section consisting of 640 acres. A quarter section became the 160-acre measure for sale under the **Homestead Act of 1862.** This system of surveying permanently marks the American landscape. Next time you're up in an airplane, particularly over the plains or the Midwest, look down on Jefferson's mark on the land. It is unmistakable.

Many early homesteaders lived at subsistence levels. Sod house preserved in Bowman, North Dakota. (Photo by Brianne McWhorter)

Land was the natural resource most available for the development of a national economy. The federal government realized that it could (a) obtain revenue through the sale of land, (b) secure its borders through the settlement of distant lands, and (c) establish economic strength as the agricultural and mineral resources of the lands were developed. Lewis and Clark's exploration from the Mississippi to the Pacific in 1804–1805 brought back important information regarding the suitability of western lands for civilization. But new settlement continued primarily east of the Mississippi until the mid-1800s.

Westward expansion exploded in the middle of the nineteenth century, when word of easily picked gold in California excited imaginations back east. Increasingly steady immigration from Europe filled eastern cities with land-hungry peasants, so that opportunities for better lives in the West became dreams on which people acted. The opening of the Oregon Territory and the migration of Mormons to Utah brought settlers west. Silver and gold strikes in Nevada, Colorado, Arizona, and later the Black Hills and Alaska brought a boom of rapacious settlers to the western territories.

Their mentality was not particularly tuned to low-impact camping. It was their singular thought to get rich quick and let as little as possible stand in the way of that momentum. Mining activities required large amounts of water, so water became a commodity of property to be rerouted and fouled, as was necessary, for the good of the mines. Millions of trees were felled for the construction of roads, bridges, mineshafts, flumes, and for use as fuel.

Market hunting led to decimation of many wildlife species. Here a hunter in California's Central Valley poses with a day's work. (John Cowan Collection)

Game wardens enforce hunting regulations. Here wardens pose with confiscated ducks, taken from market hunters in 1936. (John Cowan Collection)

Market hunting brought virtually every form of edible bird and mammal to the stores and restaurants of towns and cities. On the plains, bison were slaughtered for sport and also for **ecological warfare** against the tribes that depended on them. Massive herds of cattle overgrazed the rich grasslands of Texas, New Mexico, and Arizona, their market potential realized by the ability to reach railroad transportation in Kansas. Native Americans were slaughtered or rounded up to be moved out of the way. And all of the exploitation was righteously justified by the morals and ethics of the day, the legacy of Americans' European ancestry.

The Wild West was wild because of conflicts over the exploitation of resources. Farmers dependent on soils despised ranchers for overgrazing. Ranchers didn't

Estimates of bison populations before their wholesale slaughter in the mid-1800s range from 30 to 75 million. By 1884, when bison hunting was outlawed in Yellowstone NP, only about 300 remained. (Courtesy of Library of Congress)

like farmers who erected fencing. Sheepherders and cattle grazers were at odds. Miners fought over claims to minerals and water. Homesteaders scrapped for water rights. Then there were the survey's squares; settlement of a complex crooked landscape was restricted to square plots bearing little resemblance to landforms. Throw into these mismatches the ethnic and religious separatism between groups of settlers and between settlers and Native Americans, and we had a pretty wildly boiling melting pot. And everywhere there was the battle against the land, for it was always considered necessary to subdue the land to obtain its fruits.

Era of Preservation: Changing Views of Natural Resources

Without this melee on the land, it is unlikely that the eventual backlash of preservationism would have occurred. But exploitation brought about small and large disasters that pointed directly to the need for a revised relationship with the land. Coupled with the words and pictures of new-thinking writers and artists, the era of exploitation melded into a new era of preservation and conservation, where the foundations of present-day resources management were laid.

Environmental Disasters

Several cataclysmic events painted exploitative resource practices in a negative light. Included among these were the massive forest fires named **Peshtigo, Miramichi**, and **Hinckley**; the extinction of the **passenger pigeon** and near-extinction of the **bison**; the **Johnstown Flood**; and the pointless destruction of a single **giant sequoia**.

The legend of Mrs. O'Leary's cow has kept the history of the Great Chicago Fire alive, but few people know about the three-times-deadlier 1.3 million acre forest fire that erupted the same night to the north around the small mill town of Peshtigo, Wisconsin. America's deadliest forest fire killed 1,182 people in a conflagration caused by the burning of settlers' fires during a late-summer drought in October 1871. Settlers' fires were used to clear stubble from harvested farms and to beat back the encroaching forests from which the farms had been carved. Winds whipped the fires into the forest, and nothing could control the onslaught. Other fires, such as the giant Miramichi Fire in New Brunswick (1825) and Hinckley fire in Minnesota (1894), also destroyed millions of acres. These disasters brought about the realization that America's forests were not necessarily endless, and that their mismanagement could leave them forever ruined.

The passenger pigeon once flew in flocks so large that their passing overhead could literally darken the skies for hours. An eastern species, the passenger pigeon was an easy mark for settlers who would randomly shoot skyward and collect what birds fell nearby. By the turn of the century, they were all but gone from the wild, and by 1914, completely extinct. This very noticeable disappearance could be directly attributed to habitat loss and unregulated hunting, for it was found that even a small percentage drop in flock size could alter breeding patterns that could not be reprogrammed. The passenger pigeon became part of the fossil record, and people started to wonder why.

Best known among environmental idiocies of the era of exploitation was the intentional decimation of the American bison. Once roaming over a third of the nation in herds that stretched beyond the horizon, the bison were easy targets for "sport" hunters. Railroad managers hired "buffalo hunters" to provide meat for their work crews, and when buffalo robes were introduced back east, they came into vogue as attire. More insidiously, bison were exterminated to deprive Native Americans of their source of food, clothing, and shelter. With eastern demand for robes satiated, slaughtered bison were left to rot with only their tongues removed for a culinary delicacy and their ears for bounty. Within a few short years, only several hundred bison remained, and a call went out to try to save the species.

Pennsylvania's Johnstown Flood of 1889 forewarned of the disastrous potential resulting from extensive clear-cutting and poorly constructed dams. Upstream from Johnstown, on the Conemaugh River, a 37-year-old earthen dam backed up a reservoir built as a summer retreat for Pittsburgh's wealthy industrialist elite. The dam was a privately financed endeavor, and signs of weakness in it were dismissed so as to delay expensive repairs. Further upstream, the forests of the **watershed** had been overcut and unrecovered. Heavy spring rains on deforested lands brought increased runoff into an overtaxed reservoir, melting down the weakened dam, and sweeping through the downstream city of Johnstown, killing 2,200 people. The lessons of the relationship between forests and watersheds and the dangers of privately financed dams were obvious.

Even the mismanagement of a single tree pointed to the irony of a greater stupidity. Realizing they might be looking at one of the largest living things on earth, in 1854, entrepreneurs erected scaffolding and set about meticulously removing the lower 116 feet of bark on a tree known as the "Mother of the Forest" in the Calaveras Grove of Big Trees in California's Sierra Nevada mountains. Crated and shipped to New York for display as one of America's wonders, it was later sent to London, impressing visitors to the Crystal Palace until 1866. Critics expounded that, were such a tree to have grown in Europe it would have been protected by law. But in America, such a marvel could be purchased, stripped, and shipped off "for a shilling show." Within a few years, a small fire swept through the North Grove of Calaveras *Sequoia gigantea.* The thick bark of healthy redwood trees protected them from the heat and flames. But the exposed Mother of the Forest succumbed, leaving today only a blackened 80-foot toothpick as a monument to human greed.

Sequoia gigantea, one of the largest living organisms, were toppled or carved up as curiosities, before their limited numbers were protected in national and state parks.
(Photo by Steve Dennis)

Though some of the disasters were part of eastern rather than western experience, the obvious message hit closer to home and was easily seen as a forewarning about the disastrous consequences of mistakes being repeated in the west. Beyond cataclysmic events, improvements in communications and transportation brought the west closer, and news of the rapid changes of the pioneering era was readily accessible to the educated classes of the eastern seaboard. Some of the seeds of preservationism may have sprouted in the west, but it was on the east coast that the paintings of western landscapes, the writings of influential authors, and the arguments over disposition of the western lands blossomed.

Words and Pictures

At a time when westward expansion was sweeping up adventurous Americans to try their luck in the promised land, a number of artists—painters, thinkers, and writers—were quietly going about their trades, extolling the virtues of wildness and decrying the destruction by which civilization tended to grow. Writers and painters helped to shape an evolving American culture, a culture that began to develop a unique sense of pride in the backdrop of its landscape.

George Catlin began traveling west in 1829, sketching detailed images of the Native Americans whom he encountered. Returning to his studio in the winter, he would complete the vivid paintings and keep records in his journal. By 1832, he was writing that the way of life he was seeing was on its way to irrevocable loss, that the extinction of the Indians and the nature of their habitat were imminent. Catlin proposed that the government should protect them in a "magnificent park," a nation's treasure that would be the model for such preservation. Catlin's words and even his incredible paintings received scant attention in the United States, though in retrospect, his words 40 years before Yellowstone now echo in their foresight. The imminent extinction Catlin feared came to pass. In some cases, it is his paintings that provide the only historical evidence of certain Native American tribes.

The **Hudson River School** of painters was inspired by **Thomas Cole**, an immigrant from England when he settled in the upper Ohio Valley in 1818 at the age of seventeen. Cole's paintings featured the raw, unsettled, and beautiful wild scenes he encountered on his wilderness travels. The glory of nature was displayed in grand landscapes, and human figures, if included at all, were dwarfed by the majesty of the scenery. **Asher Durand** and **Frederic Church** were among this first generation of Hudson River painters who popularized the style as uniquely American, challenging the myth that magnificence and art were the domain of the old world, and birthing an embryonic pride in things monumental and American. Following the lead of the first Hudson River crop, **Albert Bierstadt** and **Thomas Moran** ranged west across the Mississippi, painting landscapes of the Rockies, Tetons, Yellowstone, Yosemite, and the Grand Canyon. Sometimes completed on huge canvases, their paintings were

Native Americans stalk bison in this painting by George Catlin. Note Catlin under wolf skin sketching.
(Courtesy Department of Library Services, American Museum of Natural History)

Paintings such as Thomas Moran's "Grand Canyon of the Yellowstone" dramatized the magnificence of western landscapes.
(Courtesy of Library of Congress)

acknowledged as a source of national pride. They were also some of the first images of the marvels that lay to the west—landscapes on a scale unimaginable to easterners accustomed to rolling hills and mountains that rarely topped timberline.

Among writers, **Henry David Thoreau** holds a position as the preeminent philosopher of American naturalism. Thoreau and **Ralph Waldo Emerson** formed the core of a group of thinkers ascribing to transcendentalism, a philosophy that connected man, material, nature, and spirituality. Their thinking recognized man as an earthly being tied to the necessities of material living, yet whose soul set him apart, enabling him to transcend to a spiritual plane that through nature's truths, would bring him closer to God. Thoreau's famous dictum, "In wildness is the preservation of the World," proclaimed the view that nature (wild, not pastoral) was the appropriate fountain of religion. In *Walden*, Thoreau extolled the virtues of living "deliberately" for two years as a woodcutter at Walden Pond, several miles outside his hometown of Concord, Massachusetts. Transcendentalists celebrated nature as symbiotic with man's sanctity. This thinking inspired the intellectual transition that slowly began to view nature and wilderness as desirable, rather than as ungodly and repugnant.

Henry David Thoreau, author of
Walden and *Civil Disobedience*.
Thoreau set a tone for future
American nature writing.
(Courtesy of Library of Congress)

Several influential writers of the nineteenth century nature movement were better known as painters. Catlin and Cole both wrote of the losses being suffered through the over civilizing of the country, as did **John James Audubon,** whose *Birds of North America* (1827–1838) gained him fame as a proponent of natural beauty. Other writers of the era, starting with James Fenimore Cooper, included Washington Irving, Francis Parkman, Samuel H. Hammond, William Cullen Bryant, and Horace Greeley of "Go west, young man" fame. Consistent throughout all of their writings is the theme that applauds the value of nature in helping to renew the human spirit. Invariably coupled with this sentiment was the concern that the future of wildness in America was relatively bleak.

George Perkins Marsh, in writing *Man and Nature: Or, Physical Geography as Modified by Human Action* (1864) brought another dimension to the human purposes for wildlands. Besides nature's qualities for contemplation and spiritual renewal, Marsh described the benefits that wildlands bring through preventing drought, harboring wildlife, and providing opportunities for recreation. His point that excessive logging prevents effective percolation of storm precipitation—leading instead to runoff, floods, erosion, and drought—indicated that there were viable economic reasons to maintain areas in their natural state. Marsh compared the exploitation of lands in America with similar

John J. Audubon's "Hooping Crane."
Audubon may not have envisioned the
near-extinction of this species when he
made this painting in 1834.
(John James Audubon, Robert Havell,
Engraver, 1834. Gift of Mrs. Walter B. James,
Photograph© Board of Trustees, National
Gallery of Art, Washington)

George Perkins Marsh's book
Man and Nature alerted people
to the dangers of poor land
management practices.
(Courtesy of Library of Congress)

practices that led to the decline of Mediterranean empires. Preservationists embraced Marsh's theories, adding a truly utilitarian purpose to the reasons for saving the wilds.

The Era of Preservation is remembered as that point in U.S. history when a tide of exploitation was first met by waves of opponents bearing rational arguments against the status quo. True evidence of potentially impending disaster sent a wake-up call to the halls of power in Washington, D.C. After eight decades of ensuring transfer of lands to private ownership, the federal government slowly and timorously initiated an experiment in exercising governmental control over certain lands. The Era of Human Management was officially born with the withdrawal of Yellowstone National Park in 1872. Arguments over the best uses of lands, however, split the preservationists, bringing utilitarian conservationism forward as the politically viable compromise position between preservation and development.

Era of Human Management: Evolving Methods of Natural Resource Stewardship

Governmental control of natural resources was a unique concept that was slow to gain favor. For almost a century, the United States had followed a very deliberate policy of putting lands under private ownership. The right to property was deeply imbedded in the Constitution, and property ownership was considered a strong motivation for individuals and groups to seek prosperity. Sale of lands helped feed the federal Treasury in a time before the birth of income taxes. So the idea of withdrawing lands from disposal required some fairly convincing arguments.

All of this calls for a quick explanation of withdrawal and disposal. When the United States acquired territory through purchase or treaty, the federal government automatically became the owner and landlord of those lands. But the government considered it appropriate to turn property over to private ownership, because (a) private property owners would be responsible and motivated to use their land productively, thus stimulating the national economy; (b) land was the most valuable commodity the government possessed, and selling it provided a source of revenue; and (c) the "right to property" was one of the tenets of our Constitution, in itself a rejection of old-world monarchist systems. Disposal was the term used to describe the selling or rededication of government lands to private parties. **Withdrawal,** on the other hand, meant withdrawal from disposal. To withdraw meant either to set aside for government management, or simply to withdraw from entry, meaning "settlers stay out."

During the era of human management, two movements arose, each espousing its vision as the best way to ensure resource viability for the future. Both of the movements were shaped by a larger **progressive movement**, a wave of new thinking that believed in people's ability to combine efficiently scientific methods with industrial and technological innovation to better their lives. Reform movements were sweeping the nation in the latter half of the nineteenth century, including the abolition of slavery, child labor, and labor movements, and the push for better conditions for the urban poor and society's diseased and disadvantaged. Caught up in these social movements of change, those who held preservation and conservation philosophies established followings and forever changed Americans' relationship with their land.

The Preservation Philosophy

The preservation philosophy grew from the backlash against unregulated exploitation, the images in words and pictures of the magnificence of the American landscape, and the guidance of people who tied nature to spirituality.

The philosophy held that resources should be valued in their natural state, that people would be uplifted and invigorated by venturing into wild areas. Practical benefits of wildlands included the security of water resources and wildlife habitat. And **monumentalism**, an exercise in national pride, extolled the virtues of the distinctly American landscape and its wonders. The eventual manifestation of the preservation movement became America's National Parks as well as the many park systems of states throughout the nation.

No single person seems to embody the preservation movement as charismatically as **John Muir**. A Scottish immigrant, Muir was 11 in 1849 when his family moved to a homestead in central Wisconsin. Sternly raised, Muir was taught to farm by beating back the wilds with ax and plow. Hard work and mechanical devices could accomplish this mission, and Muir became adept at labor and designing mechanical agricultural tools. Though he was effective as a farmer and manufacturer, it was the wilds that beckoned Muir, creating an inner struggle that resolved itself in a nearly catastrophic accident. Muir was working in a carriage factory in 1867 when a file slipped from his hand and hit his right eye. His other eye went into sympathetic shock, and he became completely blind. Bandaged and resting in a darkened room, Muir spent six weeks wondering about his future without sight. But his vision recovered, and he was soon off to his true love, the wilderness. Of this turning point in his life, Muir wrote, "God has to nearly kill us sometimes, to teach us lessons."

Muir started out simply by heading south, walking 1,000 miles from Indiana to the Gulf of Mexico, keeping a journal along the way. Malaria kept him from tracking up the Amazon, and he sailed for San Francisco, arriving in 1868. Aiming for "anyplace wild," he was pointed across California's central valley to the Sierra Nevada, the mountains that would become his "range of light" and his celebrated cause for preservation. Muir's writings began to attract a readership, and eventual popularity. His exploration, naturalist's observations, and philosophizing on wildness occurred at a time when America was debating the management of unsettled lands. He was to become one of the most influential

John Muir, founder and first President of the Sierra Club, was a staunch advocate of preserving wild places.
(Courtesy of Library of Congress)

proponents of wilderness preservation, traveling extensively to rally the cause and serving as president of the Sierra Club from its founding in 1892 until his death 22 years later.

Governmental actions were slow in coming. One of the earliest moves was the creation of a preserve in 1832 to protect the warm mineral waters of Hot Springs, Arkansas. This, however, was not a move to preserve nature for the nation's citizens. That distinction has fallen to **Yellowstone** and **Yosemite**, two parks that vie for the title of America's first national park.

In 1864, Congress passed the Yosemite Act, transferring ownership of Yosemite Valley, its immediate surroundings, and the Mariposa Redwood Grove to the State of California for "public use, resort, and recreation." It was stipulated in the act that the valley and big trees be held "inalienable for all time" (U.S., 1864). It took California two years to accept the transfer with its conditions. Fourteen years later, a much larger area of Yosemite was declared a national park, and the Valley and Mariposa Grove were returned from California to federal management as part of the park in 1906.

Yellowstone claims first national park status, having been established by Congress in 1872 to be "dedicated and set apart as a public park or pleasuring ground for the benefit and enjoyment of the people" (U.S., 1872). Yellowstone was massive in size—some 3,300 square miles carved from the Wyoming territory. Congress based its decision on the natural wonders described by the Hayden Survey of 1871 and also upon strategic arguments stating that the high plateau of the Yellowstone region was "worthless" for anything except scenery and tourism. This **worthless lands argument** would be used frequently to defend the park concept against detractors who objected to tying up valuable natural resources for scenic enjoyment alone (Runte, 2010).

Despite its seeming contradiction, the worthless lands argument was necessary to sway staunch resource-developing interests toward the parks idea. Given that commodity extraction and development had dominated land policy in North America for two and a half centuries, the establishment of Yellowstone marked a significant detour from business as usual. For a variety of reasons and causes, America had begun to protect its most cherished monuments.

In the latter years of the nineteenth century and early in the twentieth, Congress would pass legislation creating national parks such as Sequoia (1890), Mt. Rainier (1899), Crater

John Muir shared his vision of preservation with President Teddy Roosevelt during a trip to Yosemite in 1906.
(Courtesy of Library of Congress)

Lake (1902), and Glacier (1910). But for some, the inevitable delay associated with acts of Congress was too slow to ensure protection of resources fast being targeted by tourism promoters and extractive resource developers. Because the political thrust behind national parks still relied on scenic nationalism, protection of less scenic, but certainly important, natural wonders lagged. John F. Lacey, an Iowa congressman, sought to streamline the process of protective designation by pushing a bill through Congress in 1906 that became known as the **Antiquities Act**.

The Antiquities Act was designed primarily to empower the president to withdraw lands and designate them as national monuments through **executive order.** Originally, passage of this act was intended to offer more immediate protection of valuable resources such as the archaeological sites being discovered and overrun by looters in the Southwest. The Antiquities Act noted the preservation of artifacts and objects of scientific value as distinct from scenery and natural marvels. The term **national monuments** was clearly intended to signify the nationwide importance of these areas, and their importance as sources of national pride. And as if timing was everything, the power of the Antiquities Act was delivered smack-dab into the hands of President **Theodore Roosevelt.** Roosevelt interpreted scientific qualities as having geological significance and set about withdrawing large tracts of land for monument designation. Devils Tower, Cinder Cone (later Lassen V.N.P.), Grand Canyon, and Mount Olympus (later Olympic N.P.) were proclaimed under Roosevelt's pen, together with a host of Southwestern cliff dwellings. Preservationists hailed Roosevelt for breaking the tortoise's pace of Congress in withdrawing lands for preservation status. As many national monuments have since been converted to national parks, Roosevelt can be credited with taking the longest strides in establishing a parks system of national and worldwide significance.

Forty-four years after the establishment of Yellowstone, an agency to manage the national parks and monuments was finally organized under the **National Park Service Act of 1916** (more on this later). Preservationism in the era of human management was reaching its golden age. But preservation did not coast to popularity. In the latter nineteenth and early twentieth centuries, the more utilitarian philosophy of conservationism also gained a foothold, and under its own charismatic leadership, eventually led to what we know today as the **national forests**.

The Conservation Philosophy

The conservation philosophy, by its very nature, is as simple to grasp but harder to apply than the clear-cut mandate of preservation. Conservation was equated with wise use. It went beyond preservation to provide for the wise use of resources for the benefit of present and future generations. Best use would be determined by economic, social, aesthetic, and ethical considerations, as appropriate to assure the long range and continued viability of natural resources. The conservation view held the people would forever need forest products, water, minerals, and grazing areas, and opportunities to hunt and view wildlife and engage in outdoor recreation. That these types of uses can at times be incompatible did not stop the conservationists who rallied behind the slogan "to provide…the greatest good for the greatest number for the longest time," which was adopted by the movement's head honcho **Gifford Pinchot.**

It is virtually impossible to tell the story of conservation's rise without describing the activities of Gifford Pinchot. Born into a well-to-do Connecticut family in 1867, Pinchot's father was an early member and vice president of the **American Forestry Association**. Pinchot gained his dad's enthusiasm for forestry and decided on it as his career. The only problem was that there was not a single school of forestry in the United States. Scientific forestry, as it was known, had been developed in Germany, Switzerland, and France. So, ignoring advice that European forestry could not be applied effectively in the United States, but bankrolled by his father, Pinchot left for a year of study under famed forester Dietrich Brandis in Nancy, France. On his return, he immediately set out to demonstrate the newfound methods at an American forest. Pinchot was fortunate to be offered the job of forest manager at George Vanderbilt's Biltmore Estate in North Carolina. Thinking of trees as a crop, Pinchot set about a yearlong demonstration project of thinning and felling trees, selling some, and valuing those that were used for construction and fuel on the estate. Accounting a net profit of over a thousand dollars, Pinchot declared scientific forestry a success and moved on to bigger fish. He opened a forestry-consulting firm in New York and was able to impress his wealthy eastern clients that scientific forestry would work in "improving" the forest while returning profits.

During this period, Congress passed legislation that came to be known as the **Forest Reserve Act of 1891** and the **Forest Management Act (or Organic Act) of 1897.** These two works of legislation led to the withdrawal of lands that have become our national forests, and also to the establishment of an agency (eventually the U.S. Forest Service) to manage them. The Forest Reserve (or Reservation) Act of 1891 was a result of abuses of western public forestlands. Like the later Antiquities Act, it, too, gave the president the power to withdraw public lands from entry and to establish them as reservations for public purposes. Not without controversy, westerners both lauded and decried the act, with its backers claiming that it would curb abuses, and its detractors screaming that resources would be tied up by pencil-nosed-landlords of the eastern bureaucracy. The first three presidents to enjoy the power of the Forest Reserve Act—Benjamin Harrison, Grover Cleveland, and Teddy Roosevelt— withdrew over 100 million acres by 1905, more than half of our present-day national forest system.

The reserves, however, were essentially left unmanaged. Responsibility for their protection fell on the Department of Interior's **General Land Office** (GLO), an agency that, until this point, had only managed the disposal of government lands. The GLO's job had been to handle transfers of federal lands to private individuals, corporations, and states through sales, the Homestead

Act, and the many land grants made for purposes such as schools and railroads. The GLO was essentially a clerking agency not unlike a real estate broker, and the agency had no **appropriation**, expertise, or workforce to deal with the management of forest reserves. Withdrawn from entry, the reserves were legally locked up, barring trespass and use of forest resources within their boundaries. This move, of course, did not sit well at all with the folks residing in proximity to forest reserves. They had grown accustomed to using these forested areas as necessary, and in whatever fashion they saw fit. Soon, the legal restrictions of the Forest Reserve Act were being ignored.

The 1897 Forest Management (Organic) Act grew out of the disharmony resulting from the Forest Reserve Act. It was evident that some sort of regulated use of the forest reserves was necessary, yet there was no structure to perform this function. The Organic Act stipulated the management of the forest reserves and set up the first structure for their administration. The reserves were to be managed to protect their water and timber resources and to provide for the long-term survival of the forests. Timber harvesting was regulated and limited to "dead, matured, or large growth of trees," a phrase that would feature prominently in a lawsuit against clear-cutting on the Monongahela National Forest 76 years later. But still, the act left the administration of the forest reserves under the General Land Office, while over in the Department of Agriculture, a small **Division of Forestry** was soon to gain its new leader, Gifford Pinchot.

Pinchot, in his enthusiastic and relentless manner, lobbied for transfer of management of the forest reserves to his division (already renamed the Bureau of Forestry) within the Department of Agriculture. With the blessing of the American Forestry Association and President Roosevelt, the **Transfer Act of 1905** accomplished this move. Within two years, the Bureau of Forestry was renamed the U.S. Forest Service, with Pinchot serving as its first "**chief.**" Conservation, or the wise-use movement, grew with the development of the national forests and the rise of the profession of forestry to manage them. From endowing the School of Forestry at Yale to heading the agency that was his creation, Pinchot embodied the conservation movement and acted for three decades as its primary spokesman.

Gifford Pinchot with President Teddy Roosevelt. Pinchot's influence with Roosevelt helped launch the U.S. Forest Service.
(Courtesy of Library of Congress)

A Permanent Split

The preservation and conservation movements moved in tandem during the late 1800s and early 1900s. Parks and monuments answered the call of preservationists, and national forests adopted the complexities of sustainable use. Acreage designated for national forests far exceeded that set aside for parks and monuments, reflecting social sentiment that too much absolute protection would stymie economic growth. In the early enthusiasm of the era, it seemed there was room for both philosophies to happily coexist. Muir and Pinchot were even cooperative friends for a time. But preservation and conservation were bound to eventually meet head-on in controversy, and that meeting was reserved for debate over the fate of a little-known pristine and lovely valley in Yosemite National Park called **Hetch Hetchy**.

Hetch Hetchy Valley in Yosemite National Park before it became a reservoir to slake the thirst of a growing San Francisco.
(Courtesy of Yosemite Museum, National Park Service)

Hetch Hetchy, just north of Yosemite Valley, shared many of the characteristics of its southern neighbor, but was not quite as majestic or as well known. Framing the Tuolomne River, Hetch Hetchy offered a perfect reservoir site for the dam-engineering abilities of the early twentieth century. Proponents of the project were primarily the growing city of San Francisco, central valley agriculturalists, and towns looking for cheap sources of electrical power. Pitted against them in the 15-year political war over the valley were Muir and his Sierra Club, and mostly eastern preservationists opposed to the overt violation of a national park. Muir would rage:

> These temple destroyers, devotees of ravaging commercialism, seem to have a perfect contempt for nature, and, instead of lifting their eyes to the God of the Mountains, lift them to the almighty dollar. Dam Hetch Hetchy! As well dam for water tanks the people's cathedrals and churches; for no holier temple has ever been consecrated by the heart of man. (Muir, 1912)

The response of a dam-backing senator from Montana would proclaim that preservationists would rather have the babes of the community suffering anguish and perishing for want of sufficient water than destroy something that they may go once in many years and gaze upon in order to satisfy their aesthetic and exquisite taste for natural beauty. (Wellman, 1987, p. 110)

Pinchot clearly saw water management as the appropriate future for Hetch Hetchy:

As to my attitude regarding the proposed use of Hetch Hetchy but the city of San Francisco...I am fully persuaded that...the injury...by substituting a lake for the present swamp floor of the valley...is altogether unimportant compared with the benefits to be derived from its use as a reservoir. (Nash, 2001, p. 161).

At the end of 1913, Woodrow Wilson approved the bill authorizing construction of the reservoir that would fill Hetch Hetchy. Broken, Muir died a year later. San Francisco got its water and power and would grow to be one of the great cities of the world. Wise-use sentiment had won out, but the loss of Hetch Hetchy spurred the preservation movement to push Congress into establishing the **National Park Service** in 1916. Preservationism would remain forever skeptical of the conservation movement, heeding Muir's warning: "Nothing dollarable is safe, however guarded" (Muir, 1908 in Sierra Club, 2008).

The building of the dam across the Tuolumne River at the entrance to Hetch Hetchy Valley. (Courtesy of Yosemite Museum, National Park Service)

Hetch-Hetchy after flooding, in its new role as reservoir. (Courtesy of Yosemite Museum, National Park Service)

Eras of Multiple Use and Ecosystems Management: Stewardship in the Modern Era

The era of human management spanned the period from Yellowstone's establishment to the early 1960s, when the concept of multiple use was legislated as policy for the U.S. Forest Service. During these years, the federal land estate was carved from the western United States and disposal came to an end. A look at a public lands map of the United States clearly portrays the pattern of the country's settlement and shows that the western portion of the nation was the recipient of the policies of withdrawal. In the West, resource managing agencies such as the National Park Service, U.S. Forest Service, Biological Survey (later the U.S. Fish & Wildlife Service), Bureau of Land Management (from the old GLO), Reclamation Service (later the Bureau of Reclamation), and U.S. Army Corps of Engineers flourished during this era, left to manage lands and resources by a nation generally satisfied with their expertise.

Industrialization, technological know-how, and population increased dramatically in the United States during the twentieth century. The West was officially "closed" and the pioneer period declared over early in the century. The West of the imagination grew to become the West of reality, as Americans' migration continued following the advice of Horace Greeley. Railroads, roads, seagoing access spurred by the canal across the Isthmus of Panama, and eventually airplanes opened the West to the touristing and suburbanizing masses. The twentieth-century settlers came to stay and play, placing new demands on the resources of the West to meet their needs for food, water, housing, electricity, security, and recreation. The federal government responded to these demands, authorizing agencies to build dams, irrigation works, and hydroelectric stations; to cut timber, graze livestock, lease land for vacation cabins, and build trails and campgrounds. In many cases, these developments moved forward with little controversy. In others, such as Hetch Hetchy and Los Angeles' raid on the waters of the Owens Valley, controversy boiled as the projects rolled on.

In essence, manifest destiny led to the evolution of the "superpower," the notion that the United States would not only occupy its slice of the western hemisphere, but also would become the dominant nation on earth. Eventually, the pressures on natural resources to meet these lofty objectives grew, bringing conflicts to a consistently louder pitch. The stakes, so to speak, grew higher. Plans to build dams in the Grand Canyon, **Rachel Carson's** (1962) eloquent warnings against the use of pesticides, outcries over clear-cutting, and near-extinctions of species all spoke to a system of resources overtaxed by the country's demands. A new **environmental movement** grew in the reworked soil of the ancestral progressive movement. The demand for government action was answered by legislation and regulation kindled in controversy and beckoning for compromise. The optimistic concept that natural resources could be "all things to all people" was expressed in the doctrine of multiple use, which was made the legal mandate of the U.S. Forest Service by the Multiple Use and

Sustained Yield Act of 1960. A similar mission was required of the Bureau of Land Management by the **Federal Land Policy and Management Act of 1976.** But giving everyone a small slice of the resources pie left everyone hungry. Compromise in the face of competing demands became the job and eventually the position of Congress and the resource agencies. Able to satisfy nobody, agencies have looked toward a new vision of ecosystems management.

Ecosystems management is a more recent manifestation of the evolution of our ethic toward the land and the earth's resources. In the century and a half since Catlin and Thoreau, Americans have wrestled with their perceptions and vision for a dynamic land that holds meaning to the roots of their souls. The idea that we are integrated with an ecosystem, and should manage it as a peer rather than as a master, is gaining a foothold and struggling with its own meaningful definition. Exactly where we will eventually lead ourselves is hard to predict. But we do know that our ethic toward the land continues to evolve.

Suggested Readings

Carson, R. (1962). *Silent spring.* Boston: Houghton Mifflin.

Chiras, D. D., & Reganold, J. P. (2009). *Natural resource conservation: Management for a sustainable future* (10th ed.). Upper Saddle River, NJ: Prentice-Hall.

Conlin, J. R. (2009). *The American past: A survey of American history, volumes 1 & 2* (9th ed.). Belmont: Wadsworth Publishing.

Crosby, A. W. (1986). *Ecological imperialism: The biological expansion of Europe, 900-1900.* New York: Cambridge University Press.

Dana, S. T., & Fairfax, S. K. (1980). *Forest and range policy* (2nd ed.). New York: McGraw-Hill.

Diamond, J. (1997). *Guns, germs, and steel.* New York: W. W. Norton.

Emerson, R. W. (1981). Nature. In C. Bode (Ed.), *The portable Emerson.* New York: Viking Penguin.

Engbeck, J. H., Jr. (1973). *The enduring giants.* Berkeley, CA: University Extension, University of California-Berkeley.

Gorte, R. W. (1999, October). Multiple use in the national forests: Rise and fall or evolution? *Journal of Forestry, 97*(10):19–23.

Hays, S. P. (1959). *Conservation and the gospel of efficiency: The progressive conservation movement, 1890–1920.* Cambridge, MA: Harvard University Press.

Huth, H. (1957). *Nature and the American: Three centuries of changing attitudes.* Berkeley, CA: University of California Press.

Marsh, G. P. (1965). *Man and nature: Or physical geography as modified by human action.* Cambridge, MA: Harvard University Press. (Original work published 1864)

Muir, J. (1912). *The Yosemite.* New York: The Century Co.

Nash, R. (Ed.), (1976). *The American environment: Readings in the history of conservation.* Reading, MA: Addison-Wesley Publishing.

Nash, R. (2001). *Wilderness and the American mind* (4th ed.). New Haven, CT: Yale University Press.

Pyne, S. (1997). *Fire in America: A cultural history of wildland and rural fire.* Seattle: University of Washington Press.

Robbins, R. M. (1962). *Our landed heritage: The public domain, 1776–1936.* Lincoln, NE: University of Nebraska Press.

Runte, A. (2010). *National parks: The American experience* (4th ed.). Lanham, MD: Taylor Trade Pub.

Sierra Club. (2008). Hetch Hetchy. Retrieved from http://www.sierraclub.org/ca/hetchhetchy/timeline.asp

Thoreau, H. D. (1972). *The Maine woods.* Princeton, NJ: Princeton University Press.

Thoreau, H. D. (1971). *Walden.* Princeton, NJ: Princeton University Press.

U.S., Statutes at Large, 13 (1864):325.

U.S., Statutes at Large, 17 (1872): 32-33.

Wellman, J.D. (1987). *Wildland recreation policy: An introduction.* New York, NY: John Wiley & Sons

Federal Resource Managing Agencies and Authority

Federal Lands Classifications

The evolution of our American land ethic brought forth several distinct resource management philosophies. Principal among these were preservation and conservation. In Chapter 4, the rise of the National Park Service (NPS) from the preservation movement and the development of the United States Forest Service (USFS) from the conservation movement were described. The two are probably the best known of the federal resource land management agencies. But preservation and conservation spawned a number of other specialist agencies to deal with various resource lands management functions. Let's introduce them here, and categorize them by their principal **missions**.

There are a number of other resource managing or regulatory agencies with authority over a wide variety of resource management functions. However, the agencies listed in Table 1 are the principal land-managing agencies of the federal government. Combined, they have management responsibility for roughly one third of the land in the United States, primarily located in the West and Alaska. A very brief description of each follows Table 5.1.

Table 5.1

Principal Federal Resource Management Agencies

Mission	Agency	Department
Reserved (Preservation)	National Park Service (NPS)	Interior
	U.S. Fish & Wildlife Service (USFWS)	Interior
Multiple Use (Conservation)	Bureau of Land Management (BLM)	Interior
	U.S. Forest Service (USFS)	Agriculture
Water Project	Bureau of Reclamation (BR)	Interior
	U.S. Army Corps of Engineers (COE)	Defense
Special Use	Bureau of Indian Affairs (BIA)	Interior
	Military Lands	Defense
	Department of Energy (DOE)	Energy
	National Oceanic & Atmospheric Administration (NOAA)	Commerce

National Park Service (NPS)

The NPS is responsible for national parks, monuments, historic sites, seashores, recreation areas, preserves, and other significant properties. It manages lands ranging from Haleakala Volcano on Maui to the White House. With approximately 84 million acres, the NPS ranks fourth in acreage managed among the federal lands agencies.

U.S. Fish and Wildlife Service (USFWS)

The USFWS manages the National Wildlife Refuge System and has regulatory authority for a broad array of wildlife laws and treaties, including the Endangered Species Act. Managing roughly 90 million acres, the USFWS is the third largest agency measured by acreage.

Bureau of Land Management (BLM)

The BLM manages what are known as the public domain lands. Leftover "lands that nobody wanted," the public domain includes those lands that remained in federal possession following the many disposal and withdrawal policies. Concentrated in the Great Basin of the West, these lands were not particularly attractive for homesteading, forestry, or other uses. Public Domain lands remained under the General Land Office (GLO) until the BLM was established in 1946. Managing approximately 270 million acres, and having mineral rights on 570 million acres, the BLM is responsible for more acreage than any other federal agency.

U.S. Forest Service (USFS)

The USFS manages the National Forest System. More than 150 national forests cover almost 200 million acres, making the USFS second to the BLM in acreage managed. The USFS also manages some national recreation areas such as the Sawtooth in Idaho and a national monument at Mount St. Helens on the Gifford Pinchot National Forest in southern Washington.

Bureau of Reclamation (BR) & U.S. Army Corps of Engineers (COE)

The BR and the COE are both water managing agencies significant for their programs of flood control, irrigation, hydroelectric power generation, and outdoor recreation (COE manages recreation on its water projects, while the BR generally transfers that responsibility to other agencies such as the NPS and the USFS). Both agencies are well known (and controversial) for the large dams and reservoirs they manage. The COE also manages 11 million acres surrounding the reservoirs and waterways it controls.

Bureau of Indian Affairs (BIA)

The BIA assists in the management of a number of reservations for the Native American Nations. Gradually claiming more autonomy in their resource management activities, the Nations are important producers of forest and agricultural products, minerals development, and outdoor recreation and tourism. Native American lands account for roughly 55 million acres of the national estate.

Department of Defense

The different branches of the military all manage resource lands on bases both large and small. As base closures accelerated in the 1990s, the military's presence as a land manager has been reduced in some areas, but increased in others. Currently, the Department of Defense manages approximately 30 million acres of military land. Its role as a resource manager is gradually being given greater emphasis in all branches of the service.

Department of Energy (DOE)

The DOE manages approximately 2.4 million acres of research facilities and other energy-related sites. These facilities range from nuclear reactors to research and development labs, oil reserves, and cleanup sites.

National Oceanic and Atmospheric Administration (NOAA)

The NOAA manages the National Marine Sanctuary System, consisting of 13 national marine sanctuaries and the Northwestern Hawaiian Islands Marine National Monument. NOAA also heads the National Estuarine Research Reserve System with 28 reserves functioning as laboratories for long-term research, education, and enhancing coastal stewardship.

Other Important Federal Regulators: EPA and CEQ

Environmental Protection Agency (EPA)

The EPA was established in 1970 with little fanfare. Occurring in the midst of a Nixon Administration plan to reorganize federal resource agencies, the birth of the EPA seemed a minor step in consolidating federal pollution-control efforts. Before EPA, 44 agencies in nine different departments dealt with the many pollution control and mitigation laws. EPA became the funnel through which many environmental protection laws were to be poured, ever increasing the regulatory authority of the agency. The Clean Air Act, Clean Water Act, pesticide control, and toxic waste regulation all fell under the regulatory authority of the EPA. Regulation of greenhouse gas emissions tenuously became a role for the EPA, though the Bush Administration and then the Republican-majority House of Representatives elected in 2010 have argued there is not yet sufficient science to merit EPA's authority over greenhouse gas pollution. Since its inception, the EPA has become a major presence in the regulation of natural resources. The EPA's regulatory authorities have been contentious issues, as Republican and Democratic administrations vie to limit or expand EPA's powers.

Council on Environmental Quality (CEQ)

The CEQ was established under the **National Environmental Policy Act of 1970** (NEPA). The CEQ was designed to interpret NEPA through the issuance of regulations on the act's implementation. The CEQ is composed of three members appointed by the president, plus a small staff in charge of handling mostly legal work involving the NEPA and environmental regulation. The CEQ's guidelines on the procedural implementation of the NEPA have been strongly upheld by the Supreme Court, opening avenues for environmental litigation brought against agencies for not appropriately following NEPA procedures.

Congressional Committees and Subcommittees

A number of committees in the U.S. Senate and House of Representatives have responsibility for dealing with natural resource and environmental issues (Table 5.2). Committees are the arena in which proposed legislation is first considered for adoption. It is also through committee work that Congress conducts its oversight function, monitoring the implementation of laws and regulations for compliance. Following the activities of committees provides a useful window into the workings of the legislature. Today access to information on committee work is more available than ever before, thanks to the Internet. Check Appendix A for a listing of directories that provide access to Congressional committee Web sites.

Resource Agency Functions

Land management is one of the principal responsibilities of the federal agencies noted in this chapter. Their other functions include (a) **regulatory authority**, (b) **planning**, and (c) **assistance.** An agency's land management function is considered its mission, broadly categorized in Table 5.1. Its regulatory authority is an important part of an agency's mission. Regulatory authority is the means by which agencies manage resources and activities that may or may not actually be on lands under their direct control.

Another major function of the federal agencies is planning, particularly under the requirements of the National Environmental Policy Act (NEPA) of 1970. Finally, assistance is another major duty of federal resource agencies. It is through assistance that agencies sponsor grants to other governmental and private entities for many types of research and resource development programs.

Table 5.2

*Selected Congressional Committees and Subcommittees with
Natural Resource and Environmental Responsibilities*

Senate

Committee on Environment and Public Works
    Subcommittee on Clean Air and Nuclear Safety
    Subcommittee on Water and Wildlife
    Subcommittee on Superfund, Toxics and Environmental Health
    Subcommittee on Transportation and Infrastructure
    Subcommittee on Green Jobs and the New Economy

Committee on Agriculture, Nutrition and Forestry
    Subcommittee on Conservation, Forestry and Credit

Committee on Commerce, Science, and Transportation
    Subcommittee on Oceans, Atmosphere, Fisheries and Coast Guard

Committee on Energy and Natural Resources
    Subcommittee on Energy
    Subcommittee on Water and Power
    Subcommittee on Public Lands and Forests
    Subcommittee on National Parks

House of Representatives

Committee on Energy and Commerce
    Subcommittee on Energy and Power
    Subcommittee on Environment and the Economy

Committee on Natural Resources
    Subcommittee on Energy and Minerals
    Subcommittee on Fisheries, Wildlife, Oceans and Insular Affairs
    Subcommittee on National Parks, Forests and Public Lands
    Subcommittee on Water and Power

Committee on Science, Space, and Technology
    Subcommittee on Energy and Environment

Committee on Appropriations
    Subcommittee on Agriculture, Rural Development, Food and Drug   Administration
    Subcommittee on Energy and Water Development
    Subcommittee on Interior and Environment

Committee on Agriculture
    Subcommittee on Conservation, Energy, and Forestry

chapter six

Civics 1A and the Federal Regulatory Process

In the previous chapter, a group of federal resource management agencies was introduced. These agencies manage a lot of the resources on which we depend, such as water and timber, grazing and minerals. These folks also manage many of the areas in which we recreate, or will recreate in the future. Throw in the management of much of the nation's wildlife, and hopefully you can see the value in knowing a little more about them.

Before launching into a closer view of these agencies, however, it is probably time for a very quick review of the origin of their authority, and how we as citizens are part of that authority. To get through the really hard part first, here is a quiz you need to take. No grade. You should know the answers to all of these. In case you don't, study the answers that follow!

Civics 1A Quiz

1. What is the ultimate authority over government in the United States?
2. What is the guiding document that outlines the rules of that authority?
3. What are the three branches of the federal government?
4. What are the two components of the legislature?
5. How many senators are there? How many from each state? How do they get into office? What is the length of their term?
6. How many representatives are there? How many from each state? How do they get into office? What is the length of their term?
7. What branch of the federal government is headed by the president? How does that person get into office? What is the length of the president's term?
8. What is the third branch called? How many levels are there in this branch?
9. How many members are there on the Supreme Court? How do they get into their "seats"? What is the length of their term?

10. What are the names of the other two levels of the federal judiciary? How do the members of these levels come into their seats? What is the length of their terms?
11. What is a piece of proposed legislation called? A passed legislative act?
12. What do we call a directive given by the president?
13. What do we call a directive given by the Court?
14. What is the name of the group in the executive branch that has responsibility for the administration of agencies?
15. Name 10 of these departments. What are the department heads called?
16. From where do these departments get their orders?
17. What do we call the directives that these departments and their agencies prepare in response to these orders?
18. Where would you be able to read proposed federal rules?
19. Where would you go to look for the rules of the federal government?
20. Do you, as a citizen, have any right to comment on proposed federal rules?
21. Bonus! What are the five levels of government in the United States?

Civics 1A Quiz Answers

1. The people.
2. The Constitution.
3. Legislative, Executive, Judiciary.
4. The legislative branch, or Congress, is composed of the House of Representatives and the Senate.
5. 100. 2. They are elected. 6 years.
6. 435. It is based on the population of the states. California has the most with 53. 7 states have the least, with 1 each. Washington, D.C., and 4 territories also have 1 representative each. They are elected. 2 years.
7. Executive. Elected. 4 years.
8. Judiciary. Three main levels.
9. Nine. They are appointed by the president and must be confirmed by the Senate. For life.
10. U.S. Circuit Courts of Appeals (there are 13 of them), District Courts (there are 94 of them). They are appointed by the president and must be confirmed by the Senate. For life.
11. A bill. A statute or law.
12. An executive order.
13. A decision.
14. The cabinet.
15. Departments of State, Defense, Homeland Security, Health & Human Services, Education, Commerce, Interior, Agriculture, Labor, Energy, Justice, Transportation, Housing and Urban Development, Treasury, and Veterans Affairs. Secretaries except Justice, which is headed by the Attorney General. There are 15 cabinet posts.

16. Through Statutes (Legislative), Executive Orders (Executive), and Decisions (Judiciary).
17. Federal regulations.
18. In the Federal Register.
19. The Code of Federal Regulations (CFR).
20. Yes. The opportunities to review and comment on proposed regulations are stipulated under the "notice and comment" requirements of the Federal Register Act of 1935 and the Administrative Procedures Act of 1946.
21. Federal, State, County, Municipal, Special District.

Not bad! Let's hope.... I only force you to suffer through the "Quiz of 21" because I've been amazed in the past by the number of students in my university classes who couldn't answer many of these questions. They're pretty basic—and important, too, because they are the basis of a government "by the people." A government by the people requires people who understand it.

There is much about these agency and regulatory matters that becomes important in our study of natural resources and the informed citizen. You'll see how these processes work in relation to government management of natural resources. But first, let's drop back again and have a look at how these agencies came to be, and where their power lies.

The Rise of Administrative Agencies and Regulations

Remember the founding fathers? The men who drafted and ratified the Constitution included in Article 1, Section 8, a statement to "provide for the ... general Welfare." This was a rather broad stroke, which generally meant that government could take actions that would work in the best interests of the citizens. Early on, the executive branch created the secretary of state position to specialize on matters dealing with foreign nations. Cabinet positions were also created for secretaries of war, treasury, and the interior. The General Land Office, created in 1812, was one of the early agencies given authority for dealing with government land transfers (disposal). But agencies and the regulatory process were slow to evolve. Congress was responsible for the laws of the land and their oversight. Many in Congress felt that the creation of agencies and delegation of responsibilities to them would weaken Congress' power and was not constitutionally legitimate. During its first 100 years, there were no regulatory agencies, as we now know them, in the United States.

Toward the latter part of the nineteenth century, it was becoming apparent that the job of running the country was becoming too complex. Population growth, control over distant territory and resources, increased industrialism, transportation, commerce, and a citizenry bent on social reform had turned into a cauldron of activity that was not foreseen by the founding fathers. So Congress debated its way to a change of heart and authorized the Interstate

Commerce Commission (ICC) under the Interstate Commerce Act of 1887. The Interstate Commerce Act was a response to the railroad industry's power over transportation and shipping as well as the many state regulations that varied among the railroads crossing state borders. In an attempt to handle the mess, Congress decided to let a specialist agency (the ICC) iron out the details. Regardless of the early lack of success of the ICC, Congress had opened a new chapter in its way of doing business. Administrative agencies could serve a valuable purpose, and they were here to stay.

The administrative agencies provided numerous benefits to a government overstretched by the business of running the country. Two values of agencies were particularly useful: (a) agencies could specialize and work on problems that were too complex or burdensome for Congress, and (b) agencies could be used to fill in the details of legislation that often was written in a vague and politically innocuous fashion.

Complex problems rose dramatically in the nineteenth century. Congress was increasingly called upon to deal with issues such as the regulation of railroads, labor struggles, and the management of distant lands being set aside as parks, monuments, and reserves. Passing laws could not offer the best solution to these problems as the specifics were often beyond the skills of legislators. The operations of land management, railroad regulation, and other activities required personnel with expertise and a management structure to organize their work. Agencies could meet this need. Once authorized, agencies could carry Congress' intentions into action. Agency personnel could focus on specific problems and give them their attention, whereas earlier Congress had only been able to cast a small piece of divided attention toward any one issue. Agencies, in the progressive view, would be more efficient and effective.

An obvious extra benefit of creating administrative agencies soon became apparent. If agencies were thrust on the front lines to deal with the nitty-gritty of thorny political and management issues, they could also deflect some of the political heat that elected officials generally absorbed in taking stands on issues. Agency personnel would be employed, not elected. They would not be subjected to voters' scorn and cast out of office for doing politically unpopular work. The agencies could act as the shock absorber for elected officials from the congressman representing Wyoming to the president. Legislation and executive orders could be written in a manner more politically acceptable or slippery. It was the beginning of the "Teflon effect." Congress could write and pass vague legislation and then ask the cabinet secretaries to direct their agencies to prepare regulations, or fill in the details. This practice helped insulate elected officials from their electorate. They could claim that any onerous regulations placed on their constituents were the work of the agencies, and were not their intent at all. Agencies and regulations became important aspects of the rise of the "career politicians." Further adding to Congress' ability to pass vague legislation was the use of the federal judiciary to fill in the details. When vague statutes or their explanatory regulations were directly challenged, the judiciary would be called on to make a ruling, and the details were thus provided. Judges could not be thrown out of office because they were appointed for life, and they were immune from prosecution in fulfilling their duties. The agencies and regulatory process paved the way for the bureaucratization of government. In addition, agencies developed their own mechanisms for success and survival, in effect creating a fourth branch of government: the **Administrative Bureaucracy**.

The administrative bureaucracy is an enormous block of agencies that carry out the regulatory and management functions of government. Department and often agency heads are appointed by the presidential administration, making them subject to change according to the results of quadrennial elections. But most of the personnel in these agencies are career civil service employees who are protected by the regulations of the Civil Service. Advancement, promotions, benefits, and retirement plans all provide motivations to employees who find that supporting the agency is the best means to achieve job security and progress up the career ladder. They are motivated to support their agencies and the regulations that support that mission. These personal motivations are one of the supporting blocks of agency strength. The strength and well being of the agency equates with the welfare of its employees. Thus the mission of their agency becomes the employees' prime directive. This drive helps agencies to develop their strength, and also causes them to resist change. Though governed by the people and the three branches of government, the administrative agencies are able to breathe a life of their own.

The purpose of this chapter has been to review and remind us of the structure of the federal government. Understanding the relationships between the branches of government, the people, and the Constitution is important if we're going to start dealing with the field-level implementation of federal regulations and management of natural resources. A basic knowledge of the workings of these systems will help an informed citizen better understand the issues that we face. Consequently, when you're ready to take a stand on an issue, you'll know the avenues to pursue in order to be effective.

Suggested Readings

Edwards, D. V. (1988). *The American political experience: An introduction to government* (4th ed.). Englewood Cliffs, NJ: Prentice-Hall.

Meyerson, M. I. (2008). *Liberty's blueprint.* New York: Basic Books.

Smith, Z. A. (2009). *The environmental policy paradox* (5th ed.). Upper Saddle River, NJ: Prentice-Hall.

Wilson, J. Q., & Dilulio, J. J. (2010). *American government: Institutions and policies* (12th ed.). Boston, MA: Houghton Mifflin Harcourt.

chapter seven

Federal Agencies
The National Park Service

Protector of the "Crown Jewels"

Some people have called them "America's Crown Jewels." Others have said they are "America's Best Idea." Showpieces of a nation, America's national parks include some of our most precious lands. The marks of Thoreau, Muir, and Catlin are seen in these places. To many, they are the cathedrals of a nonsecular spirituality, monuments that have helped us to define ourselves. Their protection has been entrusted to an agency created forty-four years after the establishment of Yellowstone. The National Park Service, organized in 1916, was directed

> ..to conserve the scenery and the natural and historic objects and the wildlife therein and to provide for the enjoyment of the same in such manner and by such means as will leave them unimpaired for the enjoyment of future generations. (National Park Service Act, 1916)

No clause better defines the mission of the National Park Service (NPS). Written in the statute that authorized the agency, the statement implies a pair of conflicting objectives. First, "conserve the scenery..." is read to mean keep the parks as they are, protect them. Second, "provide for the enjoyment..." tells the agency to play host, to maintain a perpetual open house for all who might shelter there. Not explained in the National Park Service Act of 1916 is how to "conserve" the parks when the "future generations" stop by to visit them more than 300 million times every year. We still wrestle with this question. For example, in 2001, Clinton Administration policy stated that when the agency's goals were in conflict, "conservation is to be predominant." Under George

Bush, the policy was altered to reflect an "even balance" between conservation and public use.

Early Development of the NPS

The birth of the agency destined to manage the national parks and monuments is in itself an interesting bit of history. Established by individual acts of Congress, 12 national parks were managed by the Department of the Interior at the beginning of 1916. Three more were under consideration in pending legislation. Additionally, 19 national monuments and two reserves had been set aside, comprising a block of federally "preserved" lands totaling 4.6 million acres. Lacking a workforce to manage them, the department had enlisted the Army to care for some of the parks, and in other cases, parks and monuments relied on the volunteer efforts of locals to keep an eye on the resources so valued by the distant federal government.

Parks had become tourist attractions from the outset. The railroad industry recognized the potential income from park-bound passengers, laying down spur rails to Yellowstone, Glacier, and Grand Canyon and constructing magnificent hotels to pamper a cash-laden clientele. In country too rough for railroads, stage lines bumped sightseers to and through the parks' gates, en route to recently built hotels and stores centered on the parks' main attractions. Tourist-based entrepreneurship flourished, spurring competition among outfits vying for visitors' bucks. Unorganized and unregulated, the first generation of park visitors and their caterers began to take a toll on the very resources they came to behold. Beyond tourist threats, parks in some cases were still open to unregulated grazing, timber, and mineral operations. And finally, the authorization of the dam across the Hetch Hetchy Valley in Yosemite National Park galvanized political interest from those who now recognized even the government as a threat to the national parks.

In 1914, a California businessman by the name of **Stephen Mather** wrote to a fellow U.C.–Berkeley alumnus named **Franklin K. Lane**, who happened to be serving as Secretary of the Interior. Mather, having made a small fortune in the mining of borax, had joined the Sierra Club and begun traveling in the Sierras as a diversion from the rigors of his business. In his letter to Lane, he angrily described the abuses and damage occurring at Yosemite and Sequoia National Parks. Recognizing that he may have stumbled on the right man for the job, Lane penned his now famous reply: "Dear Steve, If you don't like the way the national parks are being run, come on down to Washington and run them yourself." On condition that Lane grant him an assistant to handle the red tape, Mather agreed to serve the parks within the department. He and a young Berkeley-educated lawyer from Bishop, California, **Horace Albright**, went to work on the politics of establishing an agency to manage the parks and monuments. Two years later, Mather was in the high country in late August when an act to create the National Park Service was signed. Limited at first by the NPS Act's $19,500 annual appropriation ceiling, Mather and Albright would set about steering the early development of the NPS until Mather's death in 1930 and Albright's return to private business in 1933.Their vision and direction did more to chart the path of the NPS than any other influence in the nine-plus decades that have followed.

Mather recognized that the strength of his fledgling agency depended on a base of political support larger than the intellectual elite who brought the parks into being. What better way to sell the national parks to the people than to bring the people to the national parks? By raising a group of park lovers, the park service would also be establishing a group of political supporters. But bringing people to the parks presented a variety of problems in the early days of the NPS. First, there was the problem that people visiting these parks in great numbers would carelessly damage resources, and that the freedom they would choose to exercise in parks would overrun efforts at control. Second, there was the problem that civilized visitors would require civilized surroundings, needing food, shelter, and sanitation. Mather himself noted that scenery was rather unnoticeable to someone who had just

Stephen Mather was the driving force behind the establishment and early development of the National Park Service.
(Courtesy of Library of Congress)

spent a hungry, sleepless night on cold, hard ground. The accommodations that visitors would need were indeed part of the problem in the parks: competing hotels building bigger and better non-park attractions to lure customers. For Mather, the solution to these issues boiled down to controlled use, encouraging mass visitation to controllable surroundings. The proliferation of assembly-line automobiles provided part of the answer.

The automobile, Mather reasoned, provided a means of personal conveyance that would allow large numbers of visitors. These "tin lizzies" only needed roads to get to and into the parks. Once the cars got there, those roads would also provide a form of control, because autos weren't very effective at crossing wildlands without them. Thus roads would provide access corridors, leaving the majority of parklands undisturbed. So Mather went before Congress to testify in favor of appropriations to build roads. No sooner had early roads been put in place than the railroad companies and dude ranches raised objections: The automobiles, it seemed, were taking away their customers. This was the beginning of the NPS's persistent battle over access. Wilderness devotees abhorred the automobile, while the auto industry and groups such as the American Automobile Association rallied to support roads. Mather felt the brunt of the NPS Act's phrase "...in such manner and by such means..." The seesaw struggle between wilderness preservation and roads was under way.

A second thorny problem facing the NPS was the explosion of tourist "services" offered in many parks. Capitalist competition had brought numerous businesses that provided everything from food and lodging to amusements. Mather saw competition as the enemy. So long as different companies could operate in parks, they would continue to try to outdo one another competing for tourist dollars. So he proposed the concept of a "**regulated monopoly**," or **park concessions**, to reduce the number of businesses and their resultant competition within parks. Under this model, the NPS would license specific concessions, providing needed visitor services such as lodging, meals, and guiding. In return, the concessions would enjoy monopolistic rights—their ability to gouge limited only by their operating contracts with the NPS. Mather's plan produced results. Many flimflam entertainments were removed from parks. But the reigning concessionaires proved to be tough partners. Arguing for their need to turn a profit in what was often a fairly brief tourist season, concessions have continually pressed the NPS for opportunities to dish out more goods and services to ever-greater numbers of visitors. Like roads for access, concessions marked the birth of another love-hate relationship for a National Park Service charged to "provide for the enjoyment..."

Another major difficulty facing the NPS was evident in the numerous loopholes cut into legislation that authorized many parks. Specific resources were often singled out for continued development within park boundaries. In some cases, minerals could still be mined, trees logged, meadows grazed, and wildlife hunted. The worthless lands argument used to promote the creation of parks had also left an impression that scenery was the major resource on display in the parks. Bowing to political pressure, certain pieces of park authorizing legislation had protected pre-existing commodity uses. Scenery, so it was thought, could survive a little bit of continued "wise use." But commodity extraction could not be continually compatible with park purposes, as defined by the NPS Act. The agency and its supporters would turn again to Congress to amend the original legislation for many parks, restricting commodity uses and strengthening the NPS's **preservation mandate.**

Types of Management Areas

This flexibility in legislation is an important point. What Congress giveth, Congress can taketh away. We must all recognize that parks are only ideas— ideas that we, at this point in history, are supporting as a necessary part of our human landscape. How long the idea will carry into our future is hard to say. But we do know that at times in our past, parks have served purposes other than preservation and recreation, such as the reservoir in Hetch Hetchy and timber operations in Olympic National Park. Not all units of the National Park Service were created equal. Originally, parks were withdrawn by acts of Congress, and monuments were withdrawn by executive order. Over the years, the NPS has assumed management of a variety of other types of nationally significant resources, including National Historic Sites, National Recreation Areas, and Wild and Scenic Rivers. Today the NPS manages a wide variety of natural, prehistoric, historic, and recreation resources. Their types can be organized as follows:

Natural Areas: National Parks, National Monuments, National Preserves

These areas have distinctive scenic and scientific value. Natural areas include the "old line" national parks and monuments, including Yellowstone, Yosemite, Sequoia-Kings Canyon, Glacier, Hawaii Volcanoes, Crater Lake, Grand Canyon, Devil's Tower, and Mesa Verde. The natural areas also include most of the NPS-managed wilderness areas, accounting for 44 million of the U.S.'s 110 million–acre Wilderness Preservation System. Natural areas are accorded the highest levels of resource protection among NPS units. Some resource extraction has been permitted in national monuments, such as mining in Death Valley NM (now NP). The 1987 legislation authorizing Great Basin NP in Nevada (switched from USFS to NPS) provided for a 20-year continuation of existing grazing leases within the new park. In addition, hunting is permitted on national preserves such as Big Thicket Preserve in eastern Texas. Preservation within the borders of NPS natural areas is a major focus of management. Increasing visitation and resource threats from outside park boundaries (such as air pollution and water management) create some of the biggest headaches for the NPS's preservation function.

Military architecture at headquarters in Yellowstone National Park from times when the Cavalry served as the Park's first caretaker.
(Photo by Steve Dennis)

Historical Areas: National Historical Sites, National Historical Parks, National Battlefields, National Memorials, National Cemeteries

The NPS got into the custodianship of historic sites upon passage of the Historic Sites Act of 1935, which transferred management of a number of historic sites to the agency. Primarily located on the East Coast, and in the South, and the Midwest, these NPS units include historic sites such as Washington's home at Mt. Vernon, Jefferson's estate–Monticello, Colonial Williamsburg, Jamestown, and the Liberty Bell in Philadelphia's Independence Hall. Vicksburg, Gettysburg, and Yorktown are examples of military battlefield parks. National memorials include the Lincoln and Jefferson Memorials in Washington D.C., and the U.S.S. *Arizona* Memorial in Pearl Harbor. National Cemeteries such as the Gettysburg National Military Park and the Little Bighorn Battlefield National Monument are also under NPS management.

Old Faithful Geyser, a symbol of American National Parks.
(David E. Simcox Collection)

Recreation Areas: National Recreation Areas, National Rivers, National Lakeshores and Seashores, National Parkways, National Trails

Recreation areas are managed to provide recreation opportunities on lands that may not possess the magnificence of the national parks, yet are exceptional for their outdoor recreation resources. In some cases these lands have been transferred to the NPS through legislation authorizing construction of reservoirs. Glen Canyon National Recreation Area and Lake Mead NRA on the Colorado River are examples. Other national recreation areas include the newer urban and "gateway" areas consolidated from dispersed federal lands around New York Harbor (Gateway NRA) and San Francisco Bay (Golden Gate NRA). The NPS inherited many of the nation's wild and scenic rivers, originally authorized under the 1968 Wild and Scenic Rivers Act. Sections of the Upper Missouri, Rio Grande, and Snake rivers are examples of the 166 wild and scenic rivers stretching some 11,400 miles. National lake and seashores include Pictured Rocks on Lake Superior, Cape Hatteras on the Atlantic, and Point Reyes on the Pacific. National parkways include the famed Blue Ridge Parkway in Virginia, and the John D. Rockefeller, Jr. Memorial Parkway linking Grand Teton and Yellowstone National Parks. National scenic, historic, and recreational trails, authorized by the National Trails System Act of 1968, comprise thousands of miles of linear parklands primarily administered by the NPS. Best known of the NPS-managed national trails are the Appalachian National Scenic Trail, and the Lewis and Clark National Historic Trail.

(Mental exercise: Name as many units of the NPS as you can. Try not to get these mixed up with state parks, national forests, etc. How many can you name?)

Growth of the Agency and Subsequent Controversies

The NPS has experienced several growth spurts and heydays. Before the agency was established, the initial boom came with the political legitimacy of preservation by Congress that created the first parks. Roosevelt's bold wielding of the Antiquities Act increased the number of national monuments. After the NPS Act of 1916, Congress continued to pass park legislation, prompted by drives to protect the Grand Tetons, Everglades, and Great Smoky and Shenandoah Mountains. People liked their national parks, and preservationists pursued park legislation as a means to protect significant natural resources. The 1935 Historic Sites Act expanded the NPS mission to include protection and interpretation of a previously unorganized block of historic sites, many in dire need of repair. Also, in the depression era of the thirties, Roosevelt's Work Projects Administration's (WPA's) Civilian Conservation Corps (CCC) was put to work aggressively building roads, bridges, trails, and structures within national parks and monuments. Many of these developments are still in active use today. World War II brought a slowdown to the NPS, but postwar prosperity sparked a recreation boom never before encountered by the parks. Forty-hour workweeks, summer vacations, and chromed, finned gas hogs brought Americans to the parks in herds. Answering the call of the wilds, and encouraged again by the American Automobile Association, in 1956 the NPS launched "Mission 66," a system-wide expenditure and development program aimed at increasing access, visitor services, and accommodations (particularly auto campgrounds) within the parks over the next decade. As with the prior CCC projects, many parks bear the stamp of the Mission 66 developments.

Unregulated auto camping in Yosemite Valley damaged meadows and brought about new thinking in campground design.
(Courtesy of Yosemite Museum, National Park Service)

The Civilian Conservation
Corps worked on numerous
park development projects in
the 1930s.
(Courtesy of Yosemite Museum,
National Park Service)

In the early 1960s, Congress answered a national call to study the conditions of outdoor recreation opportunities in America. The resulting **Outdoor Recreation Resources Review Commission** published the **ORRRC Report** in 1962. The commission called for the establishment of a fund to finance further park and recreation area purchases and developments. The answer to this call was the **Land and Water Conservation Fund Act of 1965.** Originally built through motorboat fuel taxes, surplus land sales, and entrance and user fees to federal recreation areas, the L&WCF gave a boost to NPS land acquisitions. The addition of revenues from federal offshore oil leases improved the cash pool, and the NPS became the major resource agency beneficiary. Until 1980, the L&WCF provided a steady revenue stream to an NPS that could no longer obtain lands through simple withdrawal. Never directly buying property until the 1959 purchase of Minuteman National Historic Monument, park acquisition costs had steadily risen to a crescendo in 1978 with the $300 million purchase of mostly cut-over lands that increased the size of **Redwood National Park** in California. The L&WCF annual appropriations have fluctuated with the politics of Washington, D.C., ranging from lows of near $300 million to highs near $1 billion.

The last major expansion for the NPS occurred in 1978 through an administrative response to the Alaska Native Claims Settlement Act of 1971. Under the settlement act's section 17(d)(2), the federal government was to study some 80 million acres of lands in Alaska and have Congress recommend which should be managed under the NPS, USFS, USF&WS, and as wild and scenic rivers. The deadline for congressional action expired in December 1978, so Jimmy Carter and Secretary of the Interior Cecil Andrus set about withdrawing 110 million acres of BLM lands for a three-year development moratorium. Carter carried the process a step further, proclaiming 56 million of the withdrawn acres as national monuments, using his authority under the 1906 Antiquities Act. The three-year moratorium would expose the remaining 50 million–plus acres to future development, so once again, a legislative response to the Alaska lands was played out in Congress. During (and because of) the Reagan and

Republican landslide in 1980, Congress forged the **Alaska National Interest Lands Conservation Act**, which finalized the NPS claim to 44.7 million acres, including 24.6 million acres in parks and monuments and 19 million acres in national preserves. In "Seward's Folly," the last great frontier in America, the Alaska lands acts had more than doubled the size of the National Park System.

National parks are political entities. From the start, they have been born in controversy and forged in compromise.The "dual mission" of the 1916 NPS Act breeds an inner struggle from which the agency cannot escape. It manages itself into conflict every time the entrance gates open. Today, the issues facing the NPS are more numerous and complex than ever. Virtually every unit in the system is under some form of assault, be it over-visitation, overflights, air pollution, endangered species, exotic species, water quality, or water flow. Some of the better known controversies include the following:

- overdevelopment and air pollution in Yosemite,
- water flows below Glen Canyon Dam in Grand Canyon,
- reintroduction of wolves in Yellowstone,
- water diversion draining Everglades NP,
- tourist overflights above Grand Canyon,
- air quality at Big Bend, Grand Canyon, Canyonlands, Shenandoah, Great Smoky Mountains,
- underfunding and entrance fees, and
- multiple-use encroachment on park boundaries.

Yosemite has long had its share of sideshow attractions. In retrospect, many tourist-pleasing activities in the park are now considered to have been mistakes, almost carnival attractions more appropriate to county fairs. Fascinated by *Sequoia gigantea* and wheeled travel, it was inevitable that a number of trees in Yosemite's Mariposa Grove were tunneled for the passage of carriages and later, automobiles. Vehicle traffic, unknown to park promoters, was of course damaging the shallow root systems of the big trees. Tunneling led to their toppling, and eventually to the closure of the grove to vehicles.

For more than 60 years, the "Firefall" was dropped from Glacier Point, courtesy of the Curry Company, which had made the event a major nightly summer attraction. The glowing mass of embers would scar the mountainside and leave a wasted area at its base, in time prompting the NPS to cancel the show despite considerable Curry Company and popular protest. By 1976, the six square miles of Yosemite Valley sported almost 1,500 lodging units and three restaurants; two cafeterias; one hotel dining room; four sandwich centers; one seven-lift garage; two service stations with a total of 15 pumps; seven gift shops; two grocery stores; one delicatessen; one bank; one skating rink; three swimming pools; one pitch-and-putt golf course; two tennis courts; 33 kennels; 114 horse and mule stalls; one barber shop; one beauty shop; and 13 facilities for the sale of liquor.

Throw in the 22-bed jail, park administrative buildings, employee housing, motor pool and maintenance buildings, campgrounds, visitor centers, restrooms, roads, and parking lots, and there was no longer much room remaining for the once-lush meadows of the valley floor.

Yosemite National Park underwent a massive planning effort in the late 1970s, producing the Yosemite General Management Plan in 1980. Incorporating unprecedented levels of public involvement, the Yosemite plan called for removal of many park facilities from Yosemite Valley. Implementation costs, however, were not appropriated under the Reagan Administration. Saving dollars and preserving the business interests of the park's concessionaires, took priority over the plan's back-to-nature agenda. Though some facility reductions have taken place, the flooding of 1997 and 1998 probably promoted more change than has occurred through NPS planning actions.

Just upstream from Grand Canyon National Park, the huge Glen Canyon Dam backs Lake Powell into the canyons of what was once 195 miles of free-flowing Colorado River and its innumerable tributaries. Still scenically magnificent, the 1,500-plus miles of shoreline and waters of the reservoir draw thousands upon thousands of boaters annually. Downstream, in the vast canyons that assemble the Grand Canyon, the waters of the Colorado rise and fall with the demand for power generation from the turbines at Glen Canyon Dam. Flowing with minimal fluctuation at an artificial temperature of 46 degrees, the Colorado no longer carries massive spring floods from the snowmelt of the Rockies into the Grand Canyon. Resource managers have been noticing changes to **riparian areas**, including depletion of beaches and sandbars, increases in exotic vegetation, and endangerment of native fish. Proposals to even out the flows or open up spring flooding from Glen Canyon Dam had been made for a number of years before experimental artificial floods were tested in 1996, 2004, and 2008. Although flood testing is still under study and modification, results from the experiments appear positive.

Wolves and other predators, such as coyote, bobcat, mountain lion, lynx, fisher, and marten, were

Impressed with the immensity of Yosemite's "Big Trees," people couldn't resist the temptation to leave their mark for posterity.
(Courtesy of Yosemite Museum, National Park Service)

exterminated in national parks under NPS policy that lasted from 1918 to 1938, when conservationists forced a halt. The howl of the wolf was not heard in Yellowstone for more than five decades. In the 1980s and early 1990s, a discussion on the merits of reintroducing the endangered Gray Wolf (*Canis lupus*) brought about considerable controversy. Wolves, the neighboring livestock industry proclaimed, would exit park boundaries and prey on sheep and cattle. Some wildlife groups feared predation on park wildlife. But Clinton's Interior Secretary **Bruce Babbitt** gave the go-ahead to the Yellowstone Wolf Restoration Project, and roughly 100 wolves now roam the park. Despite a reduction in program budget, the restoration program has had moderate success, although *Canis lupus* remains on the endangered species list in Yellowstone and the Northern Rocky Mountains.

Everglades National Park occupies the southern end of a 13,000-square-mile area of South Florida described as a swamp, but more appropriately designated a vast river forty miles wide and three inches deep. Buoyed by an impenetrable layer of limestone known as marl, the waters ride slowly south on the massive Floridian Plateau. These are also the waters that made possible the rapid development of South Florida, one of the fastest-growing regions of the country. Coupled with intentional drainage for building development, flood control projects, and the continuing use of water for irrigation, pressure on the river of the Everglades has put the future of the park in jeopardy. Home to the greatest concentration and diversity of wildlife of any region in the nation, the Everglades habitat is changing and shrinking. Reduced flows of freshwater allow saltwater to intrude, ponds to dry. Between 1945 and 1975 the population of large wading birds dropped from an estimated 1.5 million to 50,000. The long-term survival of Everglades National Park is not in the hands of the NPS. Rather it is the Corps of Engineers and the water districts of South Florida that hold the valves to a water system that no longer runs nature's course. The Comprehensive Everglades Restoration Plan, approved by Congress in 2000, has increased funding for lands acquisition around the Everglades, but has fallen short of targets, and Everglades National Park returned to the list of endangered World Heritage Sites in 2010. What happens in the Everglades provides a glimpse of how parks are to survive in our increasingly human-controlled systems.

Viewing the Grand Canyon from the sky has become a popular tourist activity that supports a $200 million-a-year industry for planes, choppers, and flyers in Tusayan, Page, Flagstaff, and Las Vegas. Occasionally succumbing to the force of gravity, or sightseeing their way into one another, has made the safety record of tourist "overflights" rather shabby, bottoming out in 1986 when 25 people died in a midair collision over the abyss. Besides the safety issue, overflights are loud and disruptive of the magnificent silence of the Canyon. Backcountry users have been particularly incensed by the echoing racket of passing planes and helicopters. But again, the NPS is not in charge of the air above the Grand Canyon. The agency can only request that the **Federal**

Aviation Administration (FAA) restrict overflights to specific corridors. Following the largest fatal accident above the Canyon, the FAA restricted altitude to no lower than 7,000 feet above the Canyon rims, halting the practice of buzzing the Canyon depths. But flight companies have vehemently protested further regulation of their access to the skies, noting the dangerous precedent of restricting airspace, and boasting about the numbers of tourists served, and dollars generated by the thrilling experience of flying over the Canyon. Park Service officials have sought to control ambient noise levels and have discussed the need to manage parks as three-dimensional "columns" that include not only the land surface, but also the air above parks and the ground and minerals below.

Unable to control the prevailing winds, many national parks are threatened by air pollution once reserved for urban areas. Acid precipitation is problematic in parks on the East Coast, and also for Yosemite and Sequoia-Kings Canyon in the California Sierras. Smog is sometimes the direct result of an industry such as coal-fired power generation and copper smelting in the Southwest, or it can be the accumulated toxicity of industry, agricultural burning, and myriad automobiles, such as the mix of pollutants in California's Central Valley that wafts eastward into the Sierra Nevada. Though regulation is out of the NPS's hands, the agency and parks supporters often produce the outcry that brings air problems to the attention of legislators and regulators. It was complaints of reduced views over Grand Canyon that in 1992 prompted George Bush to make an election-year gesture of reducing the output of the giant coal-fired Navajo Generating Plant near Page Arizona. By 2008, the NPS was reporting little improvement in air quality. Park health and politics continue to be nervous bed partners.

Park officials have long known that fees paid for entry and camping are a bargain. When one considers the expenses of a trip to Yellowstone, the five bucks it used to cost to get in was a drop in the bucket. Yet there has been great resistance to elevating park fees, because parks were supposed to be *for the people!* Recognition that federal tax dollars were going to become more limited, plus arguments that visitors should bear the brunt of park operations expenses, have led to a softening of the hard line against fee increases. Congress answered with the Federal Lands Recreation Enhancement Act in 2004. Fees have gone up at many parks ($25 now at Yellowstone), together with a pledge to keep the fees at the park unit of origin, rather than pouring them back into the Treasury. This will hopefully allow busy parks to meet their needs for visitor services, operations, and maintenance. But there is still a long way for the NPS to go in meeting its $3 billion budget allocation each year.

Park boundaries were often drawn to protect specific resources, and were often also limited in size to meet the political necessities and compromises that would allow park establishment. As a result, many parks function as mere sections of larger, complex ecosystems. Everglades provides a prime example of this, but even parks as large as Yellowstone were not sized sufficiently to fully protect their resources. At Yellowstone, Forest Service lands are at times clear-cut to the park boundary; "slant drilling" threatens to exploit geothermal resources under the park from outside; reintroduced gray wolves roam beyond park borders; and bison carrying brucellosis at times exit the park onto neighboring ranchlands, threatening the livestock industry. Attempts to expand park boundaries to include whole ecosystems have included the Greater Yellowstone Ecosystem Coalition, which is an effort to consolidate adjacent lands from federal, state, and private owners under the management of the NPS. Such attempts have generally failed, partially because of a lack of baseline knowledge of what would actually comprise an "intact" ecosystem. Better examples of methods to protect ecosystems include the rings of USFS **wilderness areas** that surround parts of Yosemite and Sequoia-Kings Canyon, and a good portion of all but the western border of Yellowstone. Multiagency planning that incorporates all public managers and private landowners will be a major component of parks preservation well into the future. Dedication to these activities will be a measure of our will to preserve "America's Crown Jewels."

Suggested Readings

Albright, H.M. (1985). *The birth of the national park service: The founding years, 1913–33.* Salt Lake City, UT: Howe Brothers.

Chase, A. (1987). *Playing god in yellowstone: The destruction of America's first national park.* New York: Harcourt Brace Jovanovich.

Conservation Foundation. (1985). *National parks for a new generation: Visions, realities, prospects.* Washington, D.C.: Conservation Foundation.

Duncan, D. (2009). *The national parks; America's best idea.* New York: Alfred A. Knopf.

Everhart, W.C. (1983). *The National Park Service.* Boulder, CO: Westview Press.

Foresta, R.A. (1984). *America's national parks and their keepers.* Washington D.C.: Resources for the Future.

Kluger, J. (1998, January 19). The big (not so bad) wolves of Yellowstone. *Time, 151*(2).

National Park Service Organic Act of 1916. 16 U.S.C. §1, 2, 3, & 4.

Outdoor Recreation Resources Review Commission. (1962). *Outdoor recreation for America.* Washington, D.C.: U.S. Government Printing Office.

President's Commission on Americans Outdoors. (1987). *Americans outdoors: The legacy, the challenge.* Washington, D.C.: Island Press.

Runte, A. (2010). *National parks: The American experience* (4th ed.). Lanham, MD: Taylor Trade Pub.

Sax, J. L. (1980). *Mountains without handrails: Reflections on the national parks.* Ann Arbor, MI: The University of Michigan Press.

chapter eight

Federal Agencies

The U.S. Forest Service

The Conservation Movement's Star:

An Agency Symbolized by Smokey

Beginnings of the USFS

The national forests were created in response to turn-of-the-century thinking that the country could do better with its natural resources. Policies of disposal had turned most of the nation's land over to private ownership, but huge tracts of western forest, mountain, and desert lands remained unclaimed. Crises such as the Peshtigo fire, the dire warnings of George Perkins Marsh, and changes in the modus operandi of the federal government all helped set the stage for the creation of the **forest reserves.** The Forest Reserve Act of 1891 was only a piece of a larger 1891 Land Law revision that passed both houses of Congress in the closing days of the 1891 legislative session. The key Section 24 was tacked on in a conference committee report reconciling the senate and house versions of the bill, violating committee rules against such additions. The author of the key Section 24 remains anonymous to this day, perhaps from fear of the grammar police, who would not have approved. When passed, the law that would become known as the Forest Reserve Act gave the president sweeping powers, originating solely in sneaky Section 24, which read:

That the President of the United States may, from time to time, set apart and reserve, in any State or Territory having public lands wholly or in part covered with timber or undergrowth, whether of commercial value or not,as public reservations, and the President shall, by public proclamation, declare the establishment of such reservations and the limits thereof. (Forest Reserve Act 1891, p. 1103)

Within a month, President Benjamin Harrison withdrew the Yellowstone Park Timber Land Reserve bordering the National Park on the east and southeast. Circumventing the slow process of congressional action, the Yellowstone Reserve was intended primarily to expand protection to Yellowstone. Recognizing the strength of the act, Harrison set aside fourteen more forest reserves in his next two years in office, bringing the total to 13 million acres. Grover Cleveland put the power to use by declaring another 4.5 million acres as reserves. But the Forest Reserve Act made no provisions for managing or administering the reserves. In effect, they were locked up, which was a situation that could not long be tolerated.

It took six more years before Congress pounded together a bill for the administration of the forest reserves. Referred to today as the **Organic** (for organizing) **Act of 1897**, this 110-year-old law forms the statutory basis for the operations of the U.S. Forest Service. The act defines three basic purposes of the forest reserves:

1. to "preserve and protect the forest within the reservation"
2. "for the purpose of securing favorable conditions of water flows"
3. "to furnish a continuous supply of timber for the use and necessities of the people of the United States"

A month later, the Department of the Interior produced the first set of regulations governing administration of the reserves. But no appropriation was made for their enforcement until Congress earmarked $75,000 for protection of the forest reserves in fiscal year 1899.

Forest reserves were administered through the Interior Department's General Land Office, but the new "foresters" were employed in the Department of Agriculture. The Department of Agriculture was authorized to spend $2,000 to hire a scientist with knowledge of forests in 1876. Congress established a Division of Forestry in Agriculture in 1886, and the Division was renamed the Bureau of Forestry in 1901. Gifford Pinchot headed the Department of Agriculture's Bureau of Forestry, and was busily building political support for transfer of the reserves to the Department of Agriculture, and ultimately his control. Pinchot and others feared the political susceptibility of the GLO, its history of handling transfer of lands, and its overly bureaucratic methods. The management of reserves, they felt, required action, and a stodgy old Washington agency was not the place to forward a movement. The Transfer Act of 1905 concluded both a divorce and a marriage. The reserves were removed from Interior's General Land Office, and were re-wed to the Department of Agriculture's Bureau of Forestry. Finally, the forest reserves were to be managed by an agency with the necessary expertise in the "new" methods of scientific forestry. Pinchot had his plum. Within a few years, the bureau became the U.S. Forest Service, and the reserves were renamed the "National Forests."

The government had created a new form of land management, and with it had planted the seeds for a new profession: forestry.

Building a Forest Management Program

For the next 50 years, the USFS performed its task of managing the national forests. Building a workforce of hardy woodsman "**rangers**," Pinchot laid the groundwork for a system of forest management that flourished. Through his close ties with Teddy Roosevelt, Pinchot exercised influence that allowed the establishment of forestry experiment stations while Roosevelt liberally applied the Forest Reserve Act to withdraw 86 million more acres for the system. Six million more acres of land in the eastern U.S. were purchased and added to the national forest system by the **Weeks Act of 1911**. The early USFS set about the primary tasks of enforcing protective regulations. Timber theft, illegal mining, and water diversions required vigilant rangers. To protect forests from fires, a network of observation platforms was set up to look out for the first signs of smoke. Construction of trails and roads was undertaken to provide access for management activities. "**On the ground**" management was preferred, as **local conditions** varied and required **local decision makers**. Because forest exploitation was reduced, the rangers of the USFS were a success story. It was the agency's good fortune to be for half a century pretty much ahead of its time. But just as the conservation movement's star thrived during the era of human management, social and economic change and the rise of a new environmental movement would thrust new challenges at an agency with its boots firmly planted in decades-old tradition.

When Forest Service rangers enforced restrictions on timber removal, many lumber companies reconsolidated their focus on private lands and continued to seek new timberlands from private owners such as railroads. The supply of privately owned timber was considerable, and demand for wood from national forests could remain relatively low. Where practiced, the USFS's scientific forestry showed good results. New vigorous stands of trees often replaced removed **old growth** stands of trees. Early on, the agency was confident that it would assure the permanence of a national timber supply. And indeed, as long as demand remained low, prospects were good. The demand for timber products slowed further during the Depression, a time when the Forest Service (like the NPS) made use of Civilian Conservation Corps workers, building roads, trails, fire lookouts, campgrounds, and a host of other developments. The forests remained apart from the national consciousness, as economic hard times and then World War II captured the public's attention. Pinchot had exited the agency in a 1910 controversy with President Taft and Secretary Ballinger. Lacking the charisma embodied in its founder, the USFS stayed on the sidelines for a number of years. But the concern about forests continued, and the considerations born during these quiet years would have profound implications for the agency's future stewards.

Ecology and Wilderness

Upon graduation from the Pinchot-endowed Yale School of Forestry, **Aldo Leopold** went to work for the USFS in 1909 in the Forest Service's Region 3, eventually the Gila National Forest in New Mexico. Typical of early USFS rangers, Leopold enforced regulations, hunted predators to "protect" game species, and lived the life of the woodsman. But in Leopold was an aspiring naturalist and gifted writer who would speak of the interconnectedness of things, of the foundations of what would come to be called ecology. Leopold witnessed the results of planned predator extirpation. He saw that the new abundance of deer created no hunter's paradise. Instead, human intervention had created a deer population nightmare, leading huge and starving herds to defoliate the landscape and open it to erosion. In his classic essay, "Thinking Like a Mountain" (1944), Leopold described the results of the "hoped for deer" dying in the eyes of a mother wolf he had shot. Leopold proposed, and obtained designation of, the first USFS "**primitive area**," the 500,000-acre Gila Roadless Area, in 1924. By the time *A Sand County Almanac* was first published in 1949, Leopold had been rearranging some of the thinking about forest management for over two decades. "Saving all the cogs and wheels" as the first rule of "effective tinkering" was beginning to make sense to a new generation of forest watchers ready to question the few tenets of "scientific forestry."

Aldo Leopold's study and writing on the ecology of forest management influenced the practice of modern forestry. This 1910 photo shows Leopold early in his career as a Forest Assistant and reconnaissance party leader on the Apache National Forest in Arizona. (Forest History Society, Durham, N.C.)

The increased emphasis on wilderness management within the USFS received another boost in 1937 when **Robert Marshall** moved in as head of the Recreation and Lands Division. Marshall, at 36, had long been a champion of the wilderness concept. A Ph.D. in plant physiology, Marshall wrote a famed "minority rights" argument for the preservation of wilderness. Citing the physical, mental, and aesthetic benefits of wilderness, Marshall extolled the development of stamina, the retreat from the stresses of modern life, and the sensations of immersion in natural beauty that flow through the wilderness experience. Marshall proposed legislative protection of wilderness areas in the 1930s, a generation prior to passage of the Wilderness Act in 1964. As head of forestry for the Bureau of Indian Affairs, Marshall set aside 12 roadless areas of over 100,000 acres each on Indian reservations where Native Americans could escape modern civilization and build tourism. In 1935, Marshall, Leopold, and Robert Sterling Yard were three of the charter members who founded **The Wilderness Society.** By 1937, Marshall had surveyed and recommended the preservation of over 55 million acres of wilderness on national forest land. Legendary as a hiker, Marshall proceeded to explore as much of his recommended wilderness as he could. Frequently hiking more than 30 miles in a day, Marshall's undertaking a personal field inventory endeared him to those agency employees who met him. But Marshall's stamina could not keep pace with his raging enthusiasm. He died of a heart attack at age 38 in 1939. Today the 80 million-plus-acre National Wilderness Preservation System includes a vast stretch of western Montana known as the Bob Marshall Wilderness. The fight launched by Marshall became one of the USFS's most contentious issues in the 1970s and 1980s. The preservation movement had resurfaced within Pinchot's wise-use agency.

Get the Cut Out

Pinchot's forestry had taught that young, vigorous stands of trees were more productive for timber than old growth stands, which were considered decadent, diseased, and slow growing. Converting old growth to second (or new) growth was the first step in **silvicultural** management. The art-science of silviculture even used an interesting spin on the practice of harvest, referring to cutting as **regeneration methods.** Harvesting allowed the regeneration of new, fast-growing, vigorous trees. This conversion was not one of destruction, but one of improvement.

Several trends united in the post–World War II years to bring greater pressure on the national forests. In the West, abundant timber on private lands had been steadily cut for years. Many of these once-cut stands were not ready for reharvest, or else they had been poorly managed and were not yet close to recovering. Because of its vast holdings, the USFS provided the most accessible supply of quality timber in the postwar era. Foresters trained in silviculture knew how to regenerate stands of trees, and local timber industries were more than willing to help with the process. Economically, maintenance of timber-dependent rural communities grew to depend on federal logs. Federal lands generated no local tax revenues, so rural counties were compensated with payments of 25% of USFS timber receipts for the development and maintenance of schools and roads. And, much to the delight of Congress' voracious appetite, timber harvesting made the USFS one of the very few agencies that actually returned

A young pine grows to replace trees on harvested U.S.F.S. land.
(David E. Simcox Collection)

money to the Federal Treasury. Coupled with these economic incentives for timber production, postwar prosperity brought on a housing boom in the American suburbs. Wood-frame houses could eat up a lot of two-by-fours, and the mills went to work supplying the demand. This symbiosis of timber need, economic growth, and agency ability to partner in the enterprise led to a focus on wood products as the major social benefit of the national forests. A doctrine of **dominant use** permeated the agency's works without ever officially being declared. Within the Forest Service, aspiring career employees marked their progress through their ability to administer timber sales. Locating, measuring, price estimating, harvest planning, road engineering, and putting loggable stands up for competitive bidding from timber companies became the measure of achievement for agency personnel. The incentive for managing the forests became to **"get the cut out,"** to keep the flow of wood traveling toward the nation's prosperity.

Scientific forestry made good economic sense. Its adherents held strongly to the cause, creating a **"Forest Service culture"** of which Pinchot would have been proud.

The Second Half of the 20th Century: Gifford Pinchot Rolls Over in His Grave

The greatest good might have seemed to the USFS to be the production of timber, but society hadn't reached the same conclusion. Other trends would also propel influence in the direction of the national forests, but they would come from opposing positions that weren't necessarily easily accommodated by the culture the agency had developed. The happy postwar generation was booming in houses and babies. Shiny cars and roads to drive them on snaked closer to the woods, and Americans took their weekends to the national forests. Forever battling the National Park Service for recognition, the USFS launched **Operation Outdoors** in 1957, a year after the NPS had kicked off Mission 66.

Adhering to Mather's thinking about roads and access, the USFS felt it could accommodate outdoor recreation in campgrounds near recreational features, while the hunting, fishing, woodsy types would access the boonies on logging roads. Recreation could coexist with wood production. And to a point, it did. But recreationists from urban America had eyes, and their aesthetic sense could not reconcile the beauty of a clear-cut as a regeneration method. Discovering such cuts on federal lands that they thought were protected, recreationists began to question the wisdom and rationale behind USFS activities. And then came the 60s. The decade of Kennedys, Martin Luther King, Viet Nam, hippies, and Lyndon Johnson's **Great Society** would turn conventions on their collective ears. The U.S. Forest Service would not remain immune from the upheaval of a new environmental movement that scrutinized and questioned everything that had to do with the land. The agency found itself faced with demands from every conceivable corner as people pulled to get what they wanted out of the national forests. The Forest Service culture was in for a shock.

Smokey Bear brought the Forest Service's message "Only YOU can prevent forest fires" to all Americans. (Courtesy of U.S. Forest Service)

The first winds of change became noticeable when the Forest Service launched the *"Smokey Bear"* campaign in 1945. Having actually found a bear cub likely orphaned in a wildfire, the agency adopted him as a mascot named Smokey. Playing on the public relations opportunity, the Forest Service saw in Smokey a potential crusader who would implore forest recreationists to be careful with fire. The big ranger-capped bear was an immediate success, especially with children. The USFS had found a new public image that worked with the recreating masses, a save-the-forests mascot from the preservationist fold. The need for a Smokey had not existed until after World War II. Postwar prosperity, increased economic efficiencies in the timber industry, and greater dependence on national forest timber had worked in concert to raise the amount cut and point the agency further in the timber management direction. But the preservationist call for wilderness and the mass migration of vacationers to the forests presented a counter to silviculture as practiced in the Pinchot tradition. Although big, the National Forests would not be big enough to handle these competing demands without conflict. Half a century of slow but inexorable change in America's relationship with its national forests would be capped legislatively by Congress' passage of the **Multiple Use and Sustained Yield Act of 1960**. The Multiple Use and Sustained Yield Act sought to capture changes in the national forests and redecree their purposes. The agency authored the bill itself, and lobbied for its passage. In relatively unclear language, the act stated that consideration would be "...given to the relative values of the various resources, and not necessarily the combination of uses that will give the greatest dollar return or the greatest unit output." This statement was interpreted to mean that values such as wilderness and recreation would be considered on an equal footing with timber production, an obvious acknowledgment to the sentiment of the times. However, the Multiple Use and Sustained Yield Act also granted greater decision-making authority to the USFS, increasing the agency's discretionary license to practice the production-oriented management institutionalized within agency culture. The recognition that timber, water, minerals, grazing, wildlife, and recreation should be considered on an equal footing did not necessarily mean that they would be. The Multiple Use and Sustained Yield Act was an early reaction to the Forest Service's sense that it was losing control of its way of doing business. The act was unable to mollify the ever-growing storm on the horizon, and even with Smokey Bear working for them, the next two decades would brew up a hurricane.

In the 1960s and 1970s, several controversies, court cases, and legislative enactments would forever change the complexion of the USFS. Significant among these were the Wilderness Act of 1964, the National Environmental Policy Act of 1970, the **Endangered Species Act of 1973**, the **Forest and Rangeland Renewable Resources Planning Act of 1974 (RPA)**, and the **National Forest Management Act of 1976 (NFMA)**. Originating from a wide variety of social arguments over values for natural resources, these acts would greatly alter the playing field occupied by the preservation and conservation movements. The legislation would grow from long-term arguments, or it would pop up in response to crises. In the case of the USFS, the RPA and NFMA were direct responses to crises that made their way into the public arena. One was the **timber mining** accusations arising from the Bitterroot Controversy, and the other was the **Monongahela decision** from the case of *Izaak Walton League v. Butz*, which effectively outlawed clear-cutting based on the language of the **Organic Act of 1897.**

Structure of the USFS

Today, though struggling with change, the USFS remains a major agency that manages nationally significant natural resources. The 193 million acres managed by the USFS account for roughly 25% of America's public lands. The agency manages approximately 20% of the nation's commercial forest land, provides home for about half of the big-game animals in the country, permits grazing of 3.5 million cattle and sheep, maintains the world's largest road (250,000 miles) and trail (100,000 miles) network, provides over 300 million visitor days of recreation annually, and manages over a third of the nation's wilderness preservation system, three-quarters of the total in the lower 48 states. As mountains gather rainfall, Forest Service lands are where 75% of the nation's freshwater supply originates, and the agency manages three million acres of lakes and reservoirs and over 83,000 miles of streams.

To manage this vast estate, a decentralized agency structure put line officers on the ground at the field level. The district ranger is the decision-making authority closest to the resources of a ranger district within a given national forest. Each national forest, (of which there are 155), is headed by a forest supervisor. National forests are then grouped into nine Regions, each headed by a regional forester. These line officers then report to the head of the USFS. Currently, Tom Tidwell serves as the Chief of the USFS. This hierarchy involves a mere four levels from Washington, D.C., to the field—a structure that has provided for some autonomy on local questions, yet a tight rein on issues of national significance. Interestingly, it is the ranger position that is most often used to describe employees of the USFS. In fact, only the head of a ranger district, the district ranger, bears that title. Other USFS employees are designated as staff and are specialized to manage a variety of agency **functions,** including timber management, fire management, recreation, lands and resources management, minerals, and engineering, and administrative activities such as planning and public information. These management functions are headed by **staff officers**, who are referred to as *timber management officer, public information officer,* etc. It helps to know who to look for when seeking answers to questions about forest management in your area.

(Time for another quiz break: Are there national forests in your state? What region are they in? How many are there, and what are their names?)

Let's look at California as an example:

California is distinguished in the USFS by comprising its own Region, known as Region 5 and headquartered in Vallejo. The national forests in California are the:

Six Rivers NF	Eldorado NF
Klamath NF	Stanislaus NF
Modoc NF	Sierra NF
Shasta-Trinity NF	Los Padres NF
Lassen NF	Angeles NF
Plumas NF	San Bernardino NF
Mendocino NF	Cleveland NF
Tahoe NF	Inyo NF
Sequoia NF	Tahoe Basin Management Unit

Controversies

The U.S. Forest Service is embroiled in about as many controversies as there are values for forest resources. The agency is constantly mediating competing demands while trying to meet the "assure permanence" mandate of Gifford Pinchot, written over a century ago. We'll visit a number of these controversies individually in later chapters, but for now, here's a list to get you thinking:

- Endangered species protection (one very notable one: the Spotted Owl)
- Timber harvest practices
- "Below-Cost" timber sales
- Support for local rural economies
- Harvest quantities
- Old-growth forests and "biodiversity"
- Riparian zone management
- Herbicide and pesticide use
- Budget expenditures for roads vs. trails
- Increasing demand for outdoor recreation opportunities
- Wilderness designations
- Livestock grazing
- Surface waters management
- Fire management, fuels buildup from past suppression, and the wildland-urban interface
- Law enforcement and increased crime on national forests
- Public participation in planning
- Increased litigation
- Internal affirmative action

This is just to name a few. For its first 50 years, the Forest Service kept reasonably busy protecting the federal forests. The major incursion into their mostly primitive settings occurred as the result of Roosevelt's CCC and other Depression-era work programs. Robert Marshall had protested these works as part of his advocacy for wilderness. But the second half of the 20th century would become a new order for the USFS. Operating in a fishbowl under the public eye, the agency has changed its course from pressures both external and internal. As society and natural resources evolve, so too does the U.S. Forest Service.

Suggested Readings

Clary, D. A. (1986). *Timber and the forest service.* Lawrence, KS: University Press of Kansas.

Culhane, P. J. (1981). *Public lands politics: Interest group influence in the Forest Service and the Bureau of Land Management.* Baltimore: Johns Hopkins University Press for Resources for the Future.

Dana, S. T., & Fairfax, S. K. (1980). *Forest and range policy* (2nd ed.). New York: McGraw-Hill.

Flader, S. (1994). *Thinking like a mountain: Aldo Leopold and the evolution of an ecological attitude toward deer, wolves, and forests.* Madison, WI: University of Wisconsin Press.

Hays, S. P. (2009). *The American people and the national forests: The first century of the U.S. Forest Service.* Pittsburgh, PA: University of Pittsburgh Press.

Kaufman, H. (1960). *The forest ranger: A study in administrative behavior.* Baltimore: Johns Hopkins University Press.

Knight, R. L., & Bates, S. F. (Eds.). (1995). *A new century for natural resources management.* Washington, D.C.: Island Press.

Leopold, A. (1972). *A Sand County almanac: With essays on conservation from Round River.* New York: Ballantine.

Lewis, J. G. (2005). *The forest service and the greatest good: A centennial history.* Durham, N.C.: The Forest History Society.

Nash, R. (2001). *Wilderness and the American mind* (4th ed.). New Haven, CT: Yale University Press.

O'Toole, R. (1988). *Reforming the forest service.* Washington, D.C.: Island Press.

Runte, A. (1991). *Public lands, public heritage: The national forest idea.* Niwot, CO: Roberts Rinehart.

U.S. Statutes at Large, 27 (1891): 1095-1103.

Wellman, J. D., & Propst, D. B. (2004). *Wildland recreation policy* (2nd ed.). Malabar, FL: Krieger Publishing.

Wilkinson, C. F., & Anderson, M. A. (1987). *Land and resource planning in the national forests.* Washington, D.C.: Island Press.

Federal Agencies

The Bureau of Land Management

The Public Domain: "Lands that Nobody Wanted?"

The **Bureau of Land Management (BLM)**, under the Department of the Interior, was a late arrival among natural resource managing agencies. Organized as an agency only in 1946, the BLM's roots go back to the beginnings of U.S. land management, from the days when Thomas Jefferson and Alexander Hamilton debated the disposition of the federal estate. Article IV, Section 3, Clause 2, of the Constitution gave Congress the "Power to dispose of and make all needful Rules and Regulations respecting the Territory and other Property belonging to the United States." Land Laws passed in 1796, 1800, 1803, and 1804 redefined the methods of the rectangular survey system originated in 1785, and the Department of the Treasury supervised local land offices set up to convey title and receive payment for sales of federal lands. The Louisiana Purchase put the U.S. into a rapidly growing public lands business, so Congress created the General Land Office (GLO) within the Department of the Treasury in 1812. The GLO subsequently transferred to the new Department of the Interior when it was created in 1849. Continually tinkering with methods of land disposal, Congress enlisted a variety of measures to transfer lands to settlers, institutions, and nationally significant enterprises such as railroad companies. Lands were given to soldiers in payment for their service to the country. Settlers on unsurveyed lands who had occupied and cultivated farms were given the right to claim those lands after survey through the Preemption Law of 1841. The 1862 Homestead Act offered land in 160-acre quarter sections if settled for five years, or prior to that, for the minimum price of $1.25 per acre. Also in 1862, the **Morrill Act** provided each state with 30,000 acres of public lands for each senator and member of the House of Representatives, for the purpose of financing agricultural and mechanical arts colleges, later to become known as the **Land-grant Universities.** To finance the construction of railroads, Congress granted vast tracts of land (128 million acres!) to railroad companies. The **1872 General Mining Law** gave settlers the opportunity to claim ownership of "valuable" mineral deposits in chunks of 20 acres, or in 160-acre blocks for associations or groups. The law required that $100 worth of assessment work be done annually, and $500 worth of improvements had to be in place before the claims could be patented. The law made mineral entry a legitimate and recognized use of the public domain. The belief that trees would bring rain to the semiarid West prompted Congress to pass the **Timber Culture Law of 1873**, which deeded land to those who kept 40 acres of trees (later 10) planted and "proofed" after up to 13 years. The **Desert Land Law of 1877** provided for similar granting of land to those who would irrigate and plant crops on 640-acre sections within three years. The disposal of the public domain eventually slowed as preservation and conservation interests moved for withdrawals of national parks, forest reserves, and national monuments. Homesteading had pretty much run its course by the end of World War I. After that, the federal land left over consisted primarily of arid parts of the West, land that was of interest mostly to ranchers and miners.

What homesteaders didn't want, ranchers certainly did. Unrestricted grazing on a first-come, first-served basis led western ranchers to overgraze the public lands. Grazing policy was debated for a generation before the **Taylor Grazing Act of 1934** passed in an attempt "to stop injury to the public grazing lands by preventing overgrazing and soil deterioration; to provide for their orderly use, improvement and development; to stabilize the livestock industry dependent upon the public range." The law permitted the Secretary of the Interior to place lands into "**grazing districts.**" Secretary Harold Ickes then established a **Division of Grazing** and appointed Colorado rancher Farrington Carpenter as its head. In order to administer the grazing districts, Carpenter set up district **Grazing Advisory Boards**, which were later given legal authority by Congress in 1939. These boards were entrusted with giving advice on policy regarding permits for livestock grazing within the grazing districts. The boards were stocked by ranchers, providing local knowledge and advice to the Division of Grazing. In effect, the livestock industry controlled the Advisory Boards, making it difficult for conservation measures such as reducing herd sizes to take effect. The fox had been put in charge of the henhouse.

Restoration of the western range, however, remained an important conservation priority for Roosevelt's **New Deal** administration. Drought and the dust bowl of the late twenties and early thirties, coupled with depression and overgrazing, had left the public rangelands in a sad state. Roosevelt brought the Civilian Conservation Corps to work on the range, improving water sources, fencing, and taking measures to reduce soil erosion. The Division of Grazing became the **U.S. Grazing Service** in 1941. After World War II, the Grazing

Service made the first of what would become many attempts to raise the fees paid by ranchers for livestock grazing. The "**Animal Unit Month**" (AUM) had been set after the Taylor Grazing Act at five cents per animal (one cow, one horse, or five sheep) per month. This was deemed the average cost of providing forage for livestock. The Grazing Service found this charge lower than the actual costs of grazing and proposed tripling the fee in 1941. Big mistake. Western senators supported the ranchers and saw to it that the Grazing Service would be gutted through the appropriations process. The Truman Administration recognized the conflict and duplication of efforts between the General Land Office and the Grazing Service. Both agencies managed resources on the public domain, but it was unclear at times who did what. The logical conclusion, despite an Interior Department recommendation against it, was to merge the GLO and the Grazing Service. As part of his administration's reorganization plans, President Truman combined the GLO and the Grazing Service on July 16, 1946, into a new agency called the Bureau of Land Management.

The Bureau did not get off to an auspicious start. The Grazing Service was down to 86 employees managing 150 million acres of grazing lands at the time of the merger. To keep the managers in place, the grazing advisory boards put up money themselves to back the salaries of range managers. It was an interesting move, considering that the regulatees pay the regulators' salaries! Low morale was relieved with the appointment of Marion Clawson to the BLM directorship in 1948. A Nevadan and an able administrator, Clawson pursued the decentralization of the agency and the development of a sense of mission, which happened to be multiple use. Change from Truman's Democratic to Eisenhower's Republican administration ended Clawson's tenure, and brought Edward Woozley to the head of the BLM from 1953 to 1961. Further pursuing several of Clawson's programs, the BLM continued to look more and more like a resource-managing agency. Recognizing accelerated career opportunities, a number of USFS employees shifted to BLM, strengthening the background training of the agency. Gradual increases in grazing fees brought the AUM to 22 cents by 1960. Busy with the largest acreage holdings of any federal agency, the BLM strengthened its internal philosophy of multiple-use. This mission was legally endorsed by the **Classification and Multiple Use Act of 1964**. As the BLM lands further faced the demands and scrutiny of America's new environmental and outdoor recreational focus, the agency struggled to meet the many conflicts that multiple-use management engendered. For 30 years as an agency, the BLM had managed lands "pending disposition." The public domain lands were, in effect, still available for disposal. Recognizing that the agency managed 485 million acres and was charged with implementing more than 3,000 public land laws, Congress finally authorized the BLM to manage the "public lands" as a permanent part of the federal estate. The Federal Land Policy and Management Act of 1976 gave the BLM the recognition and marching orders it needed. But no legislation could cure the controversies in which the agency would continue to be embroiled. The last of the great public estates of the

United States was now officially governed by an agency with the authority to implement the multiple-use mission. Like its multiple-use neighbor the USFS, the BLM would find confusion in its direction. The political seesaw between competing influences continued to be a mainstay of public lands administration.

Issues and Controversies for the BLM

The agency that supposedly managed a bunch of "land nobody wanted" actually holds huge tracts of resources valued for minerals, energy, grazing, outdoor recreation, timber, wildlife, water, and archaeological significance. Because the BLM manages these resources in trust for the common good, the people of the U.S. offer no shortage of opinions on how they ought to be handled. As the traditional pressures on public domain resources came from the livestock and minerals industries, the BLM originally worked mostly with these two constituent groups. Indeed, laws such as the General Mining Law of 1872 and the Taylor Grazing Act of 1934 assured that public domain lands were used for these purposes. But as moods and opinions toward natural resources morphed through the years of postwar prosperity and the environmental movement, new players came forward to stake their interest in the lands managed by the BLM. Groups protecting wildlife, water, archaeological and Native American heritage sites, recreation opportunities, and old-growth forests stepped up to the plate and took swings at the agency they symbolically dubbed the "**Bureau of Livestock and Mining**." Thrown into the pressure cooker with the rest of the government resource agencies, the BLM faced numerous controversies, some of which include:

- Forest management on the O&C Lands
- Management of wild (feral) horses and burros
- "Hard rock" and energy minerals leasing
- Grazing allotments and fees
- "Areas of Critical Environmental Concern"
- Playing checkers
- Continued "withdrawals"

The **O&C Lands** in western Oregon had originally been granted in 1866 to the California and Oregon Railroad and the Coos Bay Wagon Road companies to finance a railroad from California to Washington and to construct a connecting wagon road to the coast at Coos Bay. Granted nonmineral sections in a checkerboard pattern of alternating square miles for 20 miles on either side of the roadway, the companies were to sell lands to actual settlers in 160-acre quarter sections at no more than $2.50 per acre. Being entrepreneurial, the companies soon found the timber value of these lands far exceeded what they could get selling them to settlers. So they held on, and in as many as 45 cases sold blocks as large as 1,000 acres to private timber interests. Congress was less than pleased. In 1908 they authorized legal proceedings that went all the way to the Supreme Court, who then threw the issue back into their own lap. In 1916 Congress passed legislation to "revest" the companies' lands back to the United States, in this case the General Land Office. The 2.5 million acres of reclaimed lands, spread in a checkerboard across Western Oregon contained about 50 billion board feet of Douglas fir and old-growth forest. When the GLO became the BLM, ready or not the agency was in the timber business. And what a business! Some of the most valuable timber in the world, surrounded by small communities who profited not only from timber production, but also from the 50% of gross receipts paid to counties in lieu of taxes. Eventual harvests reached as much as one billion board feet annually. But BLM could not quietly participate in the timber industry of the Pacific Northwest. Changing attitudes toward the industry shaped a controversy from which BLM could not escape. Fluttering about on the O&C lands was a little bird that would become the spear-point of a lance thrown by the environmental movement: the **Northern Spotted Owl.** By the latter 1980s, virtually every BLM timber sale on O&C Lands was blocked by litigation The BLM was transferred by society's pressure from the timber business to the owl-sitting business.

Management of feral horses and burros on public lands is a contentious issue.
(Photo by Jennifer Moxley)

Feral horses and burros are **exotic species** that have made the western landscape of BLM their home. Originally discarded or escaped, "wild" horses and burros adapted to the Western rangelands and proliferated in numbers. Presenting competition for forage to the livestock industry, ranchers and "mustangers" hunted feral horses and burros for years, selling them for pet food and hides. Enter Nevadan Velma Johnston. Later dubbed "Wild Horse Annie," Velma single-handedly led a drive to protect wild horses that eventually became the **Wild and Free-Roaming Horses and Burros Act of 1971**. Congress was telling range managers what to do with a specific species, setting the stage for a new era of wildlife management. This public will, of course, didn't do much for BLM's efforts to improve conditions on the Western rangelands. Horse and burro populations doubled in seven years, an event that was partial reason behind passage of the **Public Rangelands Improvement Act of 1978**. In this Act, Congress returned some discretion in managing feral horse and burro populations back to the BLM. The agency had already engaged in "**Adopt-a-Horse**" and "**Adopt-a-Burro**" programs, but demand for "pet" horses and burros could not keep up with supply. The animals multiplied and tempers rose. Wild horse herds were found slaughtered in Nevada, and perpetrators escaped. The issue remains highly controversial. BLM is joylessly riding the range fence between wildlife protectionists who would leave horses and burros alone, and ranchers who want to keep available forage for their livestock.

"**Hard rock**" and **energy minerals** offer up another problematic resource issue for the BLM. Charged to administer the 1872 General Mining Law, the agency has been continuously accused of catering to the minerals industry in a lands "giveaway" that disposes of federal property to mining companies for ridiculously low prices. Countering the argument, the minerals industry points out the high development costs of putting a successful mine into operation. Opponents cite the environmental damage caused by mining, and the industry's lack of compliance with environmental regulations and reclamation laws. Secretary of the Interior Bruce Babbitt went on record in the 1990s, calling the 1872 Mining Law a giveaway. Meanwhile, back at the BLM, the agency is governed both by a 125-year-old law and the swinging pendulum of political opinion. This topic will be further discussed in Chapter 22.

The BLM has been administering **grazing permits** since its inception. Ranchers with small private holdings adjacent to BLM lands rely on the federal range to graze their cattle and sheep. Representing only 4% of the nation's cattle supply and 25% of the sheep, livestock on public lands is a "traditional" use not easily rearranged by environmentalists who claim grazing constitutes a "dominant" use **subsidized** by the federal government. Ranchers point out that grazing has been going on since prehistory when ungulates roamed ancient America. They also argue that grazing fees are not artificially low, as the quality of forage on sparsely vegetated BLM lands is marginal. Attempts to raise grazing fees invariably encounter a political whirlwind kicked up by Western Senators and Representatives who recognize the clout of the livestock industry. And there is old BLM, caught in the middle again. There will be more on this topic too, in Chapter 20.

The BLM has begun closely watching areas of **critical environmental concern** that support ecological diversity and cultural heritage. Such areas include riparian zones, wildlife migration corridors, habitat for threatened and endangered species, unique geological and scenic resources, and archaeological areas. The Bureau often prepares special management plans for areas of critical environmental concern, evidence of the agency's commitment to long-term stewardship of the public lands resources entrusted to them.

The **checkerboard pattern** of many BLM lands (such as the O&C Lands in southwestern Oregon) is the direct result of government disposal policies from the last century. Granting odd or even sections (square miles) to companies such as railroads, or to states, produced a checkerboard pattern of intermixed federal and private or state lands. In effect, each square mile of federal lands in these granted areas became an island, connected to other federal lands only at the tips of each of the four corners. Right of way and access to these lands were frequently challenged by private landowners on adjacent sections. The checkerboard became a headache to manage, as there was little continuity between activities on adjacent sections. This furthered BLM's incentive to sell off or trade isolated sections to build consolidated management units. Today the checkerboard is still with us, and it is still a management pain.

In the last few years, BLM has experienced some Congressional and Presidential activity reminiscent of the withdrawal days of earlier this century. In 1976, the **California Desert Conservation Area** was established under the Federal Land Policy Management Act. BLM went to work developing a management plan for the CDCA that was approved in 1980 following a massive public involvement process. Included in the plan were special management areas for off-road vehicle enthusiasts, a Desert Tortoise Natural Area, and the East Mojave Scenic Area. But preservationists remained unsatisfied with the multiple use programs of BLM, and California Senator Dianne Feinstein pressed legislation in a California Desert bill that would transfer a sizable chunk of BLM land to the National Park Service as the **Mojave National Preserve** in 1995. Congress had once again withdrawn lands from the public domain for preservation. Not to be outdone, in an environmentalist gesture in 1996, Bill Clinton invoked the Antiquities Act to declare 1.3 million acres of Southeastern Utah BLM land as the **Grand Staircase-Escalante National Monument**. Remaining under BLM control, the new National Monument covers a vast region connecting lands of the Dixie National Forest with Glen Canyon National Recreation Area, Canyonlands, and Capitol Reef National Parks. Clinton proceeded to designate nearly five million more acres as national monuments before the end of his second term, much of that on BLM lands. These withdrawals inevitably exacerbate the contentious perspectives of ranchers, recreationists, mineral companies, local communities and environmentalists.

Caretaking a huge portion of the nation's public lands, the BLM has been directed to manage for multiple use while frequently being ordered to manage special areas for specific purposes. As a result, BLM's repertoire of skills and knowledge needs to be extensive. BLM's job has become only more complex and challenging as Congress passed on new responsibilities and constituent groups stepped up pressures on the agency to meet their specific agendas. Even though BLM's lands provide considerable revenue to the federal budget, primarily through energy leases, the agency suffers from political maneuverings in the budgetary process, and enjoys less than half of the annual appropriations granted to the NPS. Today BLM continues to struggle a bit with its underdog latecomer image. The measure of BLM's success will certainly come as our values for the resources of the public lands increase, and the agency referees the social will in providing for their use.

Archaeological resources, such as this large pictograph in Utah, are important management concerns of the BLM. (Photo by Steve Dennis)

BLM manages the wilderness study area at Grand Gulch, Utah. (Photo by Steve Dennis)

Agency Structure

The BLM is housed under the Department of the Interior. The head administrator is the Director, followed by two Deputy Directors. Assistant Directors head divisions of 1) Renewable Resources and Planning, 2) Minerals and Realty Management, 3) Information Resources Management, 4) Communications, 5) Business and Fiscal Resources, and 6) Human Capital Management. Field operations are broken down into field offices, first at the State level, then into districts, or field offices. For example, Utah's State BLM Office is headquartered in Salt Lake City. The BLM District and field offices in Utah are organized as follows:

- West Desert District
  -Salt Lake Field Office
  -Fillmore Field Office
- Green River District
  -Vernal Field Office
  -Price Field Office
- Canyon Country District
  -Moab Field Office
  -Monticello Field Office
- Color Country District
  -Cedar City Field Office
  -Kanab Field Office
  -St. George Field Office
  -Richfield Field Office
- Grand Staircase - Escalante National Monument
- Henry Mountains Field Station

What has been discussed thus far is just the tip of the iceberg about BLM. Next time you're out recreating, or reading an article about a resource controversy, keep an eye out for the BLM. This agency will be much more noticeable once you start looking.

Suggested Readings

Culhane, P. J. (1981). *Public lands politics: Interest group influence in the forest service and the bureau of land management.* Baltimore: Johns Hopkins University Press for Resources for the Future.

Dana, S. T., & Fairfax, S. K. (1980). *Forest and range policy* (2nd ed.). New York: McGraw-Hill.

Robbins, R. M. (1962). *Our landed heritage: The public domain, 1776 - 1936.* Lincoln, NE: University of Nebraska Press.

Skillen, J. R. (2009). *The nation's largest landlord: The bureau of land management in the American west.* Lawrence, Kansas: University Press of Kansas.

U.S. Department of the Interior, Bureau of Land Management. (1988). *Opportunity and challenge: The story of BLM.* Washington, D.C.: U.S. Government Printing Office.

Wilkinson, C.F. (1992). *Crossing the next meridian: Land, water, and the future of the west.* Washington, D.C.: Island Press.

Federal Agencies

The U.S. Fish and Wildlife Service

The Wildlife Specialists

Origins

Wildlife was one of the abundant natural resources abused by European settlers in the New World. Wildlife harvest practices (taken to excess) such as trapping, hunting, and fishing took a toll on wildlife that offered a product useful to humans. The fur trade in beaver pelts that led to a good deal of exploration of North America was driven by a demand for felt hats in Europe. Feathered plumes, also for the decoration of hats, created a demand for pelicans, herons, and egrets, which were also severely over-hunted. Bison robes created initial demand for trade in harvesting the American Bison, a trade that became an epidemic of greenhorn sport hunters seeking some last connection with the "old" West. Extinction of the passenger pigeon, reduction in the stocks of whales, seals, and otters, and damage to fisheries were all brought on by market demand for wildlife products from feathers and fur to meat and oil. "Market hunting" was widely practiced during the 19th century, and hunters avidly brought to restaurants and markets the bounty of the American habitat: cougars, bears, antelope, bighorn sheep, deer, elk, moose, ducks, geese, cranes, turkeys, partridges, and on and on. Regulation of such hunting was nonexistent, but the eventual depletion of certain species caught the attention of sports hunters and fishers, who began to fear the loss of their quarry.

Well-to-do gentlemen of the industrializing nation enjoyed their opportunities to travel to vacation lodges and partake in a bit of hunting and fishing. The recreational benefits of sojourns in the woods were extolled in the popular press of the time, and more and more successful citizens sought refreshment and revival in the "manly" pursuits of hunting and fishing. Reduction of wildlife habitat and over-harvest reduced wildlife populations, conflicting with the newfound values for wildlife held by the nation's elite. From their perspective, the unruly masses of settlers and entrepreneurs were exploiting wildlife to imminent ruin. They began to consider the use of political influence to push for the regulation of hunting, fishing, and trapping. Politics had created Yellowstone in 1872, and wildlife was to be protected as part of the park's attractions. The **Boone and Crockett Club**, established in 1888, had a membership of influential industrialists and politicians, including one of its founders, Teddy Roosevelt. Fishers grouped into another powerful club, the Izaak Walton League. These groups began to press their pro-wildlife agendas, becoming charter members of the resource-related citizen organizations. Their work began to pay off.

Market hunters with kills and cages, Butte County, California, c.1912-1914.
(John Cowan Collection)

Federal Wildlife Regulation

The **Lacey Act of 1900** marks the beginning of federal wildlife regulation in the U.S. Prior to this act, wildlife had been designated among the resources to be preserved within national parks, but no structure for federal regulation of species outside withdrawn lands had been built. Congress got into the wildlife business through its power to regulate interstate commerce. The Lacey Act prohibited interstate transportation of wildlife killed in violation of state law. In direct response to the plight of the passenger pigeon, the Lacey Act also authorized the Secretary of Agriculture to adopt measures necessary for the "preservation, distribution, introduction, and restoration of game birds and other wild birds." This federal mandate remained subject to the wildlife laws of the states and territories, where wildlife regulation primarily resided.

In 1905, a **Bureau of Biological Survey** was established in the Department of Agriculture, the grandparent of the U.S. Fish and Wildlife Service. In the years that followed, Congress somewhat regularly passed legislation aimed at protecting wildlife. President Teddy Roosevelt kicked off the national wildlife refuge idea by establishing **Pelican Island National Wildlife Refuge** on a little five-acre island off the Florida coast in 1903, and 53 three additional refuges by the time he left office. In 1918, the **Migratory Bird Treaty Act** protected migratory birds by controlling their possession, sale, importation, and transport. The **Migratory Bird Conservation Act of 1929** authorized acquisitions and development costs for wildlife refuges. The **Migratory Bird Hunting Stamp Act of 1934** required hunters to purchase the now famous "duck stamp," funneling money into the acquisition of more migratory bird refuges. The **Pittman-Robertson Act of 1937** and the **Dingell-Johnson Act of 1950** placed excise taxes on guns and ammunition, and fishing tackle, respectively, adding large amounts of money to the management of areas for game species and fisheries. The Bureau of Fisheries in the Commerce Department, and the Biological Survey in Agriculture were transferred to the Interior Department in 1939, where they were combined as the Fish and Wildlife Service in 1940. In 1956, the Fish and Wildlife Act defined national fish and wildlife policy, but re-separated the Fish and Wildlife Service into bureaus of Sports Fisheries and Wildlife, and Commercial Fisheries. In 1970, the Bureau of Commercial Fisheries was transferred to the new **National Oceanic and Atmospheric Administration (NOAA)** in the Commerce Department and became known as the National Marine Fisheries Service. Sports Fisheries and Wildlife dissolved within the U.S. Fish and Wildlife Service. Major wildlife management responsibility at the federal level falls on the U.S. Fish and Wildlife Service and the **National Marine Fisheries Service**.

There are a host of other laws and a number of international treaties regulating the export and importation of marine and terrestrial wildlife, and requiring the provision of refuges. When the Endangered Species Act of 1973 is thrown in, the Fish and Wildlife Service turns into the most powerful conservation agency in the nation, as it is the major agency charged with its implementation.

The National Wildlife Refuge System

Approximately 150 million acres are designated as the 500-plus National Wildlife Refuges managed by the USF&WS. Several types of refuges are categorized as (a) migratory bird refuges, (b) waterfowl production areas and wetlands management districts, (c) big game refuges, (d) wildlife ranges and game ranges, and (e) coordination areas or wildlife management areas. Additionally, the USF&WS manages 71 national fish hatcheries, seven fish technology centers, and nine fish health centers.

A real "Bambi." The Disney version carried a powerful anti-hunting message.
(John Cowan Collection)

Wildlife Management

The key to management of the wildlife resource is the provision of **habitat.** Refuges are designed and, in many cases, intensively managed to produce optimal habitat. Regulation of land use, both public and private, is another, and far more controversial, means to provide habitat. The difficult side of wildlife management is that "everybody knows what's best for wildlife." The American public, increasingly urban and raised on media images of talking animals from Mickey Mouse to Mr. Ed, has anthropomorphized wildlife, (i.e., given human characteristics and emotions to animals). This has created an extremely strong affinity for wildlife in America, and a very emotional one that wildlife managers frequently refer to as the "**Bambi Syndrome.**" This is not so bad in and of itself, but the Bambi Syndrome strikes when game managers use harvest (hunting and trapping) as a means to regulate wildlife populations to keep them within the carrying capacity of their habitat. Many wildlife protectionists are unable to reconcile hunting as a method that is good for wildlife. Because of these factors, wildlife management is one of the most controversial of the varied natural resources regulatory efforts. The power of the Endangered Species Act (ESA) over the different uses of public, and in some cases, private lands, has made non-game species of animals and plants into protected resources. When species are officially designated as threatened—or endangered—a host of habitat protective regulations are invoked, often setting off a firestorm of protest from land users feeling the brunt of the change. As a preservationist tool, the ESA has become the most controversial of all natural resources legislation.

Enforcing hunting and fishing regulations is a
primary task of state wildlife agencies.
(David E. Simcox Collection)

Suggested Readings

Bean, M. J., & Rowland, M. J. (1997). *The evolution of national wildlife law* (3rd ed.). Westport, CN: Praeger.

Bolen, E. G., & Robinson, W. L. (2003). *Wildlife ecology and management* (5th ed.). Upper Saddle River, NJ: Prentice-Hall.

Sinclair, A. R. E., Fryxell, J. M., & Caughley, G. (2006). *Wildlife ecology, conservation, and management* (2nd ed.). Malden, MA; Oxford: Blackwell Publishing.

chapter eleven

Federal Agencies

The Bureau of Reclamation and U.S. Army Corps of Engineers

The Water Managers

The water resources of the U.S. are extensively developed for purposes of **flood protection**, generation of **hydroelectric energy**, **"flatwater recreation,"** and **storage** for agricultural, industrial, and domestic uses. At the federal level, two major agencies provide management of water resources: the Bureau of Reclamation under the Department of the Interior, and the U.S. Army Corps of Engineers, under the Department of Defense. These two agencies carry very different histories, but each has at times functioned in a manner much like the other.

Reclamation

The Bureau of Reclamation traces its beginnings back to the **Reclamation Act of 1902** or "Newlands Act," after its originator, Francis Newlands. Newlands was a successful San Francisco lawyer and beneficiary of his father's Nevada silver mine who spent three years, from 1888 to 1891, losing half a million dollars on a venture known as the Truckee Irrigation Project. Switching from water to politics, Newlands gained a congressional seat and served in the same era as conservationist president Theodore Roosevelt. Both Roosevelt and Newlands believed that the waters of the West were going to waste and that private enterprise could never sustain the level of development necessary to bring these waters under control. The Reclamation Act was a distinct departure from federal government policy of the day. It brought the federal government into the resource development business in a manner not previously attempted. The newly created **Reclamation Service** went to work in several western states, establishing water projects and irrigation works with little regard for the agricultural businesses that would come to depend on them. But nowhere was the Reclamation Service's program more noticeable than in the massive undertaking dreamed up to bring water from the Eastern Sierra's **Owens River** to the budding metropolis of Los Angeles, 250 miles to the southwest.

The **Los Angeles Department of Water and Power**, established by the privately held Los Angeles City Water Company in 1904, saw the Owens River as the only answer to its two biggest problems: (1) the city's population had doubled to 200,000 in the past four years, and (2) the L.A. basin was a desert. **William Mulholland**, head of the LADWP, Fred Eaton, former mayor under employment of the Reclamation Service; and Joseph Lippincott, regional engineer of the Reclamation Service, went to work stealthily acquiring the water rights and reservoir sites necessary to bring ownership of most of the Owens River under their control. At times both legendary and infamous, the story of LA's "grab" of the Owens River would set the stage for an era of wheeling and dealing over water in the West that rivaled some of the best cowboy and Indian tales. L.A. got its water, and the Owens Valley went into decline. Land speculators such as Harry Chandler and newspaperman Harrison Gray Otis became enormously wealthy buying un-irrigated farmlands and selling them at huge profit when Owens water began flowing into the San Fernando Valley in 1913. By 1924, Owens Valley residents took to insurrection, first blowing up sections of the aqueduct, and then arming themselves and opening up gates that fed aqueduct water back into Owens Lake, cutting off the supply to L.A. in 1927. Infuriated, Mulholland convinced the city to send a trainload of heavily armed detectives to quell the battle. Miraculously, without bloodshed, Owens Valley residents backed down, and order, by L.A.'s definition, prevailed.

Shasta Dam, a large multipurpose Bureau of Reclamation project on California's Sacramento River. (Courtesy of the Bureau of Reclamation)

The next crisis quickly fell in March 1928 when the 11.4 billion gallons of water stored behind the project's flawed **Saint Francis Dam** tore down San Francisquito Canyon and the Santa Clara River into Castaic Junction, Piru, Fillmore, and Santa Paula before hitting the sea at Ventura. Estimates counted the dead at 450. Mulholland's dam had failed. Engineers would not again make an error this horrendous until **Teton Dam** 50 years later. For all the benefits provided by water development in the West, the ambitious L.A. Aqueduct project, early on, demonstrated the reality of the potential costs.

Beginning in 1933, Franklin Roosevelt's New Deal assured that an era of water development would make its mark on the American landscape. The Work Projects Administration (WPA) allied with the Bureau of Reclamation and Corps of Engineers to construct enormous development projects on the major river systems of the West, including the Columbia, Colorado, and Missouri. On the Columbia River watershed in Montana, Idaho, Oregon, and Washington there are no fewer than forty-four federal dams. The works of the Bureau of Reclamation would provide cheap electricity to the Pacific Northwest and enable the economic development of the western states.

The Bureau of Reclamation partners with a variety of agencies to manage outdoor recreation at 289 recreation areas attached to BR water projects. Turning most of the provision of outdoor recreation management to the federal NPS, USFS, USF&WS, and BLM, the Bureau of Reclamation also partners with non-federal agencies and organizations, and manages solo at 33 recreation areas. Well-known national recreation areas managed in partnership between BR and NPS include the Glen Canyon NRA surrounding the Bureau's Lake Powell on the Colorado River, and Lake Mead NRA, further downstream behind Hoover Dam.

Massive turbines driven by gravity-powered water generate hydroelectricity. (Courtesy of the Bureau of Reclamation)

Waterways

The U.S. Army Corps of Engineers found a less direct route to the water business, becoming established more than a century before the Reclamation Act. The Corps' origin dates to 1775 when George Washington established the Corps of Engineers as part of the Continental Army. The work of this unit consisted of building battlements, fortifications, and roads for military purposes. During peacetime in 1824, Congress assigned the first civil works functions to the Corps, removal of sandbars and snags from the major **navigable rivers** of the East and Mississippi watershed. Comprehensive river basin resource development was planned in 1890, and in 1936 the Corps was given responsibility for **nationwide flood control**. On the West Coast, the Corps improved harbors and inland waterways such as the navigation projects in San Francisco Bay and the Sacramento River. Often referring to their dams and reservoirs as "projects," the Corps manages the water as well as the surrounding lands, making the Corps a major provider of outdoor recreation in the U.S. The authority to develop and manage outdoor recreation sites was granted to the Corps in the 1944 Flood Control Act. Since that time, **economic values** of water-based recreation have come to be included in **cost-benefit analyses** used in justifying water project expenses.

Cumberland Dam and Locks on the Ohio River, waterways management by the U.S. Army Corps of Engineers. (Courtesy U.S. Army Corps of Engineers)

Fish ladder scaling Ice Harbor Dam on the lower Snake River. Mitigation measures such as these have slowed, but not halted the decline of the northwest salmon fishery. (Courtesy U.S. Army Corps of Engineers)

Pork

Congress, the two big water agencies, and regions bolstered by the development of water resources formed a powerful political structure to advocate more dams and irrigation works. Coupled with the abilities of engineers to build ever more challenging dams, the Corps of Engineers and Bureau of Reclamation entered into a sort of interagency rivalry that heralded the era of big dam development dubbed the "pork barrel."

Pork barrel politics is a reference to the antebellum (pre-Civil War) practice on many plantations when, on some holidays, a barrel of salted pork was rolled out for the slaves. The ensuing frenzy, where ill-nourished slaves grabbed all the pork they could, provided entertainment for the plantation owners balconied above. The pork barrel was later used as a metaphor for the Federal Treasury, full of money and frenzied over by congressmen eager to carry off "pork" to their constituencies back home. Big water projects became a method to secure huge appropriations that would be spent in areas where dams and irrigation works were built. What better way to assure reelection, congressional leaders thought, than by bringing loads of money back to the home district? Citizens back home were served by the flood control, electrical, and irrigation benefits of the projects, the Bureau of Reclamation and the Corps made out big, and politicians got to put their stamp on things larger and more permanent than themselves. This triangle of back-scratching held sway for years, slowed only when environmentalists began to question the merits of some obviously political "make work" development projects.

Flood control is a primary mission of the U.S. Army Corps of Engineers.
(U.S. Army Corps of Engineers)

Tennessee Valley Authority

The Tennessee Valley Authority (TVA) was established in 1933 by President Franklin Roosevelt as a quasi-governmental private corporation aimed at developing the water resources of the Tennessee River watershed covering much of Tennessee and small parts of Virginia, North Carolina, Georgia, Alabama, Mississippi, and Kentucky. One of the poorest regions of the country during the Depression, much of the region remained without electrical power. A series of large dams brought flood control and electricity to the region, and an economy came out of the doldrums. The TVA never quite became the self-sufficient corporation its founders had hoped for, but with federal subsidies, the experiment was marked a success. Together with the regional presence of the Corps of Engineers, the TVA is a major provider of resource management and outdoor recreation opportunities.

The TVA has not been without its environmental detractors. So much water development was bound to rearrange the nature of the Tennessee River watershed. In the 1970s, the TVA once again reached national prominence—not for the proud, progressive development of water resources, but for its unrelenting drive to continue dam building for benefits that were questionable. The TVA became the object of the first and best-known battle for the protection of endangered species under the 1973 Endangered Species Act. The Department of the Interior and citizen groups invoked the act to save the supposedly endangered

snail darter from the construction of **Tellico Dam** on the Little Tennessee River. In TVA v. Hill (437 U.S. 153, 1978), the Supreme Court ruled that TVA violated the Endangered Species Act, temporarily halting completion of the dam. Subsequent congressional and administrative actions allowed TVA to finish and operate the dam, despite the judicial decree. To this day, critics use the snail darter story as an example of environmentalism gone awry.

Controversies

The image of big dams has become synonymous with the industrial might of the U.S., as well as an environmental symbol of the costs that water development brings to free-flowing riparian systems. The era of big dam building slowed to a crawl in 1977 when President Jimmy Carter placed a moratorium on the continued funding of eighteen federal water projects. Serious questions had been raised about

The remnants of the Bureau of Reclamation's Teton Dam, which failed in 1976. (Photo by Steve Dennis)

the benefits such projects were bringing. And other questions asked whether the environmental alterations were worth it. Standing up against big water during a drought year in the West was not among Carter's more brilliant political moves. He got slammed. But the slowdown brought a new look at a number of projects and left them in limbo for years. Auburn Dam, on the American River upstream of Sacramento in California, was under construction in 1977. In the 30-plus years since it was counted among the 18 projects to be cut, Auburn Dam has moved no further than the drawing board and debating tables.

The collapse of the Bureau of Reclamation's Teton Dam in June of 1976 likely weighed on Carter's mind when he made his politically disastrous move to slow the rolling barrel of pork. Killing 11 people and destroying an estimated $2 billion in property and agriculture, the Teton Dam was a project of doubtful value and was constructed in a questionable site. It is frequently used as an example of the worst-case scenario that can unfold in developing water resources. Forty-eight years after Mulholland's Saint Francis Dam failed, Teton again pointed the finger at overzealous dam proponents. But the collapse of a dam is only one of the aspects of water development that raises controversy. The following provides a partial synopsis of pro and con arguments on dams and water projects:

Pro

- Dams, levees, and other structures offer flood control in regions frequently inundated by uncontrolled rivers and streams.
- Dams provide a relatively cheap and clean source of electrical power.
- Dams have allowed the irrigation and agricultural development that have made the U.S. the "breadbasket of the world."
- Reservoirs provide enormous opportunities for outdoor recreation; and controlled flows provide for recreation that might otherwise not exist, such as a trout fishery or whitewater opportunities.

Con

- Dams inundate natural riparian systems, altering ecosystems and burying valuable cultural heritage sites.
- Dams hold back waterborne silt that regenerates floodplains with valuable soil.
- Dams block the movements of migratory fish, particularly **anadromous** species such as salmon and steelhead.
- Reservoirs cannot replace lost white-water floating recreation.
- Reservoirs will eventually "silt in," becoming useless for water storage.
- Dams and irrigation projects have brought too much agriculture into action, mucking up the markets for some commodities and requiring federal price supports and subsidies.
- Many dams and reservoirs have cost more than they're worth; costs of development and operation exceed benefits.
- Dams and reservoirs alter wildlife habitat.

This list is by no means complete, but it should give an idea of the arguments involved in controversies over water development. Considering that the Bureau of Reclamation has in the past planned for dams and reservoirs in the Grand Canyon, one can imagine the fever-pitch level to which such controversies can escalate. Battling dams on the Colorado River in the 1950s and 1960s, environmentalists (led by a growing Sierra Club) halted dams in the Grand Canyon and at **Echo Park** in Dinosaur National Monument. In a compromise, however, **Glen Canyon Dam** was built, flooding Lake Powell into 195 miles of the Colorado River in some of the most remote and unique canyon country on earth. Still a sore point, Lake Powell is considered among the most beautiful reservoirs in the world. The Sierra Club, however, advocates dismantling the dam and letting the Colorado flow through Glen Canyon again. Expressive of the symbolism of battles over dams, the Bureau of Reclamation once pointed out that a reservoir in the Grand Canyon would allow motor-boating recreationists the chance to see the canyon close up. In retort, the Sierra Club bought full-page ads in *The New York Times, Los Angeles Times*, and *San Francisco Chronicle* asking: "Should we also flood the Sistine Chapel, so tourists can get nearer the ceiling?"

Suggested Readings

Barcott, B. (1999, February). Blow up. *Outside*, 70–79, 102–104.

Linenberger, T. R., & Glaser, L. S. (2002). *Dams, dynamos, and development: The Bureau of Reclamation's power program and electrification of the west.* Washington, D.C.: U.S. Department of the Interior, U.S. Government Printing Office.

Murchison, K. M. (2007). *The snail darter case: TVA versus the endangered species act.* Lawrence, KS: University Press of Kansas.

Pisani, D. J. (2002). *Water and American government: the Reclamation Bureau, national water policy, and the west, 1902-1935.* Berkeley, CA: University of California Press.

Reisner, M. (1988). *Cadillac desert: The American West and its disappearing water.* New York: Penguin Books.

Rowley, W.D. (2006). *The Bureau of Reclamation: origins and growth to 1945.* Denver, CO: Bureau of Reclamation, U.S. Department of the Interior; Washington, D.C.: U.S. Government Printing Office.

Sipes, J. L. (2010). *Sustainable solutions for water resources: policies, planning, design, and implementation.* Hoboken, N.J.: John Wiley.

Wilkinson, C. F. (1992). *Crossing the next meridian: Land, water, and the future of the West.* Washington, D.C.: Island Press.

chapter twelve

State Government Involvement in Natural Resources

States and Natural Resources

States have been in the resource management game from the time that their predecessors, the colonies, began to control use and access to insure resource supplies. The Great Ponds Act, passed by the Massachusetts Bay Colony in 1641, set aside 2,000 bodies of water covering 90,000 acres as public resources available for fishing and hunting. The **"state's rights"** 10th Amendment of the U.S. Constitution gives states the authority for resource management, stating: "The powers not delegated to the United States by the Constitution, nor prohibited by it to the States, are reserved to the States respectively, or to the people." Thus, the management of resources not specifically under the authority of the U.S. belongs to the states, and then to the local governments. Of course, the lines between authorities are not distinct. States have frequently challenged federal authority over their resources, particularly in western states that contain large amounts of federally managed land.

States often contain agencies that look very similar to their federal models. Many states have state park systems patterned after the National Park Service example. State fish and game, forestry, water development, and regulatory agencies govern resources under laws that are the primary source of authority in the absence of federal regulations. In a number of cases, state laws are actually more powerful than federal laws, particularly when they are more restrictive or demand higher standards for legal compliance. California's **Environmental Quality Act**, for example, requires the documentation of environmental impacts on nonfederal and even private developments, surpassing the powers of NEPA, its federal counterpart.

Lands Management

States manage lands under a wide variety of designations. Perhaps the two best examples are areas managed as parks and those managed as game refuges. Some states also manage forests under multiple-use guidelines, often as areas for experimental, or demonstration forestry. Minnesota, for example, manages 58 state forests covering nearly 4 million acres. States also manage water resources, in some cases on a massive scale, such as the **State Water Project** in California.

A state-managed recreation and resource area. (Photo by Steve Dennis)

Speaking of California, this state provides a good example of the ways in which states are involved in resource management. Structurally, lands management is housed under the state's "umbrella" super-agency, **The Natural Resources Agency.** In a way, the Natural Resources Agency would be like the federal Department of the Interior if all lands managing agencies were housed under its single roof. The following major state agencies function under the Natural Resources Agency:

- Department of Parks and Recreation (DPR) manages the State Park System. Similar to the NPS, California operates a statewide system of parks, wilderness areas, recreation areas, scenic and scientific reserves, historical units, beaches, wayside campgrounds, underwater parks, and off-highway vehicle recreation areas. Beginning with California Redwood State Park (Big Basin Redwoods) in 1902, California's park system has grown to encompass 1.25 million acres in more than 270 units of significant natural, scenic, cultural-historical, and recreational values. The DPR also functions as a major planning and assistance agency, funneling federal and state grant dollars for state and local park development and providing planning expertise.

- Department of Fish and Game (DFG) is the state agency regulating California's wildlife resources. The DFG operates an extensive system of wildlife refuges, reserves, and "management areas," and runs a number of fish hatcheries. DFG provides for enforcement of regulations using game wardens and investigative officers. The department's specific objectives are to (a) maintain all species of fish and wildlife for their natural and ecological value, (b) provide for varied recreational use of fish and wildlife, (c) provide for an economic use of fish and wildlife for the state, and (d) provide for scientific and educational uses of fish and wildlife.

- Department of Water Resources (DWR) manages the State Water Project, called the eighth engineering marvel of the modern world. One of the few states with the fiscal resources capable of tackling such a huge project, California built the SWP in the 1960s, harnessing the Feather River with Oroville Dam. Huge pumps send water south from the Delta via the California Aqueduct, and then up and over the mountains into the L.A. Basin. The vast network of 34 lakes, reservoir and storage facilities, 20 pumping plants, five hydroelectric power plants, four pumping-generating plants, and over 700 miles of canals and pipelines has led many to observe that California is the most extensively plumbed area on earth. The SWP provides water to 25 million Californians and 750,000 acres of irrigated farmland. Avoiding people management, DWR turns over surface waters and surrounding lands management to other state agencies, usually DPR or DFG. DWR is also responsible for programs in floodplain management, flood control, and drinking-water quality.

- California Department of Forestry and Fire Protection (CalFire) is the agency primarily concerned with fire prevention, suppression, and other emergency services. CalFire also manages California's eight State Forests and a State Forest Tree Nursery program. Similar to the fire management function of the USFS, CalFire maintains fire-ready crews and regularly inspects rural areas for compliance with fire safety regulations. In many rural areas, CalFire is a principal provider of emergency services, responding to accidents and medical emergencies. Additionally, CalFire (a) regulates logging practices on private forest land, (b) provides advisory assistance to small landowners on forest management, (c) regulates controlled burning of brushlands, and (d) provides for assessment of the state's forest and rangeland resources.

- California Department of Boating and Waterways (DBW) is the state agency involved with boating, waterways, marinas, and harbors. The agency (a) makes grants for the development of small craft harbors and launching facilities, (b) promotes boating safety and education, and (c) licenses yacht and ship-brokers to protect consumers from fraudulent acts.

- California Department of Conservation (DC) is primarily a regulatory agency whose stated objective is to protect, conserve, and ensure informed development of the state's earth resources. DC's major divisions and offices include (a) Land Resource Protection, (b) Mine Reclamation, (c) California Geological Survey, (d) Oil, Gas and Geothermal, and (e) State Mining and Geology Board.

- California's Department of Resources Recycling and Recovery (CalRecycle) is the state's authority on recycling, reduction, and re-use of products. Responsible for implementation of California's Integrated Waste Management Act and the Beverage Container Recycling and Litter Reduction Act, CalRecycle Boasts that California leads the nation with a 59 percent recycling rate for all materials.

Regulation

In addition to its resource-managing agencies, California sports a number of regulatory and advisory boards and commissions. These groups are appointed to provide advice and make policy decisions regarding management of resources under their control:

- The State Board of Forestry governs forest management practices within the state through its charge of implementing the California Forest Practices Act.
- The State Parks and Recreation Commission oversees the operations of the Department of Parks and Recreation.
- The State Fish and Game Commission sets policies for regulation of fish and wildlife in California.
- The California Coastal Commission regulates private and public development within the coastal "zone" established under the Coastal Zone Management Act of 1976. Additionally, the commission is the state agency involved in federal outer-continental shelf oil and gas drilling decisions.
- The State Lands Commission manages parcels of undedicated lands received from the federal government including (a) beds of naturally navigable waterways, (b) tide and submerged lands from the mean high tide line seaward to the three-mile limit, (c) swamp and overflow lands, (d) vacant school lands, and (e) granted lands.
- The Wildlife Conservation Board is primarily responsible for acquiring property for the purpose of protecting and preserving wildlife while providing fishing, hunting, and recreational access.
- The California Energy Commission plays a strategic role in the planning and development of state energy policy.
- The San Francisco Bay Conservation and Development Commission works to meet broad public concern over the future health and vitality of San Francisco Bay.

- The Delta Protection Commission is chartered to ensure orderly, balanced conservation and development of Delta land resources and to improve flood protection.
- The Colorado River Board of California was established in 1937 to protect California's rights to Colorado River water, and to represent the State in negotiations over the river and its management.
- The Central Valley Flood Protection Board cooperates with the U.S. Army Corps of Engineers and other state and local agencies to control flooding and to develop and maintain flood control works.
- The State Mining and Geology Board, under the Department of Conservation, represents the State's interest in the use and conservation of mineral resources, in the reclamation of mined lands, and in the development of geologic and seismic hazard information.
- The Native American Heritage Commission assists local and federal agencies, citizens, educational institutions and Native Americans with the protection and preservation of cultural resources.
- The State Historical Resources Commission is responsible for the identification, registration, and preservation of California's cultural heritage.
- The State Off-Highway Motor Vehicle Recreation Commission cooperates with the State Parks and Recreation Commission and advises with regard to OHV plans and applications for grant funds for new and expanded recreation areas.

It should be clear by now that states are deeply involved with the management of natural resources. Most states will show a resource management structure similar to that of California's, if not quite as extensive. We are all involved, in one way or another, with state-level regulation and management of natural resources. Informed citizens will want to make themselves familiar with the structure of their state's resource management agencies and regulatory bodies. In the next chapter, government gets even closer to home, in describing special districts, county, and municipal governance of natural resources. Also discussed will be private lands and governmental regulation of privately held resources.

Special Districts, County, and Municipal Involvement in Natural Resources

Special Districts

Special districts have been created to deal with a variety of governmental functions that are not well served by traditional federal, state, county, or municipal jurisdictions. Special districts, like these other governmental structures, are able to collect taxes and make expenditures in support of their missions. Generally, special districts have been created when county and municipal boundaries do not effectively govern people's service needs in a region. For example, a cluster of small towns within a large county all have needs for education. People reside within these municipalities, and in the unincorporated (non-city) areas in between. The cluster of population does not match either the borders of the cities or the boundaries of the county. It may be more efficient for the education function to be administered by a special district, with new boundaries drawn encircling the service area that will best meet the needs of the regional population. Because a new special district will have the power to tax, residents within the service-area boundaries must vote to create the district. If the district is voted into existence, its governing body, usually called a board of directors, will also be elected and given authority to manage the affairs of the district. A special district's directorship may also be appointed if it is entirely within a county's jurisdiction, or a city council may be given directorship authority for the district's purpose.

Special districts are created to meet service needs such as education, water management, police and fire services, sewage and waste disposal, flood control, transportation, conservation, historical preservation, parks, open space, and recreation. Creation of special districts is dependent on state enabling legislation. State legislatures provide for the establishment of numerous

Special Districts are created to provide services to areas that are not well represented by county or municipal boundaries. (Photo by Steve Dennis)

types of special districts. Some examples of resource managing special districts in the San Francisco Bay Area include: (a) The East Bay Regional Parks District, (b) Midpeninsula Regional Open Space District, and (c) the Marin Municipal Water District. Each of these districts provides open space for outdoor recreation, aesthetic, and resource benefits. Facilities development varies. The East Bay District is intensively developed for high levels of use in some park units, more primitive in others. The Midpeninsula Open Space District is virtually undeveloped, and the Marin Water District maintains trails and limited access to reservoirs. Though their issues seldom make national news, operations on special districts are of great importance to residents within their taxing jurisdictions. One example of a hotly contested policy has been the persistence of off-road bicyclists to gain access to the lands managed by the Marin Municipal Water District. Managing trails that are open to hikers and equestrians, the MMWD has not allowed legal access to mountain bikers. The meteorically rising popularity of mountain biking has brought great pressure on the district to open its trails. The district has maintained that cyclists exacerbate erosion, reducing water quality. Its compromise position has been to restrict mountain bikers from 130 miles of hiking trails, while allowing them on 90 miles of fire roads.

Counties and Cities

Both county and municipal jurisdictions have the authority to manage natural resources on lands they may own. Additionally, many counties and cities enter into cooperative agreements to effectively deal with cross-jurisdictional resource management concerns. Cities and counties operate extensive park and recreation systems throughout the U.S. The establishment of **Boston Common** in 1634 as pasturage for town residents is held as the first city park on what was to become U.S. soil. Still a park today, Boston Common is a swath of parkland in central Boston. The designs of Savannah, Georgia, and Washington, D.C. incorporated park and open spaces that remain features of these cities to this day. Most famous among city parks, New York City's **Central Park** was designed in 1858 by landscape architect **Frederick Law Olmsted**, who later collaborated on planning for Yosemite Valley when it was deeded to the State of California. County and city parks and open-space areas are important contributors to the recreational and aesthetic qualities of urban landscapes throughout the country. But by far the most important role played by cities and counties in the natural resources management system lies in the power of these jurisdictions to govern the uses of private land.

Most of the land in the U.S. is held in private ownership. This form of possession was favored by the founding fathers and was the impetus of the era of disposal that marked the first century of our existence as a nation. Any public lands map of the U.S. clearly portrays the westward pattern of settlement. Compared with the western U.S., very little public land exists east of the Rockies. It was

Frederick Law Olmsted designed New York City's Central Park and was instrumental in the early parks movement in the U.S.
(Courtesy of Library of Congress)

the lands from the Rockies westward that remained in government ownership at the time withdrawals began in the late 19th century. Approximately 60% of land in the U.S. is privately owned. Except for a smattering of powerful state and federal regulations, authority for natural resource-related decisions is reserved for the property owner, and the power of "**local government**" to make land-use decisions.

Powers: Corporate and Police

Perhaps the most noticeable power of local government (county and municipality) is the **corporate power**, or the power to tax and spend. Special district, city, and county jurisdictions, like the state and federal governments, have the power to levy taxes on residents within their borders and to spend monies for the benefit of citizens. Property owners are well accustomed to the annual property tax bills being assessed by their counties. This tax collection often includes assessments for city dwellers and taxes required by special districts. The other place we see the corporate power of local government is on our income tax statements, where there is often a tax deduction for local taxes due. Beyond taxation and other revenue-collecting mechanisms, the corporate power also allows local governments to spend. This power would include the authority to purchase lands for park, open space, or other natural resource values. In order to spend, local governments can also borrow. Bonds are the means frequently used by local governments to gather enough capital to finance purchases and projects that would otherwise be too expensive for the usual budgetary process. When a local government floats a bond, it must put a ballot measure before the voters, asking if they're willing to assume the financial obligation to pay it back. In other words, the government is asking if the citizens would be willing to pay higher taxes until the bond is paid off. If they get approval, the local government borrows money from a financial institution, which in turn offers the bonds for sale to investors. The local government gets the money it needs, pays back the loan in interest and principal using the taxes it collects from residents, and the residents get a new city park, or open space, or fire engine, or whatever it was they voted for.

Local government is empowered by many states to regulate land use under the police power. Police power is, in effect, the power of local governments to control the behavior of people within their jurisdictions. Power over behavior includes acts ranging from spitting on the sidewalk to running a stop sign to developing a parcel of private land. Regulation of land use at the local level is often referred to as zoning, and it has not been easily granted. For years, the right to property under the Constitution was interpreted to mean that owners were to enjoy virtually unregulated use of their land. In the early 1900s, however, communities began adopting zoning ordinances that placed restrictions on certain types of land uses within specified "zones." These ordinances were generally passed by citizens of influence, who didn't want certain noisy, smelly, and ugly land uses taking place near their homes. It made sense, they argued, to keep residential areas residential. Conflicting uses such as commerce and industry should have areas where these activities could be grouped. Under local governments' police power, land use zoning was thus enabled. But it did not happen without challenge.

In the landmark 1926 ***Euclid v. Ambler Realty Co.***, 272 U.S. 365 case before the U.S. Supreme Court, Ambler Realty brought suit against the Village of Euclid, an upscale suburb of Cleveland, arguing that the city's zoning ordinance constituted a "**taking**" of Ambler's property without "**due process**" of law and without equal protection under the law. The Village of Euclid defended its 1922 zoning ordinance, in effect saying that the quality of life in the community was dependent on the ability of the local government to regulate certain land uses. The real estate industry had selected Euclid as a test case, hoping to neutralize zoning practice by winning a precedent-setting decision before the U.S. Supreme Court. It was expected that the conservative court of the day would side with Ambler Realty. Wrong. With former President William Howard Taft at the helm, the court backed Euclid and zoning in a 6-3 decision. It seems the justices were swayed by arguments that urban conditions were becoming increasingly complex. Crowded cities needed to be able to regulate land uses. Recognizing the Supreme Court precedent set in this case, cities throughout the country began actively planning for land uses and adopting **zoning** ordinances. The most common types of zones used by cities and counties include the following:

- Residential

- Commercial

- Industrial

- Agricultural

- Open space

Of course, property rights advocates were not particularly pleased that their local government could plan and zone, regulating the free use of their property. Regulation of private land use has always been a contentious issue. Over time, people have generally grown accustomed to zoning, and in most cases appreciate the way that zoning can help to separate incompatible uses of land. However, the balance between the regulatory powers of government and citizens' rights to property is a precarious one. The foundation of citizens' right to property begins with the Fifth Amendment to the Constitution, which says property shall not be taken without "just compensation." The 14th amendment states that no state shall deprive a person of property without "due process" of law. On the government's side, certain takings of private property are legally justified when necessary for the "**public good**." Takings have always been controversial, but communities would often see the wisdom in usurping the individual's objectives for the needs of the group. Of course, the usurped individual had rights to just compensation. In other words, if government wanted a person's property for some collective benefit, it had to pay for it, and at "fair market value."

Best known among the types of taking is the process known as "eminent domain." Under eminent domain, governments have the right to "condemn" private property when some publicly necessary project needs that specific chunk of land. Originally, eminent domain powers applied only to schools, roads, and other publicly owned projects. Recently, eminent domain has been more liberally interpreted to include redevelopment projects, where a city would acquire lands and then resell them to a developer who would build the type of development desired by the community. Though the lands would become private, the public benefit derived from the new development, as interpreted by the Supreme Court, is sufficient to justify the use of eminent domain. Thus an area deemed as "blighted" can be condemned, owners bought out, and the lands then redeveloped by new owners, who purchase the property from the local government. The owners in the area designated as "blighted," however, may not see it that way. They may be quite content where they are. When condemnation proceeds, they are often offered prices for their property lower than they think is appropriate. It may not be enough money to buy other property in the area without inducing financial hardship. The local government, of course, wants to be on the cheap side of fair market value. So along come the lawsuits from the property owners alleging that they are not being offered just compensation under the Fifth Amendment.

The use of eminent domain to directly transfer private land to another private owner was contested to the Supreme Court in **Kelo v. City of New London**, 545 U.S. 469 (2005). New London (Connecticut) claimed the transfer and subsequent redevelopment of waterfront property would add 3,000-plus jobs and more than a million in annual tax revenues. The court ruled in a 5-4 decision that governmental taking of property to transfer ownership between private parties in the interest of economic development is a permissible "public use" meeting the requirements of the Fifth Amendment. Kelo's house was eventually moved and New London paid higher compensation to landowners, but the redevelopment was never built. The case elevated paranoia over takings, and 42 states passed legislation limiting municipalities' power to use eminent domain for economic purposes.

Eminent domain transfers title to property from a private owner to government ownership. It's pretty straightforward, if controversial. **Land use regulation** such as zoning, however, does not transfer title. It alters the "bundle of rights" to property enjoyed by the landowner. Considering that 60 percent of the nation's land is in private ownership, it was inevitable that society's push for environmental protection would eventually flop into the backyards of private citizens through the regulatory processes. The U.S. started managing lands by designating un-owned property as parks, monuments, and reserves. Over time, the "free" public lands were pretty much used up. Continuing the trend of managing property for public benefit eventually required the purchase of properties, and that started getting unrealistically expensive. So land use regulation, following the example set by zoning, began being used as a means to move toward socially beneficial objectives. Regulation basically would "take" some of the property owners' rights, and repossess them for the common good. In this manner, environmental benefits could be obtained without cost. But it wasn't that simple, particularly if the rights taken from the bundle deprived the individual property owners of use, enjoyment, or economic value of their property. When this happened, property owners would claim that their property values were being taken without either just compensation or due process or both. Thus began an era where the precarious balance between guaranteeing the property rights of individuals and providing for the socio-environmental welfare of the community would be weighed in the courts.

Euclid v. Ambler set the stage for zoning regulations, and from the 1920s until the 1980s, planners generally assumed the ability to limit property rights through zoning and regulation. In 1987, however, two cases from California moved the U.S. Supreme Court to limit regulators' authorities over private property rights. In the case ***First English v. Los Angeles***, 482 U.S.304 (1987) the First English Evangelical Lutheran Church of Glendale challenged L.A. County's decision to disallow the church's reconstruction of a retreat and camp for handicapped children that had been destroyed by floods in Tujunga Canyon. The county maintained that buildings should not be rebuilt within the flood zone, and so it passed a regulatory ordinance to that effect. Property rights advocates saw the test case opportunity and pushed First English to the Supreme Court. In a 6-3 ruling, the Court sided with the church, stating that the landowner whose property has been taken by regulation is entitled to just monetary compensation. Six decades after Euclid, the court began to slow a trend of regulatory authority over the property rights of citizens. Even though regulation was seen as necessary to protect the welfare of society, the court was now saying that not all regulation came free. In First English, the Supreme Court was now saying that government would have to pay for the taking of certain rights from the property owner's bundle.

Two and a half weeks later, the court decided in the case ***Nollan v. California Coastal Commission*** 483 U.S. 825 (1987) that the commission could not demand a public easement across Nollan's property as a condition of allowing Nollan to replace the house on his beachfront property. In Nollan, a regulatory authority known as exaction was challenged. Exactions were essentially exchanges of certain property rights for permissions to use or develop land. The court decided that the regulatory agency must show some relationship (or nexus) between the permissions sought, and the exaction demanded. In 1992, the case ***Lucas v. South Carolina Coastal Council*** 505 U.S. 1003 (1992) came to the Supreme Court when David Lucas claimed damages against South Carolina for taking his property. Lucas had spent almost a million dollars in 1986 for two beachfront lots on which he intended to build. Two years later, the South

Carolina Coastal Council forbade construction on the lots under a development ban aimed at reducing beach erosion. The court ruled that the regulation aimed at preventing public harm (beach erosion) did not justify the removal of Lucas' rights to economic or productive uses of his land. In overruling South Carolina's Supreme Court, which had backed the regulation, the Supreme Court was saying either to change the regulation or pay Lucas the $1.25 million he demanded had been taken. In 1994, in ***Dolan v. City of Tigard*** 512 U.S. 374 (1994), the court used the precedent set in the Nollan case to uphold the claims by a plumbing store owner that her request for a permit to expand her store led the City of Tigard to attempt to "take" some of her property for a drainage greenway and pedestrian/bicycle path. These cases have brought the property rights versus public welfare argument before a Supreme Court markedly more conservative than the courts under which government regulatory authority expanded in the 50 years or so preceding it. But the struggle will never be over, and the property rights and regulatory authority questions will be major players in the game of resource management in the future.

Organization of Cities and Counties

The decisions over local land use questions fall to counties and cities organized in a variety of different ways. Generally, their structure contains

1. a planning department or public works department that reviews development proposals and checks to see if the proposal is in line with state or local laws and codes. Additionally, the planning department will look for consistency with the local general plan, if there is one. The planning department then advises the planning commission.

2. a planning commission is composed of a group of citizens usually appointed by the local government to review plans and make recommendations to the local legislative body.

3. a local legislative body at the county level is often called a county board of supervisors. County Supervisors are elected. They have the power to make land use decisions regarding private lands and pass laws that are usually called ordinances. At the municipal (city) level, the legislative body is usually called a town or city council. They too make land-use decisions regarding private land within the city limits, and pass laws that are also usually called ordinances.

It is at these levels that citizens come most frequently into contact with government over issues relating to the management of natural resources. That's why it is important to understand the structure, functions, and powers of local government.

Private Lands Managers

Though the average owner of private land is a family with a house on a residential lot, there are a few individuals and a number of large corporations that own significant blocks of natural resource lands. First, railroads are still owners of large tracts of land. Having obtained lands through grants, railroads such as Union Pacific still hold lands that remained after selling properties to help finance their operations. Second, wood products companies such as Weyerhaeuser, Georgia-Pacific, and Boise-Cascade own considerable chunks of private timberland. Managing for forest products, these companies often also conduct and allow other multiple uses such as grazing, wildlife conservation, and outdoor recreation. Utility companies such as California's PG&E own lands surrounding reservoirs and impoundments intended for production of hydroelectric power. In some cases, utilities still own lands that have not yet been developed for energy production. Similar to wood products companies, these corporations often manage their lands for multiple uses and benefits. In real estate circles, a number of development companies have moved toward integrating wildlands with their planned communities and subdivisions. Keeping attractive lands in their "natural" state provides an additional value to adjacent nearby properties; it also may appease the conservation interests of the local regulatory authority judging the merits of development plans. **Private non-profit organizations** also may get into the land ownership and management business. Notable for property ownership and management among these groups are the **Nature Conservancy**, which acquires critical and significant environments for preservation purposes, and **Ducks Unlimited**, which has acquired tracts of land to provide important habitat for waterfowl.

Private lands managed by the Nature Conservancy. (Photo by Steve Dennis)

Suggested Readings

Bowman, A. O., & Kearney, R. C. (2009). *State and local government: The essentials* (4th ed.). Boston: Houghton Mifflin.

Fulton, W. (1999). *Guide to California planning* (2nd ed.). Point Arena, CA: Solano Press Books.

Ibrahim, H., & Cordes, K. A. (2008). *Outdoor recreation: Enrichment for a lifetime* (3rd ed.). Champaign, IL: Sagamore.

Jensen, C. R., & Guthrie, S. P. (2006). *Outdoor recreation in America* (6th ed.). Champaign, IL: Human Kinetics.

McCarthy, D. J., & Reynolds, L. (2003). *Local government law in a nutshell* (5th ed.). St. Paul, MN: Thomson/West.

Nolan, J. R., & Salkin, P. E. (2006). *Land use in a nutshell.* St. Paul, MN: Thomson/West.

Ruhl, J. B., Kraft, S.E., & Lant, C. L. (2007). *The law and policy of ecosystem services.* Washington, D.C.: Island Press.

chapter fourteen

Citizen Involvement in Natural Resources Issues

The "Environmental Movement"

The American land ethic, as an evolutionary social phenomenon, is best characterized as one that is constantly changing. Beginning with its European anthropocentric roots, the view of nature and nature's resources was forced to change because conditions in the New World were significantly different. Americans' paternal outlook toward the land slowly but dramatically shifted during the century from 1850 to 1950 from a lightly regulated free-for-all to a condition of guided management. Segments of society had begun to voice their concerns for the land, and their new philosophies were answered by government activities directed to provide new forms of stewardship. Innocent at first, this relationship between social groups and government would grow to become the dominant influence on American natural resources policy. Citizens learned that by banding together and standing for what they could describe as "right" for the environment, they could petition and succeed in directing the government agenda. Aided by the power of a visual media that itself evolved during this period, activists brought newsworthy images of environmental degradation into the living rooms of America. Brewing in the 1950s, blossoming in the 1960s, exploding in the 1970s, splitting in the 1980s, attempting to rediscover itself in the 1990s, and under assault in the new millennium, a new environmental movement evolved, captured the nation's attention, and indelibly marked the land and our minds.

Publics

We so often use the word *public* with "*the*" in front of it that we lose all track of its inherent diversity, mix of varied and conflicting values, and even its humanity. When we drive by a public works project under construction, invariably we ask what "they" are doing, disassociating ourselves from the we-ness of the project, which probably is siphoning off some small part of our paychecks and may even provide some small benefit to us as individuals during our lives, or at minimum, some cost. "The public," in our minds, becomes "they," not "us." We seem never able to agree with "them" because the public never exactly expresses our own individual set of values. The closest we get to agreement is in settings like sporting events where huge numbers of fans cheer in unison for their favored side. But then there is another side of "thems" cheering for a team that's dedicated to upsetting ours. In our localized agreeableness, "they" are still out there being disagreeable.

So, the term "the public" is an overused misnomer. *Webster's* provides a couple of definitions for "public." One is "the people as a whole." The other is "a specific part of the people." Fazio and Gilbert, in *Public Relations and Communications for Natural Resource Managers* (2000), defined "a public" as "two or more people with a common interest and who may be expected to react similarly to a particular situation or issue (p. 37)." Fazio and Gilbert take *Webster's* "specific part of the people" down to a group size as small as two people! The defining characteristics of Fazio and Gilbert's publics are that (a) people share at least one common interest, and (b) they will react to at least one issue similarly. This definition seems to fit the example of united sports fans pretty well. It also provides a useful definition of the innumerable facets of the environmental movement. Where we have so commonly thrown around the term "*environmentalists*," we have treated an extremely diverse set of people and values just as if we had called them "the public." Environmentalists in this way have also become "they." We're not sure what environmentalists are, but they must generically be just a little more inclined to hug a tree than we are. By categorizing people as preservationists, ecologists, conservationists, greens, environmental activists, or eco-freaks, we have made a feeble attempt to bring a little bit of clarity to the movement. But more likely, like sports fans, we're just picking the team for which we wish to cheer. Non-environmentalists are even harder to pin down. What is a non-environmentalist? We throw around terms like *developer, industrialist, logger, miner,* and hang tags on these people as non-environmentalists. But are they? A look at a past controversy with a bit of theory laid on top should help us get started looking at publics and how they effect natural resources management.

Publics and the Bitterroot Controversy

Fazio and Gilbert (2000) defined publics of importance to natural resource managers as fitting into two major categories: (1) internal publics and (2) external publics. Viewed from the eyes of employees of natural resource managing agencies, these distinctions make sense. The internal publics are comprised of the people who work for the agency. Additionally, people who work in similar resource agencies would be considered part of the agency's internal public because they often work with each other and are basically in the same line of work, in the same boat. Another segment of the agency's internal public are the folks who set policy and make budget decisions at higher levels of government, the legislators. Particularly close to the agency are legislators who sit on key committees that oversee the agency's operations. Certain legislative staff members would also be part of the internal publics. The agency's external publics, by Fazio and Gilbert's definition, would be all groups interested in the activities of the agency but not members of the internal publics. These publics would consist of residents living in proximity to the resource area, recreation visitors, community groups, industry groups, and environmental organizations. Their distinguishing characteristic is that they are not part of the agency's more easily defined internal publics.

Now, just to be difficult, it is necessary to make an improvement on Fazio and Gilbert. It seems that there are other publics that don't necessarily fit well into the dual distinction set up by Fazio and Gilbert. There are publics that know too much to be clearly left outside the agency in the *"external"* category. Let's call these the inside-outer publics. Inside-outer publics would be groups that are not part of the internal publics, but they work closely with them, and have influence that may stretch beyond that of the average external public. Inside-outers would include members of the media who might specialize in natural resource issues. University professors conducting research for resource agencies would not exactly fit either internal or external designations, so they can be considered inside-outer publics. Professional societies representing resource management disciplines would also be inside-outers. Many members of such organizations would be resource agency managers, but these societies also have many members from industry and environmental backgrounds. In short, inside-outer publics are groups that would be external, but have inside information and influence.

The **Bitterroot Controversy**, which showed the inside-outer publics theory in practice, unfolded in the late 1960s and hit the fan in the early 1970s. It was a turning point in the public relations of the U.S. Forest Service, and from the agency's eyes, not a positive turn. Remember that the USFS had been conducting Pinchot's "scientific forestry" since its beginnings. Generally, the agency's works had been successful. They enjoyed, with Smokey at the helm, a positive public image of clean-cut "rangers" roaming around in green-and-gray pickup trucks and caring for the nation's trees. In the postwar era, USFS timber harvesting increased, and this practice inevitably steered the agency on a collision course with the environmental movement. The Forest Service's crucible became the silvicultural practice of **clearcutting**. In West Virginia and

Montana, clearcutting would be challenged not for its scientific merits or flaws, but for aesthetic, economic, and legal reasons.

On the Bitterroot National Forest in Montana, the USFS had employed the practice of clearcutting to remove old-growth stands of trees, and regenerate even-aged stands of second growth that would vigorously replace the old growth timber in eighty to 100 years. Clearcutting is mildly unattractive to a forester, but to a forest lover it is ugly. The internal publics of the Forest Service saw from their "scientific forestry" perspective stands of "decadent" old growth replaced by young trees that would supply wood products for future generations. To environmentally leaning residents of the Bitterroot region, these clearcuts were scars on a landscape that was an important part of their lifestyles. These external publics didn't like what they were seeing on the public lands around them. To make matters worse, the Forest Service was **terracing** the steep clearcut slopes to provide access to logging equipment and to reduce erosion and enhance regeneration. Locals characterized the terraces as looking like Asian rice paddies clinging to hillsides—not a typical American landscape.

Expressing outrage, the external environmentally leaning publics worked on internal public member, Senator Lee Metcalf. Metcalf requested an independent investigation into the practices on the Bitterroot by inside-outers from the University of Montana School of Forestry. The UM School of Forestry released *"A University View of the Forest Service,"* which quickly became famous as the **"Bolle Report,"** named for Arnold Bolle, the forestry school's dean. The report was critical of USFS management objectives, but that was no big deal, it had happened before. What made the *Bolle Report* significant was the way another inside-outer public played up one of the report's major findings. The report had stated that the clearcut and terrace practice was quite expensive. The costs of altering the mountainsides could never be regained through the investment lifetime of the new timber. The "smoking gun" came with the report's powerful assertion that even "timber mining" (harvest with no replacement) would be a preferred practice from an economic point of view. The inside-outer press had a field day with that one. Imagine Smokey, that ursine image of forest protection and renewability, practicing mining, the truly non-renewable resource management method. *Now that was news*! Headlines, news stories, and editorials swept the media, condemning the USFS as an agency that couldn't be trusted. Here was a report from their own profession, a school of forestry (inside-outers), claiming that the USFS was deliberately wasting public resources. Then, of course, came the conjectures and theories that this malpractice was because the USFS was in the pockets of the timber industry, **captured** by them. Swept by the media, the external publics wondered how the trusted Forest Service had gone sour.

The Forest Service defended itself, explaining the silvicultural reasoning behind clearcutting to publics that did not want to listen. Agitators among the external publics became activists, and anger escalated over the perceived immobility of the Forest Service. Recognizing the opportunity to gain some political capital, legislators (internal) brewed up anti-clearcutting legislation aimed at halting the practice pending further studies. The 1972 "Church Guidelines" from the Senate came forward with recommendations that the USFS use environmental care, but fell short of outlawing clearcutting. Another sellout, railed the activist external publics. Not satisfied, they continued to push for an end to clearcutting. Litigation was in the works over clearcutting on the Monongahela National Forest in West Virginia. The Bitterroot and Monongahela controversies together would promulgate new statutes reasserting congressional authority over the Forest Service. A new era of "management in the fishbowl" of public scrutiny had dawned.

The Capture Concept

Agency personnel directed to manage public natural resources are forever stuck in the middle. They will attempt to employ scientific methods that were learned in professional education programs to do what is best for the long-term sustainability of the resource. But that attempt will look wrong to external publics leaning to either the environmental side or the developmental side. The agency will appear to be captured by the influences of the other side. This is the claim made by environmental activists against the Forest Service. Because the USFS allows timber companies to harvest national forest trees, it seems that the wood-products industry has "captured" the agency, that the Forest Service is bowing to the demands of the timber industry. On the other hand, when environmentalists succeed in securing declaration of a new USFS-managed wilderness area or in blocking a timber harvest, it looks to the timber industry as if the agency has been taken over by environmentalists. In fact, the resource agency is practicing what Theodore Lowi (2010) termed "*satisficing*." Satisfice is a word built from "*satisfy*" and "*sacrifice*." It implies that to satisfy one perspective is to sacrifice the opposing perspective. When resource managers weigh their options in decision making, they are left with three major concerns: (1) their "mission," as spelled out in legislation and regulations; (2) scientific practice that paves the way toward meeting their mission; and (3) the involvement of publics and the influence of their varying crusades. Back in the good old days, the mission and scientific practice drove decisions. Publics were not much of a factor after the first great American environmental movement around the turn of the 19th to 20th century. But in the second great environmental movement, which began in the 1950s, publics were to become the dominant force in decision-making. Publics could influence missions, even scientific thinking. But could they truly "capture" an agency?

Paul Culhane explored this question in *Public Lands Politics* (1981). He conducted an in-depth study of the U.S. Forest Service and the Bureau of Land Management to see if the agencies appeared overly influenced by some side of their deeply divided constituencies. He studied the agencies' backgrounds, interviewed agency employees, environmentalists, utilitarians (product-oriented folks), and used empirical research methods to get to the bottom of claims of agency capture. One of the most interesting of Culhane's findings came in what he termed an "**environmental-utilitarian**" (E-U) scale, on which he measured the basic values for natural resources held by environmentalists, utilitarians, and agency employees. Measuring values ranging from very environmental to very utilitarian, Culhane hypothesized that capture would show up through the leanings of the agency people. The data showed that the agency people's E-U values were right in the middle. Industry people tended to lean toward the utilitarian side of the scale, and environmentalists toward the environmental side. Holding the middle ground (at least with regard to their values) were the employees of the USFS and the BLM (Figure 14.1).

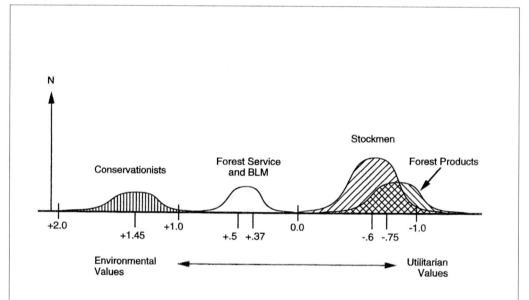

Figure 14.1. Culhane's Environmental-Utilitarian (E-U) Scale. Culhane's E-U Scale demonstrated centrist environmental values among USFS and BLM resource managers.

Culhane's findings helped build a case that these agencies are not, in fact captured by a particular clientele group. However, the *appearance* of capture is easy to see. From the utilitarians' perspective, the agencies look like they're closer to the environmentalists. Likewise, if you view it from the environmentalists' side, it looks like the agencies are leaning toward the utilitarians. Stuck in the middle, the natural resource agencies constantly compromise between the demands of their varied external public clientele groups. Compromise, Lowi pointed out, satisfies no one. To satisfice is more likely to produce a "lose-lose" than a "win-win" situation. Resource managers are thus forced to try to maintain an essentially untenable position. As publics grow more skeptical of science and find means to influence the political process, the strongest remaining guidepost for resource management becomes the struggle of interest groups to capture agencies through the hearts and minds of the people.

The "Issue-Attention" Cycle

Anthony Downs published a paper in 1972 entitled "Up and Down with Ecology: The Issue-Attention Cycle." In his paper, Downs described how issues come to people's attention and then move through a cycle of changes in interest over time. Downs used the environmental movement as one of his examples of the **"issue attention cycle**," noting that it had been through its heyday and seemed to be on the wane. Though time would prove that Downs misjudged the demise of the environmental movement, his model has frequently been used to explain the ongoing ebb and flow of environmental issues. Downs suggested that most social issues, including environmental ones, go through a five-stage process including:

1. *Pre-problem stage*, during which the problem or social ill exists, and may have caused concern among experts, but is not yet perceived as a problem by society.

2. *Alarmed discovery and euphoric enthusiasm* is the stage where society gets the message, often due to some catalyst event and extensive media coverage. An immediate reaction to fix the problem rises enthusiastically.

3. *Realizing the cost of significant progress* occurs when society begins to discover that the cost of fixing the problem is very high, thus mellowing the initial enthusiasm.

4. *Gradual decline of intense public interest* sets in as reality rears its ugly head and people start to understand the complexity and difficulty of solving the problem. People get discouraged, or they may feel threatened by the problem, or perhaps boredom sets in. Media attention falls off as some new issue comes to the front burner for a while.

5. *Post-problem stage* takes place well into the future, as new issues replace the old one, and people relegate the issue to their memory banks. Occasional recurrences bring attention back to the issue, since overall awareness has been heightened.

One can observe all kinds of problems and issues that make regular excursions through Downs' theoretical model. When you consider the British Petroleum Deepwater Horizon oil spill in 2010, for example, you can see the cycle at work. In the pre-problem stage, drilling practices in the Gulf of Mexico were potentially dangerous, requiring rigorous oversight and safety measures. The alarmed discovery and euphoric enthusiasm phase played out when the fatal accident, fire, and onset of the oil spill from the Deepwater Horizon brought an outcry including President Obama's call to drop offshore oil drilling only months after he had endorsed the practice. The cost of significant progress became clear when continued attempts to stop the oil leak proved slower than met the liking of affected publics and the media. Public interest gradually declined when the

Gulf oil spill was capped after 86 days. In the post-problem phase, the oil spill progressed into lower levels of public awareness as damages reimbursements were negotiated and the government pondered whether continued cleanup efforts would generate more environmental harm than benefit. The massive oil spill in the Gulf of Mexico stands at a higher level of awareness than in its pre-problem phase. Hindsight highlighted the ludicrousness of Vice Presidential candidate Sarah Palin's use of the "drill baby drill" slogan coined at the 2008 Republican National Convention, marking the characteristic heightened awareness that remains as the Issue Attention Cycle plays itself out over time.

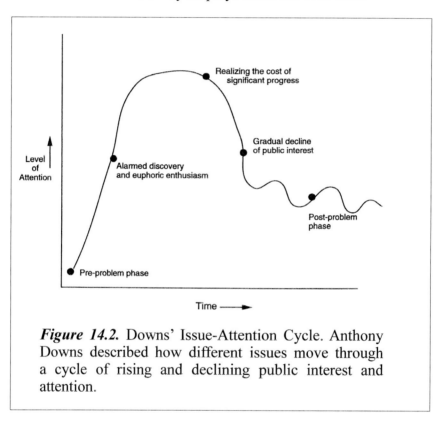

Figure 14.2. Downs' Issue-Attention Cycle. Anthony Downs described how different issues move through a cycle of rising and declining public interest and attention.

The issue-attention cycle does not apply all that well to the environmental movement as a whole. Rather, it tends to mirror the courses of specific environmental issues as they move onto the stage of public concern. As an example, **toxic wastes** were not of inordinate concern at the time Downs published his cycle, but they still represented a significant problem. In 1972 (pre-problem stage), people simply did not know that toxic wastes were a time bomb waiting to be discovered. In the city of Niagara Falls, New York, a residential subdivision and school had been built atop a landfill covering the chemical waste dump of a departed company known as Hooker Chemical. The company had been using the abandoned Love Canal bed in the 1940s and early 1950s as a convenient spot to dump steel drums containing some 20,000 tons of waste chemicals. Residents of the homes surrounding the landfill began noticing that their children's feet burned when they played in the grass. Leaking barrels became exposed in low spots, and noxious odors and "black, gooey stuff" appeared in backyards and basements. Other complaints eventually led state epidemiologists to investigate, and they discovered high rates of birth defects, miscarriages, epilepsy, liver disease, rectal bleeding, and headaches. Alarmed discovery kicked in, as the media followed the story. The Love Canal neighborhood was situated atop an environmental nightmare; something had to be done. President Jimmy Carter proclaimed the subdivision a federal disaster area in 1980 and agreed to the government purchase of contaminated homes and the absorption of relocation costs. Lois Gibbs, a Love Canal mother, founded the Citizens' Clearing House for Hazardous Wastes and went to work as the clarion call warning of toxic waste dangers. Toxic waste stayed in the news as more and more sites were discovered, and activist women stepped forward to protect working-class America from this threat. Congress passed and Carter signed the "**superfund**" legislation in 1980, creating a billion-dollar fund aimed at cleaning up the 30,000 identified toxic waste sites. By the end of Reagan's second term, only 16 of the 800 sites on the National Priority List had been cleaned. The high cost of significant progress had hit home. Intense public interest faded as attention turned to endangered species, acid rain, old growth forests, greenhouse gasses, ozone "holes," and the Exxon Valdez disgorging its ooze into the pristine waters of Prince William Sound and Alaska's gulf coast. Toxic wastes hadn't gone away; they just weren't trendy anymore. Gradually, as people grew threatened by images of deformed children and high cancer rates, toxics moved into the realm of the post-problem stage. Over time, heightened awareness has led to tighter regulation of toxic wastes, and identified Superfund sites have declined to 1,280. But the problem has not gone away. Downs' predicted recurrences have happened so we are constantly reminded that we've poisoned parts of our planet.

Citizen Organizations

Publics, it should now be apparent, will form and involve themselves with specific issues that will cycle through time. As issues come and go, so too, do the publics that became active with them. Over the long haul, certain publics maintain a reasonable level of consistency and remain stalwart in their stands on natural resource and environmental issues. Some of these organizations become household words, and their deeds became topics for discussion. Groups such as the Sierra Club and **Greenpeace** are well known to Americans, whether they agree with them or not. What makes these outfits tick? And what keeps them active in the drama played out over natural resource values? Why don't they succumb to the fading interests of Downs' post-problem stage? Go figure.

Organizing for all sorts of purposes has been called an American trait. The French political scientist Alexis de Tocqueville wrote in the 19th century that "Americans ... are forever forming associations." He found that in the U.S., people grouped for virtually anything. Proclaiming association status gave meaning to causes, pulled people together, and motivated energetic works. A quick perusal of the thousands of groups listed in *The Encyclopedia of Associations* bears witness to de Tocqueville's observation. "**Interest group politics**" has become synonymous with the American political system, even more so than the previously accepted "**pluralistic democracy**." Forming or joining citizen organizations is a favored method of generating political efficacy in the United States. It is little wonder that environmental causes have often been expressed through the activities of organized groups.

Citizen organizations are miscategorized by popular media as often as environmentalists and utilitarians are painted as good guys and bad guys, cops and robbers, cowboys and Indians. Terms such as **public interest groups, pressure groups, lobbies, special interests**, etc., are used to describe many types of groups that may be getting mislabeled. All of these types of groups can be described as citizen organizations, or organized interests. One interesting aspect of environmental groups is that they are a unique form of organization called voluntary associations. Membership in these groups is voluntary, yet they maintain considerable size and influence. How do they pull this off?

A couple of theories help to explain the persistence of groups formed to join the fray over environmental issues. Political economist Mancur Olson (1971) searched for the reasons why people would join voluntary associations. He described a "**free-rider**" problem of economically rational people who would figure there was no need to join as long as the organization did its work. Even if this rational person benefited from the efforts of the organization's political work, there remained little reason to join. This is sort of like watching or listening to public broadcasting without pledging a donation. Will it go off the air if most people don't join? That possibility is unlikely. The same free-rider logic should prevent political voluntary associations from surviving. But they have flourished, and Olson and others chased down some reasons why. First among the motivations for joining would be the **collective goods** sought by the organization. This might be clean air, more wilderness, or reduction of toxic waste. These goods are collective because they will supposedly benefit everyone, whether or not they are members of the organization. But collective goods accrue to nonmembers as well, encouraging free-riders. To understand this problem, theorists claim that voluntary associations offer selective incentives—selective because only members can get these goodies. Selective incentives include member-only benefits such as informational newsletters, magazines, discounts, travel opportunities, and a slew of other benefits from auto insurance deals to credit cards. These material selective incentives are often matched with solidary selective incentives. These are intangible rewards obtained by members that include social and psychological benefits such as feeling good, enjoying group fellowship, social interchange, and status within the group. It is no small wonder that virtually all of the major national environmental groups (a) offer members slick magazines (material selective incentives) and

(b) structure into local chapters that provide opportunities for the realization of solidary incentives.

To round out the thinking on the phenomenon of voluntary associations, and to describe the origins of group leadership, theorists have also described **resource mobilization theory**. This idea recognizes that associations begin with some group thinking similarly about an issue or a situation. Remember the definition of publics? If the issue is a big-enough deal, a social movement will begin to well up. Social movements acquire names such as the "environmental" movement, "pro-choice" movement, "antiwar" movement, "property rights" movement, etc. These movements are composed of people with available resources. They have time, money, and in some cases, political clout or name recognition. For a group to form, a cadre of entrepreneurs seizes the opportunity to organize and claims it will represent the interests of the social movement. Previously disorganized, publics sharing the organization's view rush to join up, often during the euphoric enthusiasm phase of issue attention. These entrepreneurs have "mobilized the resources" of the social movement. They have created jobs for themselves and sometimes made out pretty well in the bargain. Now for the organization to survive, they need to continue to offer incentives, both collective and selective. As their issue may fade into post-problem obscurity, their long-term survival will also be dependent on the continuing recognition and elevation of similar but new problems. A cycle of beating the issue-attention cycle is thus ensured.

Types of Citizen Organizations

A wide variety of citizen organizations have formed, thrived, and died or survived. They all share the common trait of representing the similar interests of at least one public. The environmental movement has provided fertile ground for the development of citizen organizations, because there are so many aspects of the environment that become embroiled in controversy. Consider this short list: acid rain, wetlands protection, endangered species, global warming, toxic waste, oil spills, air pollution, water pollution, native lands rights, old-growth forests, mining, cattle grazing, ground-water contamination, off-road vehicles, fisheries depletion, wilderness designation, landfills, nuclear power, and we're just getting warmed up! When you realize that all of these issues can be subdivided into geographic regions of concern, that species can be singled out for their own specific causes, that each type of mining raises concerns, that every national park and wilderness carries its own set of specific issues, then it becomes possible to fathom the massive scope of opportunities for citizen organization presented by the environmental movement.

To make at least some sense of all this, let's propose the following general list of the functions of citizen organizations:

1. Land Conveyance and Management

2. Policy Influencing

3. Litigating

4. Activity Promotion and Coordination

5. Professional Alignment

6. Specialization and Protest

A citizen organization may practice several of these functions, or it may emphasize as few as one. The functions that these citizens' groups perform will influence the type of membership they'll draw and the various strategies they will employ.

1. Organizations that focus on land conveyance and management seek to bring lands (often private) into a conservation or preservation management regime. The group may directly purchase lands or work as a broker to convey lands from private ownership to a public resource agency. The Nature Conservancy is an example of an organization that purchases and then manages "critical and significant environments" to protect habitat and unique resource types. Ducks Unlimited purchases lands to protect waterfowl habitat. The Trust for Public Lands acts as a broker, or intermediary, between private owners and public land managers, and attempts to facilitate the exchange of lands to public status.

2. Policy-influencing organizations take aim at government and attempt to push public policy toward their agenda. Utilizing a broad range of tactics to pursue their ends, groups such as the Sierra Club, the National Wildlife Federation, Greenpeace, the Wilderness Society, the National Rifle Association, the National Parks and Conservation Association, and the Audubon Society strive to convince lawmakers that society will be well served by backing the organization's agenda.

3. Litigating organizations specialize in using the judicial system to further their goals, bringing suits to delay or block specific actions or to set significant precedents. Examples in the environmental arena include the Earth Justice Legal Defense Fund, which was originally part of the Sierra Club but separated into its own organization, and the Natural Resources Defense Council.

4. Some organizations are chiefly concerned with the activity promotion and coordination of a particular form of engagement with natural resources. These groups often represent various forms of outdoor recreation, and they work to maintain or increase opportunities for the activities' enthusiasts. If

you pick an outdoor recreation activity, you're likely to find an organization representing its adherents, from the U.S Snowboard Association to the All-Terrain Vehicle Association.

5. Professional alignment organizations represent the interests of publics involved with specific professions. In resource management circles, there are a number of these professional societies, including the National Recreation and Parks Association, the Society of American Foresters, Resources for the Future, the Wildlife Society, the Society for Range Management, the American Fisheries Society, and the Western Interpreter's Association.

6. Specialization and Protest groups tend not to fit the distinctions drawn among the groups noted above. Though various forms of protest are employed by many of the previously mentioned groups, protest may not be their primary tactic. Groups specializing in protest form out of frustration with causes that are not being answered through traditional remedies. Protest groups may find themselves in a minority and thus hold no hope for achieving their desired ends without resorting to severe and headline-gathering measures. Some groups, such as Greenpeace, got their start as protest groups and then became more mainstream as their popularity increased and memberships soared. Others (e.g., as Earth First!) launched onto the national stage through dramatic (and in some cases, humorous) actions that caught the attention of the media and brought what might have been obscure environmental problems to the people's attention.

Among social movements, the environmental movement has consistently endured. Questions of how we should develop or preserve natural resources will face us as long as our species survives. In the American political context, solutions to resource problems are debated openly between people in schools, meeting halls, government chambers, courts, in print and broadcast media, and in on-site confrontation. Assembling into groups, diverse publics have found methods to increase their individual power through collective action. In the next couple of chapters, we'll look more closely at how these processes work, and attempt to explain how you will eventually take part in them.

Suggested Readings

Berry, J. M. (1977). *Lobbying for the people*. Princeton, NJ: Princeton University Press.

Coffman, M. S. (1994). *Saviors of the earth?* Chicago: Northfield Publishing.

Culhane, P. J. (1981). *Public lands politics: Interest group influence in the Forest Service and the Bureau of Land Management*. Baltimore: Johns Hopkins University Press for Resources for the Future.

Dana, S. T., & Fairfax, S. K. (1980). *Forest and range policy* (2nd ed.). New York: McGraw-Hill.

de Tocqueville, A. (1969). *Democracy in America.* J. P. Mayer, (Ed.). Garden City, NY: Doubleday.

Downs, A. (1972). Up and down with ecology: The issue-attention cycle. *The Public Interest* (28), 38-50.

Fazio, J. R., & Gilbert, D. L. (1986). *Public relations and communications for natural resource managers* (2nd ed.). Dubuque, IA: Kendall/Hunt.

Gale Group (Eds.). (2001). *Encyclopedia of associations* (38th ed.). Farmington Hills, MI: The Gale Group.

Hays, S. P. (1987). *Beauty, health, and permanance: Environmental politics in the United States, 1955–1985.* New York: Cambridge University Press.

Lowi, T. (2010). *The end of liberalism: the second republic of the United States* (2nd ed.). New York: W.W. Norton & Co.

McCarthy, J. D., & Zald, M. N. (1977). Resource mobilization and social movements: A partial theory. *American Journal of Sociology, 82* (6):1212–1241.

Mitchell, R. C. (1979). National environmental lobbies and the apparent illogic of collective action. In C. Russell (Ed.), *Collective decision making.* Baltimore: Johns Hopkins University Press for Resources for the Future.

Moe, T. M. (1980).*The organization of interests: incentives and internal dynamics of political interest groups.* Chicago: University of Chicago Press.

Nebel, B. J., & Wright, R.T. (2000). *Environmental science: The way the world works* (7th ed.). Upper Saddle River, NJ: Prentice-Hall.

Olson, M. (1971). *The logic of collective action: public goods and the theory of groups.* Cambridge, MA: Harvard University Press.

Wilson, J. Q. (1995). *Political organizations.* Princeton, N.J.: Princeton University Press.

chapter fifteen

Activism and the Legal Avenues for Public Involvement

Vehemence in Citizen Groups

Citizen organizations employ a variety of strategies to exert influence in achieving their objectives. Traditional methods such as lobbying and letter-writing campaigns have been effective at times in the past and continue to provide varying levels of success. But with natural resource and environmental issues, success is a relative concept that may range from perceptions of victory to perceptions of defeat. **Mainstream environmental organizations** such as the National Wildlife Federation, the Wilderness Society, the Sierra Club, and the Audubon Society have become large businesses accustomed to the give-and-take compromise of the political system. Still representing the values of their longstanding memberships, these organizations have begun to seem too slow, too willing to "play the game" to activists looking for fast and dramatic change. To these activists, compromise is a failed objective. Nothing less than the complete cessation of activities they perceive as environmentally degrading will satisfy their aims. In some cases, and on specific issues, these action groups have been successful in bringing about significant change. Their headline-grabbing confrontations have built followings of publics that ally with the apparent underdog. The most successful of these groups has been the organization Greenpeace, the folks who brought the plight of marine mammals to the television sets of America.

Greenpeace got its start in confrontational protest as a tiny group calling itself the "Don't Make a Wave Committee." First an antiwar group, they attempted to sail into the nuclear test zone of Alaska's Amchitka Island in 1971. Under the leadership of Paul Watson, the group changed its name first to Greenpeace Foundations, and later, to Greenpeace. They moved operations to the northern fur seal hunting grounds, where members were able to bring images of hunters clubbing snow-white harp seal pups to American TV sets and magazine racks. Gaining immediate attention, Greenpeace financed the vessel *Rainbow Warrior* and set out on the open seas in search of whalers. Positioning themselves in tiny zodiac rafts between whales and the cannon-powered harpoons of massive commercial whaling vessels, with cameras rolling, Greenpeace aroused emotions and sympathy and brought about an international outcry against whaling. Holding to its antinuclear stance, Greenpeace became a particular thorn in the sides of the French, whose giant nuclear power industry and continued nuclear testing in the South Pacific provided steady fodder for protest. Again in rafts, Greenpeacers filmed the dumping of nuclear wastes in the Atlantic, getting dangerously close to the 55-gallon waste drums jettisoned by French vessels. In the Pacific, Greenpeace would sail into the French test zone on Muraroa Atoll, eventually leading French agents to blow up the *Rainbow Warrior* in Auckland, New Zealand, in 1985, killing a passenger. Constant action and obliging media coverage made Greenpeace one of the largest and fastest-growing environmental action groups in history. By 1990, Greenpeace USA was pulling in $50 million a year and 10,000 new members a month. Action, it seemed, aroused support. But the 90s were not like the prior two decades, and by 1997, Greenpeace USA would find itself in debt, borrowing from its parent organization, Greenpeace International. The economic downturn in the 2000s was also not encouraging for environmental organizations, but in 2009, Greenpeace was holding on to a quarter of a million members in the U.S. and annual revenues over $25 million dollars.

Greenpeace, for all its activism, remained too peaceful for its founder, Paul Watson. In 1977, he protected a seal pup by forcefully removing a hunter's club. Having broken Greenpeace's prohibition against violence, Watson was tossed from the organization. Undaunted, Watson founded the Sea Shepherds Conservation Society and moved forward with more extreme activities, including coverage in the Animal Planet cable channel's *Whale Wars* series in its fourth season by 2011. Sea Shepherds was eventually gathering the types of notoriety that previously had been Greenpeace's domain, leading Greenpeace to more radical methods in an escalation of activism among environmentalists and animal rights groups. Americans began seeing video of sabotaged whaling vessels, beachhead landings to attack Russian mink farms, the liberation of animals from laboratories, and other media-broadcast stunts that kept the organizations in the news.

Using similar tactics to get its start, **Earth First!** captured attention in the early 1980s when a group of disenchanted environmentalists created a militant group that would "make the Sierra Club look moderate." Adopting the slogan "No compromise in defense of Mother Earth!" Earth First!, under the leadership of Dave Foreman, Howie Wolke, and Mike Roselle, began a cross-country "road show" interspersed with confrontational protests and occasional humorous antics. On the face of Glen Canyon Dam they unfurled a 200-foot black plastic "crack" in a gesture of protest against the dam's alteration of the Colorado River. On Bald Mountain Road, Earth First! members stared down bulldozers driven by a road-building crew, earning a spot on the evening news and some jail time. Earth First! advocates would go to New York dressed as owls to protest financier Charles Hurwitz's management of the redwood holdings of the Pacific Lumber Company. Foreman would publish the book *Ecodefense,* detailing instructions for environmental sabotage, or "**monkeywrenching**." Ecotage became an Earth First! specialty, with tactics such as pouring Karo syrup into heavy equipment, "spiking" trees, blocking roads, and disabling power lines. The mix of environmental bravado and irreverence would soon make Earth First!—like Greenpeace—a household name. But Earth First! remained essentially anarchistic in structure and never joined the money-making, membership-promoting structure of Greenpeace or the other major environmental organizations. As a result of arguments about whether to endorse or ban tree-spiking, divisions in the Earth First! movement began to grow. Today, Earth First! continues to operate in small cadres, devoid of its founders, ready to launch the next preservationist crusade. Still capable of making national news and bringing attention to the issues they pursue, Earth First! provides one of the clearest examples of a move toward vehemence among citizen action groups.

The "**animal rights**" controversy has tended to provoke extremism among citizen groups. Crossing a spectrum from the "Fund for Animals" to "People for the Ethical Treatment of Animals" (PETA), animal welfare groups have proliferated and have even spawned organizations aimed at opposing their goals. Tactics have neared the extremes witnessed in the anti-abortion movement, where abortion-performing doctors have been murdered by unrepentant "right-to-lifers." It is perhaps a peculiarly modern notion that has led to the crusade for animal protectionism. Wildlife biologists have long described a "Bambi Syndrome" at work among anti-hunting organizations and significant numbers of urban Americans. The syndrome is caused by anthropomorphism, where people begin to attribute human characteristics to animals. Bambi is used to describe this view of nature, after the Disney movie that featured a talking fawn orphaned by evil hunters. A steady stream of smart and talking animals has beamed into the theaters and TV sets of America. Cartoon characters from Mickey Mouse to Yogi Bear to Tweety Bird have portrayed animals as very human, although they are capable of taking any amount of physical abuse and snapping back to form for a laugh. Feature films and television shows with very human-like animals have included "Black Beauty," " Lassie," "Flipper," "Grizzly Adams," "Mr. Ed," and a host of mammals featured on Disney's Sunday night shows in the sixties and seventies. Our love of pets, and our treatment of them as part of the family, binds us to animals in a singular fashion, unlike the multiple purposes seen for animals by our farming forebears. This benevolent view of wildlife has helped drive anti-hunting and animal rights groups into the public arena. The outcome of this politicization of animal welfare has been to challenge the objectives of wildlife managers, who have long relied on hunting as one means to regulate wildlife populations.

Another temporarily effective protest was pulled off in the early 1970s by Mark DuBois, founder of the citizen group Friends of the River. When construction of the New Melones Dam on the Stanislaus River in California threatened to flood a pristine canyon and obliterate the most popular run of white water in the U.S., DuBois chained himself to a tree at an unknown location near the reservoir's rising waters. Issuing a statement that he was prepared to die to protect the river, DuBois put officials in a precarious position. With the officials already suffering a public relations fiasco, if DuBois was telling the truth and they proceeded to fill the reservoir, they'd have a martyr on their hands. So they stalled for negotiations, filling was halted, and DuBois came out of the woods. Inevitably, New Melones was filled, but DuBois had made his headlines and created the euphoric enthusiasm that launched Friends of the River as an environmental organization.

Unfortunately, extremism also has spawned a degree of violence in the protest arena. In October 1998, arsonists torched resort facilities at Vail, Colorado, causing $15 million in damage. Allegedly, the fires were set to protest Vail's planned expansion into undeveloped lands adjacent to the ski area. In 1999, a protester on Pacific Lumber Company land in Humboldt County, California, was killed by a falling redwood. Protesters claimed that the company dropped the tree to intentionally cause peril, while the Humboldt County sheriff planned to charge the protesters with manslaughter for putting one of their group in a dangerous, and eventually fatal, position.

Activism in its varied forms had become a mainstay among strategies employed by organizations to push their causes in the environmental debate. Extremism had the dual benefits of expressing commitment and drawing media attention. The successes and notoriety of groups like Greenpeace and Earth First! were not lost on the older and more traditional environmental organizations. In 1996, the Sierra Club, with Dave Foreman of Earth First! fame on its board, adopted a position advocating the dismantling of Glen Canyon Dam. The moderates in the Sierra Club were leaning closer to the radicals.

The somewhat blurry lines between activism, extremism, and terrorism became much more clearly drawn in the post-9/11 era. Acts that might have been considered brazen mischief or vandalism in the past are much more likely to be labeled terrorism today, leading extremists to reconsider their methods for creating splashes in the media.

Legal Avenues for Environmental Issues
and Access to the Judiciary

Activism in the environmental movement has played out in several arenas. Beyond the lobbies of Congress and the spasmodic flash of the media, environmentalists have turned to the judiciary as a means to further their causes. Also attracting headlines, famous court cases have aired the environmental agenda, testing the distances to which preservationism, government regulation, and property rights can be stretched. But the court is not like any other institution of American society. The judiciary is an institution of rules. Its procedures are strict and narrow. Its rulings can have effects that are either minimal or significant. As a venue for environmental controversy, the judiciary provides a specialized approach, and sometimes the method of last resort.

The National Environmental Policy Act of 1970 (NEPA) led to an increased use of the judiciary by parties claiming to be **aggrieved** by the actions of federal agencies. The issue of "**standing**" has been battered about with regard to whether these parties actually have the right to be heard in court. Standing, however, is only one hurdle to be overcome by a **plaintiff** seeking judicial review. As an umbrella term, standing is often incorrectly used in place of the correct term, **justiciability**. Justiciability and standing are important concepts for the informed citizen to understand, especially the citizen who may consider being a plaintiff someday.

The first concept to bear in mind is that the judiciary has a very limited focus and is relatively less powerful than the executive and legislative branches of government. With regard to environmental or natural resource litigation, the judiciary's power over public agencies lies in that peculiar branch of justice known as **administrative law.** Any prospective plaintiff should know that there are limits to what a court can do to **remedy** a situation. The two most important actions the court can take are (1) **declaratory judgments**, and (2) the provision of monetary restitution in **suits for damages**. Declaratory judgments are based on the Declaratory Judgments Act of 1934. In such cases, the court interprets the law to provide a decision in advance of an event's occurrence. In other words, the court's decision occurs before the event. Declaratory judgments are noncoercive (almost advisory), but are usually coupled with the coercive power of an **injunction**, which requires agencies or officials to alter or halt their course of action. Suits for damages, on the other hand, apply to cases brought after some alleged grievance has already taken place. In a suit for damages, the court decides whether the grievance is legitimate, and if so, then determines the appropriate sum to be awarded to the plaintiff in compensation for the damage incurred.

The concept of grounds must then be considered. Grounds essentially establish the facts relating to the nature of the alleged wrong. Two main types of grounds are most commonly considered: (1) procedural and (2) substantive. Procedural grounds are those that involve violation of the Due Process Clause of the Constitution. Specific procedures are outlined in laws that guide the activities of federal agencies. Statutes such as the **Administrative Procedures Act of 1946** and the National Environmental Policy Act guide agency actions. When these standards of conduct are not correctly followed, it may be cause for litigation against the agency's officials. Substantive issues are a little more "meaty." Substantive grounds establish that the agency action itself may be illegal or harmful to someone's rights. The proper procedure may have been followed, but the substance of the issue still generates grounds for a hearing before the court.

The next thing a plaintiff needs to know is whom he is able to sue. Certain governmental bodies cannot be sued because they are protected under the Doctrine of Sovereign Immunity. This doctrine was inherited from English law, which held that "The King can do no wrong ...." This is often an unpopular doctrine, but it can be waived under the Federal Tort Claims Act of 1946. Under such waivers (only about one-third of suits for damages are blocked by the federal government under sovereign immunity), individuals whose private legal rights have been violated by the government can still seek redress in the courts.

Agency and governmental officials can be tried as private citizens if one can prove that they are threatening to act or have acted illegally under color of state or federal law. Passed in 1871, 42 USC 1983 allows for the initiation of legal proceedings against state officers, as confirmed by the Supreme Court in *Ex Parte Young*, 209 U.S. 123 (1908). The Judiciary Act of 1875 was interpreted in *Bivens v. Six Unknown Federal Narcotics Agents*, 403 U.S. 388 (1971), to confer power on the courts to hear cases against federal officers. However, there are limits to one's rights to sue government officials. The **Doctrine of Official Immunity** protects prosecutors, judges, and legislators from suits for damages, owing to the nature of their duties and the importance of their discretionary power to protect the public interest. Executive officials (except the U.S. president) are partially protected by "**qualified immunity**." This doctrine states that the basis for a lawsuit against an executive official is "the violation of a legal right that a reasonable person should be aware of." Within the administrative structure, agency officials are considered executive; and therefore they are only partially protected by qualified immunity.

If the court can provide a remedy, and some party can actually be sued for injunction or damages, the prospective plaintiff must still gain access to the court on the strength and viability of the case and its relation to the parties involved. These access hurdles are the tests of justiciability.

The major test of justiciability comes from Article III of the Constitution. It states that any issue brought before the court must be a "real" case or controversy. This has been interpreted to mean that some legal wrong has been, or will be clearly inflicted upon an aggrieved party, and that judicial action will provide some meaningful remedy. This requirement precludes the court from providing advisory opinions. To clarify the Article III cases or controversies requirement, the Supreme Court has developed the **Doctrine of Limitations**, which mandates four tests of justiciability: (1) mootness, (2) ripeness, (3) political questions, and (4) standing to sue.

The first test under the Doctrine of Limitations is that a case must not be moot. A moot case renders a judicial decision ineffectual because a change in circumstances has precluded the need for a remedy. The exception to the Doctrine of Mootness is for cases involving "circumstances capable of repetition, yet evading review," from the decision rendered in *Roe v. Wade*, 410 U.S. 113 (1973). In this class-action suit that was brought against Texas abortion laws, mootness was ruled out because the plaintiff's term of pregnancy prior to a medically safe abortion was too short to survive the lengthy process of setting a court date, and the circumstances were certainly capable of being repeated.

The Doctrine of Ripeness concerns the timing and certainty of litigation. In essence, the court refuses to hear cases of a hypothetical nature, or review cases that "might" happen sometime in the future. In certain circumstances, court delay might force a party to suffer loss or break the law. In *Abbott Laboratories v. Gardner*, 387 U.S. 136 (1967), the court refined ripeness to include questions of (a) whether or not a case should be decided prior to the occurrence of an illegal action, and (b) what would happen to the aggrieved party if the court decided to wait.

A third limitation to judicial access is the Doctrine of Political Questions. The court will not hear cases involving questions more appropriate to the jurisdiction of the executive or legislative branch. An example of this is the court's refusal to address foreign policy questions. The court may have no judicially manageable standards for a decision, or there may be no means to enforce a decision, such as ending the Vietnam War—a case the Supreme Court dismissed as a political question in *Schlesinger v. Reservists Committee to Stop the War*, 418 U.S. 208 (1974).

Then, of course, there is the Doctrine of Standing to Sue. This hurdle to judicial access involves the question of whether a party actually has the right to a court hearing. The standing doctrine limits the broad judicial access mandated by Section 702 of the Administrative Procedures Act (1946). Section 702 is the most frequently used avenue to the judiciary; it states that "any person suffering legal wrong, or who is otherwise adversely affected or aggrieved by agency action, shall be entitled to judicial review."

The concept of standing is derived from court interpretations of the Administrative Procedures Act, other statutes, and litigation. It focuses on whether a party can show "injury in fact" when claiming to be legally wronged or adversely aggrieved. Standing has been interpreted as a concept that stretches from taxpayers' rights to challenge federal programs to nearly granting corporate rights to stand for inanimate objects. Taxpayers have limited rights to standing. In *Frothingham v. Mellon*, 262 U.S. 447 (1923), the court ruled that an individual taxpayer provides such a small increment to the sum of federal revenues that she does not have the right to sue against federal programs. However, in *Flast v. Cohen*, 392 U.S. 83 (1968), the court broadened taxpayer standing if the litigant was (a) challenging a federal spending program with a direct correlation to the litigant, and (b) invoking a specific constitutional limitation on Congress' power to spend.

Passage of NEPA was not the sole cause of increased court access for environmental purposes. The slow liberalizing of the concept of standing also has provided means for environmental litigants to seek redress before the courts. Standing's low point dates from the 1939 case *Tennessee Electric Power Company v. TVA*, 306 U.S. 118. In that case, the court ruled that the plaintiff could not claim standing, because it had not asserted property or contract rights. Because property and contract rights are not the only rights guaranteed under the Constitution, this case was viewed as an extremely narrow interpretation of the Doctrine of Standing. Among cases liberalizing standing, *Association of Data Processors v. Camp*, 397 U.S. 150 (1970), provides a glowing example. In this case, Justice Douglas took pains to write a decision that would liberalize standing and override the *Tennessee Electric* decision. In his majority opinion, Douglas stated that there are many types of legal interests beyond just property and contract rights. He went on to say that legal interests include aesthetic and environmental concerns as well! Today this decision has become the major determinant of standing over administrative agency action.

Following *Data Processors*, a number of attempts were made to further broaden the concept of standing. The Sierra Club purposely used the *Data Processors* decision to open up standing in **Sierra Club v. Morton**, 405 U.S. 727 (1972). In this "Mineral King" case, the Sierra Club claimed to have standing because of the group's long-standing concern over wilderness issues. Arguments before the courts included Christopher Stone's essay "*Should Trees Have Standing?*" which advocated that rights for inanimate objects should be represented in the same manner as those for corporate interests. However, the Supreme Court denied Sierra Club standing in its corporate capacity, because it had not claimed "injury in fact" to any individual club member. The failure to achieve standing in *Sierra Club v. Morton*, however, led to further distinction of standing to include any aggrieved individual who might have a particular interest (e.g., outdoor recreation) in an affected area.

Standing reached its most open in the case **U.S. v. Students Challenging Regulatory Agency Procedures**, 412 U.S. 669 (1973). In the S.C.R.A.P. case a group of law students studying administrative law were encouraged by their professor, John Banzhaf, to "sue the bastards" as a way to gain real legal experience and perhaps even to set a precedent or two along the way. They chose to create a tenuous link between an obscure ruling by the Interstate Commerce Commission (ICC) allowing railroads to increase freight rates, and an increase in pollution at recreation sites in the greater Washington, D.C. area. S.C.R.A.P. used NEPA to demand that the ICC prepare an **environmental impact statement** for the railroad rate increase decision. In a test of both NEPA and standing, the students in S.C.R.A.P. argued that the rate increase was a federal action, that it would raise the prices for recycled goods, that recycled goods would be less economical and would more likely be discarded, that the ensuing litter would mar the aesthetics of recreation areas in and around Washington, D.C., where S.C.R.A.P. members lived, that this would cause "injury in fact," and that the aggrieved party were the members of S.C.R.A.P. The Supreme Court agreed to hear the case, granting standing to S.C.R.A.P., and then went even further, ruling against the ICC and in S.C.R.A.P.'s favor, requiring the ICC to prepare an environmental impact statement in compliance with NEPA.

Another significant addition to standing's interpretation came in the case *Massachusetts v. Environmental Protection Agency*, 549 U.S.497 (2007), when the Supreme Court granted standing to several states and cities suing the Environmental Protection Agency (EPA) to force it to regulate carbon dioxide and other greenhouse gasses as atmospheric pollutants. In a 5-4 decision, the court recognized the states' need to represent the interests and well being of their inhabitants, broadening the definition of standing well beyond the specific interests of individuals.

Now that the aspiring litigant understands the basics of access to the courts, including the hurdles that stand in the way of determining justiciability, one must still consider two special requirements of administrative law. An agency is equipped with its own judicial process for providing administrative remedies. Before gaining access to the courts, one must exhaust these administrative remedies (if they are viable) by completing the required hearings and procedures for legal review mandated to the agency. Further, if the court and agency jurisdiction overlap, the Doctrine of Primary Jurisdiction requires that the agency remedy be sought prior to court access.

Finally, it should be noted that courts in the federal system are hierarchical. Very few cases make it to the Supreme Court (which is actually an appeals court). Litigation in the federal courts begins at the district court level and is appealed to the Circuit Courts of Appeals. Further appeals to the Supreme Court have slim chances of being heard. Of the 5,000 cases appealed to the Supreme Court annually, only about 200 are heard, and of those, 50 to 60% involve administrative law. Throw in the legal costs of sustaining cases through the court system, and judicial remedies begin to look cumbersome, slow, and very expensive. Nevertheless, the judiciary has provided a useful forum for challenges to projects and actions perceived as harmful to the environment. Environmental litigating organizations such as the Earth Justice Legal Defense Fund and the Natural Resources Defense Council have made this process their business. Countering the environmental perspective, litigating organizations such as the Pacific Legal Foundation and the Mountain States Legal Foundation represent and work to protect the rights of property owners and corporations against what they view as excessive governmental regulation of their rights for environmental purposes. The drama of society's struggle over natural resources will continue to play out on many stages. Among these, the judicial system provides one of the most interesting and definitive processes for environmental policy-making.Though time-consuming and tangled in procedure, court decisions are powerfully binding and can shape environmental policies for decades.

The next chapter will look at some historical and legal foundations for public involvement, along with some of the other strategies used by citizen organizations to influence policy.

Suggested Readings

Abbey, E. (1985). *The monkeywrench gang*. Salt Lake City: Dream Garden Press.

Aleshire, P. (1999, December). Troubled waters. *Phoenix Magazine, 34*(12), 76–81.

Anxious times on U.S. land. (1995, April 27). *The Sacramento Bee* (pp. B1, B4).

Begley, S., & King, P. (1994, October 24). Dangers of being green. *Newsweek.*

California forestry stunned by terror bombing. (1995, April–June). *Northern California Society of American Foresters Newsletter* (p. 1).

Chase, A. (1995). *In a dark wood: The fight over forests and the rising tyranny of ecology*. New York: Houghton Mifflin.

Coffman, M. S. (1994). *Saviors of the earth?* Chicago: Northfield Publishing.

Cortner, R. C. (1982). *The bureaucracy in court*. Port Washington, NY: Kennikat Press.

Dowie, M. (1995). *Losing ground: American environmentalism at the close of the twentieth century*. Cambridge, MA: The MIT Press.

Foreman, D. (1991). *Confessions of an eco-warrior.* New York: Harmony Books.

Foreman, D., & Haywood, B. (Eds). (1993). *Ecodefense: A field guide to monkeywrenching*. Chico, CA: Abbzug Press.

Gellhorn, E., & Levin, R.M. (2006). *Administrative law and process in a nutshell* (5th ed.). St. Paul, MN: Thomson/West.

Gifford, B. (1991, July). *Great green shakeout*. Outside (pp. 19, 20).

Heffron, F. A. (1983). *The administrative regulatory process*. New York: Longman.

Helvarg, D. (1994). *The war against the greens: The "wise-use" movement, the new right and anti-environmental violence*. San Francisco: Sierra Club Books.

Stone, C.D. (2010). *Should trees have standing?: Law, morality, and the environment* (3rd ed.). New York, NY: Oxford University Press.

Strauss, P. L. (et. al.). (1995). *Gellhorn and Byse's administrative law: cases and comments* (9th ed.). Westbury, NY: Foundation Press.

Williams, F. (1999, April). The old guard: Do the big dogs still have bite? *Outside,* 79–80.

Theoretical and Legal Foundations of Public Involvement

The Paths to Citizen Involvement

Freedoms of speech, of the press, to assemble, and to participate in the electoral process have taken us well along the path toward citizen involvement. As a society, we have been strongly involved in political affairs by design. A successful democratic republic is dependent on the informed participation of its populace. But not all aspects of governmental management fall conveniently under the approving gaze of the citizenry.

As originally structured, the federal government was intended to play a somewhat limited role in management. The activities of the central government were controlled by the people through representation, and representatives kept an eye out for the good of the people. But as the jobs of government became more complex, Congress delegated the authority for many functions to the administrative agencies. Agencies such as the U.S. Forest Service were given the task of management, relegating Congress to the roles of policy setter and overseer. Thus, a layer of insulation began to grow between the influence of the people and the operations of the administrative bureaucracy. This wasn't necessarily a bad thing. Agencies were trusted to work for the good of society. Talented people trained for specialist fields made up the workforce. Images such as that of the forest ranger were respected, if not admired. This approval worked to further insulate agencies from the oversight of publics. Agency personnel began to feel righteous about the work they were performing, even as society around them changed; and changes in society that were not reflected in the operations of public agencies set the stage for conflict.

We saw in the Bitterroot Controversy how publics contested the management practices of the U.S. Forest Service. Coupled with the battle over clear-cutting on the Monongahela National Forest, the USFS suddenly found itself the target of negative public opinion. Silvicultural practices long considered viable management methods did not fit the dynamic value structures of the environmental movement. The insulation effect had led to a crisis. Agencies found they could operate quite effectively while public approval was maintained. But when disapproval escalated to the point where citizens actively struggled to change agency practices, agencies found that they could no longer function effectively. The need to remove the insulation became apparent. The means to accomplish this removal seemed to be to invite publics to participate in the agencies' planning processes. If citizens were part of the plan, they would be more likely to support it.

The theoretical basis for public involvement claims that the following benefits accrue from the effective participation of citizens in the planning process: (a) public relations, (b) two-way communication, (c) convergence communication, and (d) diffusion of innovations.

Public Relations

Public relations benefits can be extremely important in maintaining a position of trust. Agencies recognize that they cannot effectively operate without the trust and goodwill of the publics they serve. This isn't the easiest position to maintain. Our society is growing ever more skeptical of government. Questions about agency credibility constantly provide material for the press, and the press is happy to pique our interest. Witness the success of TV shows such as *60 Minutes*, and *Frontline*. Good public relations are also difficult to maintain when an agency's job is to regulate. It should be noted again that agencies become the enforcing arm of federal regulations. New regulations will almost always benefit some publics, to the detriment of others. For resource managing agencies forced to "satisfice" between the divergent interests of varied publics, it is hard to win.

Public involvement is believed to benefit agencies' public relations status by "bringing people in," making them part of the planning process and demonstrating that the agency actually cares about their concerns. Public meetings put a human face on agency personnel and potentially open opportunities for improving understandings. This "outreach" by agencies is capable of building trust, and in so doing, improving public relations.

Two-way Communication

Two-way communication is another benefit of public involvement. One of the reasons agencies began to lose touch with the changes in society around them is that they were not effectively hearing the messages coming their way. For years, resource managers were notoriously ill equipped to work with publics. Resource managers sought careers to get away from people. The motivation of escaping to the woods has long been a strong reason for people to seek careers in resource management. In an era of public trust, managers were trained to improve the resources, not to deal with disaffected publics. They did not feel the need to produce information explaining management activities, nor did they seek public response to what they were doing. Everything seemed fine. Managers were trained to do the right thing and people pretty much bought in. Because of trust, this lack of two-way communication wasn't an issue. However, when trust began to break down, agencies were not prepared for the negative one-way communication they received, nor were they in any way prepared to respond. Agencies were sitting ducks, armed with quack voices against protests as strong as speeding lead shot.

Opening a forum for improved communications is a major purpose of public involvement programs. Agencies are able to actively listen to the concerns of people in meeting settings, or to digest solicited written correspondence. Effective public involvement programs also create opportunities for agencies to explain their perspective, to elaborate on their mission or to detail the reasoning behind specific management objectives. Communications flowing in both directions will, at a minimum, increase awareness. At best, two-way communications can lead to convergence.

Convergence Communication

Convergence communication is the process of bringing divergent points of view a little closer together. Its benefit is the reduction of polarization and extremism among publics. The outcome is to broaden the operating range for management. In a widely polarized setting, any agency action will look objectionable to some publics, because their perspective is so much different from the proposed actions of the agency. Suspicion and zero credibility are the dominant factors that publics use in taking a position, rather than a realistic assessment of agency proposals. Communication that leads toward convergence, some limited sharing of values and perceptions, enables a slightly broader scope of activities. Convergence reduces suspicion and allows a modicum of tolerance. It can provide a foundation for rebuilding trust. It is the product of successful two-way communication. Not a panacea, convergence can at least bring thaw to frozen positions and encourage people who are normally at odds with each other to work together.

Diffusion of Innovations

Diffusion of innovations is a communications theory well described by Rogers (2003). It states essentially that changes move through societies in identifiable patterns. Generally resistant to change, people will not commonly adopt an innovation and embrace it. We tend to want to see the results of experimentation, but not necessarily conduct the tests on ourselves. So people wait until someone convinces them that the innovation is truly beneficial. These convincers, known as "early adopters," are people a little more willing to take a risk. They are the experimenters. If they are also viewed as trustworthy and knowledgeable, people with shared objectives will follow their lead. As more people adopt the innovation, it diffuses into common understanding and use. We deal with innovations all the time. Some are accepted, some rejected. Some may not even be recognized. Falling behind the pace of innovation is one reason why resource agencies have been caught off guard in the past.

Public involvement programs help to increase awareness of innovations. Seeing things coming down the tracks allows room for analysis and experimentation. It provides people with the awareness they need to make a choice to climb aboard, get off the tracks, or switch the train to another track. In the absence of public involvement, the danger of being rolled over is real. In the Bitterroots and on the Monongahela, the Forest Service was caught by changes in social values that the agency had failed to recognize. Closer ties with public constituencies might have changed the complexion of those controversies.

Legal Requirements for Public Involvement

Public involvement in the planning process of resource managing and regulatory agencies seemed to be such a good idea that Congress began to specifically require it in resource-related legislation such as NEPA. Prior to NEPA, public involvement mandates began with the "**notice and comment**" requirements of the **Federal Register Act (1935)**. The **Federal Register** was established to house regulations set by administrative agencies. Prior to this act, no specific repository for cataloging federal regulations existed. New regulations were simply filed in the agencies that wrote them. Filing systems and recovery of documents were wildly variable, and in some cases, existing regulations could not even be found. To clean up this mess, the Federal Register became the organizer of the regulatory process. As the daily newspaper of the federal government, the Federal Register would publish proposed regulations, as well as house regulations that had been accepted and passed into law, in the Code of Federal Regulations (CFR). "Notice and comment" was set up to provide agencies and other interested parties with the opportunity to review proposed regulations and comment on them, thus paving the way toward citizen involvement.

The Administrative Procedures Act (APA 1946, PL 79-404) further clarified citizen opportunities to become involved in rule-making procedures. The following excerpts from **Statutes at Large** show how the APA integrates public involvement in the regulatory process:

APA 1946, PL 79-404
Section 3
(a) "Every agency shall separately state and publish in the Federal Register (1) descriptions of its central and field organization . . . and the

established places at which, and methods whereby, the public may make submittals or requests . . ."

(b) "Every agency shall publish or, in accordance with published rule, make available to public inspection all final opinions or orders in the adjudication of cases . . ."

(c) "Save as otherwise required by statute, matters of official record shall in accordance with published rule be made available to persons properly and directly concerned ...."

Section 4

(a) "General notice of proposed rule making shall be published in the Federal Register . . . and shall include (1) a statement of the time, place, and nature of public rule making proceedings . . ."

(b) "After notice required in this section, the agency shall afford interested persons an opportunity to participate in the rule making through submission of written data, views, or arguments . . ."

(d) "Every agency shall accord any interested person the right to petition for the issuance, amendment, or repeal of a rule."

The APA further became the major avenue for citizens to litigate over the federal regulatory process through Section 10 (a), which states: "Any person suffering legal wrong because of any agency action, or adversely affected or aggrieved by such action within the meaning of any relevant statute, shall be entitled to judicial review thereof." Section 10 of the APA has become the most frequently invoked law defining access to the courts over issues of administrative law, and thus is a major point of access to the judiciary over issues concerning natural resources and the environment.

The National Environmental Policy Act (NEPA 1969, PL 91-190) became a major focus for environmental litigation and citizen involvement. The NEPA requires that agencies use a planning and decision-making process that thoroughly considers environmental impacts. Additionally, NEPA requires that the planning process be documented and made available for public review. Both of these regulations are broadly described in NEPA, Section 102:

NEPA 1969, PL 91-190

(A) ". . . all agencies of the Federal Government shall utilize a systematic, interdisciplinary approach which will insure the integrated use of the natural and social sciences and the environmental design arts in planning and in decision making which may have an impact on man's environment . . "

(C) ". . . include in every recommendation or report on proposals for legislation and other major Federal actions significantly affecting the quality of the human environment, a detailed statement . . copies of such statement . . . shall be made available to the President, the Council on Environmental Quality and to the public . . . and shall accompany the proposal through the existing agency review processes."

Planning laws specific to the U.S. Forest Service and Bureau of Land Management were passed by Congress in response to controversies that embroiled the agencies in the early 1970s. These laws specifically mention public involvement and require that the agencies take measures to insure that citizens have the opportunity to give input to the planning and decision-making processes. There are two laws that pertain specifically to the U.S. Forest Service:

The Forest and Rangeland Renewable Resources Planning Act (RPA 1974, PL 93-378) mandates an "interdisciplinary" and "comprehensive" planning process for national forest lands in accordance with the Multiple Use-Sustained Yield Act of 1960 and the NEPA of 1969. Therefore, RPA includes NEPA provisions for public involvement. The RPA however, has generally been considered a failure in implementing the "rational-comprehensive" planning process.

The National Forest Management Act (NFMA 1976, PL 94-588) effectively amended RPA to make it work better. The NFMA specifically prescribes citizen involvement through

NFMA 1976, PL 94-588
Section 3

(d) "In developing the reports required under subsection (c) of this section, the Secretary shall provide opportunity for public involvement and shall consult with other interested governmental departments and agencies." Additionally, NFMA paints a pretty clear picture of what is required of public participation in
Section 6

(d) "The Secretary shall provide for public participation in the development, review, and revision of land management plans including, but not limited to, making the plans or revisions available to the public at convenient locations in the vicinity of the affected unit for a period of at least three months before final adoption, during which period the Secretary shall publicize and hold public meetings or comparable processes at locations that foster public participation in the review of such plans or revisions."

Clearly, the NFMA is intended to tell the Forest Service that it had jolly well better get the public involved!

Similarly, the Bureau of Land Management was instructed by Congress to get in the public involvement business through the Federal Land Policy and Management Act (FLPMA 1976, PL 94-579). In this act, direction is given through Title II:

Section 202

(f) "The Secretary shall allow an opportunity for public involvement and by regulation shall establish procedures, including public hearings where appropriate, to give Federal, State, and local governments and the public, adequate notice and opportunity to comment upon and participate in the formulation of plans and programs relating to management of the public lands."

Subsequent to FLPMA, the Public Rangelands Improvement Act (PRIA 1978, PL 95-514) further specifies BLM management of the "public lands" and Forest Service management of "rangelands" as they relate to grazing fees, range inventories, grazing advisory boards, and allotment management plans. PRIA reemphasizes the public involvement mandates of NEPA, FLPMA, and NFMA.

The federal Freedom of Information Act (FOIA 1966, PL 89-554) offers further public access to agency activities. The FOIA has frequently been used to expose sensitive or controversial documents. The law has been subsequently amended to ensure citizens access to their personal records (Privacy Act of 1974, PL 93-579), and to make records available by electronic media (Electronic Freedom of Information Act Amendments, 1996, PL 104-231).

Although these statutes and their attendant regulations appear complex, the bottom line is that citizens have the right to be involved, and agencies are required to involve them. All of the detail that's been presented in this chapter is intended to bring home the point that, both theoretically and legally, your purpose and right to be involved in natural resource planning and decision-making is assured. Most people don't even know that they have these rights, and may discover them only if they hire a lawyer to defend themselves when they think they're being abused by an administrative agency. The interesting thing about these laws and the theories that drive them is that they are intended to increase pro-activity and reduce reactionary backlash. Involving publics in planning should reduce cases in which agencies ignore or are ignorant of public sentiment. By involving publics early in the process, costly mistakes can be avoided. At least they should be. The door to citizen involvement is open; use it!

Suggested Readings

Adams, D. A. (1993). *Renewable resource policy: The legal-institutional foundations.* Washington, DC: Island Press.

Coggins, G. C., Wilkinson, C., Leshy, J., & Fischman, R. (2007). *Federal public land and resources law* (6th ed.). New York, NY: Foundation Press.

Dana, S. T., & Fairfax, S. K. (1980). *Forest and range policy: Its development in the United States* (2nd ed.). New York: McGraw-Hill.

Fazio, J. R., & Gilbert, D. L. (2000). *Public relations and communications for natural resource managers* (3rd ed.). Dubuque, IA: Kendall/Hunt Publishing.

MacDonnell, L. J., & Bates, S. F., (Eds.). (1993). *Natural resources policy and law: Trends and directions.* Washington, DC: Island Press.

Rogers, E. M. (2003). *The diffusion of innovations* (5th ed.). New York: Free Press.

Wilkinson, C. F., & Anderson, M. A. (1987). *Land and resource planning in the national forests.* Washington, DC: Island Press.

chapter seventeen

Effective Avenues for Public Participation

Commitment and Representation Problems in Public Involvement

We saw in the last chapter how citizen involvement has been legally mandated. Legal requirements, however, do not necessarily guarantee that effective citizen participation programs are carried out. Actively engaging publics to provide meaningful input is not a simple matter. There are two major obstacles to quality citizen involvement: (a) a lack of commitment to the effort on the part of agencies, and (b) under-representation of all publics, interests, and values.

The requirements for participation set a legal minimum for compliance. Agencies can choose to aim for that minimum or expand their efforts to openly engage in active interchange with citizens. Minimum efforts are usually rather obvious. In such cases, an agency might prepare a plan that includes two or three alternative management strategies. The agency makes notice that drafts of the plan are available for review by the public, and then schedules one or several open meetings in the area affected by the plan. At these meetings, the plan might be discussed, or citizens might simply be invited to make verbal comments. The latter format is usually referred to as a **hearing**. One-way communication dominates at hearings. It is as if verbal letters are being collected. Once the legal requirements for public participation are met, the agency then proceeds to incorporate the comments obtained into the plan and moves on. In this minimal compliance model, participation is underappreciated and underutilized. In the extreme, agencies occasionally will intentionally avoid active participation by scheduling meetings at inconvenient times and by providing notice of the availability of a plan in an obscure manner. These methods have been used for those plans that are particularly controversial. The effort to downplay participation, however, can backfire when activist citizens recognize an agency's effort to avoid them. When the agency's intentions are revealed, its public relations can suffer in ways more powerful than if it had encouraged participation in the first place.

On the other hand, agencies have also made extensive efforts to involve citizens in their planning efforts. In the late 1970s planners at Yosemite mailed out over 50,000 "workbooks" designed to gather citizen input on the problems and management direction for the park. Agencies have established **steering committees, stewardship committees**, and **stakeholder groups** in order to bring **opinion leaders** into the planning process. These opinion leaders are akin to the "early adopters" of diffusion of innovations theory. They are entrusted to represent the thinking of their groups and to be able to effectively articulate their points of view. Rather than being asked to simply comment on the two or three alternatives already designed by the agency, these committees and groups are invited to participate in the setting of goals and objectives and to become more aware of the issues and procedures tackled throughout the planning process. Generally more time-consuming and challenging, intensive involvement of citizens can produce benefits that simple compliance efforts will miss. Agencies have begun to recognize groups as **partners** in the management mission. This acknowledgment of the importance of citizens builds trust and improves cooperation. It provides a far better management environment than one marred by distrust and divisiveness.

Agency personnel and participating citizens meet to discuss stream bank restoration in Modoc County, California. (David E. Simcox Collection)

Even when an agency is committed to active inclusion of citizens, problems of **representation** can limit the effectiveness of their efforts. Participation in government and natural resource management planning requires time and commitment on the part of interested citizens. Not everyone who might like to be involved can be. Public involvement programs have been criticized because they are not readily available to everyone who might want or need to make input. People have limited amounts of time and money. They may not be able to travel to an evening, weekday, or weekend meeting because of commitments at work or home. Some cultural groups are simply distrustful of government, or it might not be part of their value structure to become involved in government-related activities. The environmental burden borne by African Americans and socioeconomically disadvantaged groups is at least partly the result of their lack of representation in planning processes. The people who showed up at meetings kept the waste dumps and power lines out of their neighborhoods, leaving the underrepresented to bear the brunt of environmental impact. And those who show up tend to consistently be those with (a) a high stake in the planning process at hand, (b) higher levels of education, (c) better informational connections with the planning agency, (d) more available time (often seniors or professionals), and (e) the financial ability to either attend or send representatives.

These limitations to adequate representation are a thorny problem for agencies trying to effectively involve all people with a stake in the planning issue. Stakeholders are easier to identify than they are to include. As mentioned before, resource agencies were not made up of talented communicators or personnel with expertise in marketing. As public involvement becomes more important and agencies recognize the value of quality involvement programs, people with communications, social research and marketing skills become part of the workforce. Citizen involvement is improving. Its long-term benefits outweigh the costs of organizing its effective implementation. We can all expect to be part of such efforts in the future.

How to Be Heard: Methods and Strategies
Used by Citizen Organizations

Citizen organizations from labor unions to voluntary associations have developed an arsenal of techniques over the years. At times their methods have stretched the limits of social acceptability. Radicalism is occasionally effective and sometimes self-defeating. Some methods that may have been considered radical in the context of their historical period may be perceived as tame by today's standards. Certain organizations specialize in particular strategies. Others employ a variety of methods. Among the most common strategies are the following:

- Lobbying

- Information Dissemination and Communications

- Letter-writing, Telephone, FAX, E-mail, Internet, Social Media Campaigns

- Cooperative Programs

- Litigation

- Letters and Testimony (Hearing Process)

- Protests and Demonstrations

- Position and Advocacy Statements

- Campaign Endorsements

- Public Meetings

- Citizen Initiative and Referendum

- Oversight Monitoring

- Boycotting

Lobbying

Lobbying is one of the oldest methods of influencing public policy. The name derives from the practice of influence peddlers hanging about the lobbies of legislatures, waiting to catch representatives to give them a piece of their mind. In the worst cases, lobbyists and crooked politicians have not been above the occasional bribe. More often, however, lobbyists work to show politicians the benefits of certain courses of action. Those courses of action, obviously, are in the best interests of the lobbyist's organization. It is the lobbyist's job to demonstrate how that course of action will benefit the politician, the greater welfare, and their organization. Lobbyists are experts at demonstrating the "win-win" situation.

Information Dissemination and Communications

Information dissemination and communications are used by organizations to get the word out and convince people that they should be concerned. Organizations use newsletters, magazines, the Internet and e-mail to broadcast their points of view and bring issues to people's attention. Larger organizations are able to afford television productions such as the Audubon Society specials. Communications are designed to alert and inform and then provoke people to take action ranging from keeping informed to joining the organization to spreading the word to becoming active.

Letter-writing, Telephone, Fax, E-mail, Internet, and Social Media Campaigns

Letter-writing, telephone, fax, e-mail, Internet and social media campaigns are all versions of the original letter-writing strategy used by organizations to influence policy. An organization has the advantage of usually being focused on a specific issue or set of issues. Because the organization's membership is generally of like mind on those issues, the membership can be encouraged to blast an impressive quantity of letters or other communications toward key lawmakers on specific issues at certain times. The receipt of thousands of letters can have an impact on a politician or the manager of a national park, national forest, or other resource management area. At minimum, a politician is inclined to count votes in those letters. Today, technology has brought electronic communications into the old letter-writing campaign. People can automatically sign on to send emails and Faxes to public officials through the Internet. Whether the abundance of communications sent through these media is having a diluting effect is uncertain, though probable. The simplicity of communication does not easily demonstrate the true commitment on the part of the sender. Quantity may be replacing quality, and the impact of the message may be softening.

Cooperative Programs

Cooperative programs are used by many organizations as a means to build rapport and to work with agencies toward shared values. Sponsorship of funding for habitat improvement, species recovery, and land acquisitions can prove very effective in influencing the agenda of resource agencies. Agencies are frequently underfunded and wish to accomplish tasks that are simply impossible without outside assistance. Cooperative efforts, also called partnerships, provide agencies with means to move forward on projects that might otherwise be neglected. Organizations further their objectives and also increase cooperation by engaging in partnerships.

Protest at a Bureau of Land Management Public Meeting
(Courtesy of the Bureau of Land Management)

Litigation

Litigation is a tool used to achieve specific objectives under particular circumstances. Seeking judicial review can be expensive and quite contentious, but it can be an effective implementation of oversight, and can lead to the setting of important long-term precedents.

Letters and Testimony

Letters and testimony are essentially part of the managed public involvement programs operated by agencies and governmental bodies. Hearings are required by law, as are opportunities to provide written comments. Many organizations pay special attention to planned public participation programs because they are legally able to express their concerns through these processes. To ignore or shun such opportunities would be to alienate the organization from the agency or governmental body that it's trying to influence. Letters and testimony also are read or heard by an audience larger than just the agency. Other stakeholders, whether they agree or disagree, are able to hear or read the opinions of the participating organizations, thus expanding the overall level of awareness about issues and controversies.

Protests and Demonstrations

Protests and demonstrations are tools used when others are considered too slow or ineffective. Protests and demonstrations are often symbolic in nature, but carry a confrontational element that makes them valuable as news items. Protests at the World Trade Organization (WTO) meeting in Seattle in 1999, and their extensive media coverage, have been given some of the credit for bringing down what is considered to have been a "failed" meeting. Groups such as Greenpeace and Earth First! have specialized in protest. Radicalism in the 1980s, 1990s, and 2000s became more acceptable than it had been in decades past. Organizations that failed to maintain the hairball edge even began to drop in favor, while the "crazies" gained followings. Occasionally, protests can have dramatic effects and even foment significant change. Remember the civil rights and anti-war demonstrations of the 1960s, the lone man facing down a tank in Tiananmen Square in China in 1989, and the campaign of civil resistance and disobedience that led to the overthrow of President Hosni Mubarak in Egypt in 2011. Protests and demonstrations may or may not succeed, but they invariably draw attention to the grievances of the participants.

Position and Advocacy Statements

Position and advocacy statements are used by organizations to make their positions clear and to indicate the organization's stance on particular issues. Organizations will frequently take a stance on issues before voters, such as propositions on ballots. Openly committing to positions on court cases, resource management practices, and even strategies of influencing agencies are all techniques used by groups to define themselves and what they stand for. Standing for or against clear-cutting, tree spiking, and whether to dismantle Glen Canyon

Dam are all examples of strategies that organizations have employed. Often containing considerable thought and explanation, some position statements such as the Society of American Foresters' "Code of Ethics," aim to develop logic and garner acceptance. Other position statements are reduced to slogans such as Earth First!'s catchy "No compromise in defense of Mother Earth!"

Campaign Endorsements

Campaign endorsements are similar to advocacy statements, but directed at candidates for office. Endorsements imply the backing of certain candidates, but negative endorsements are also used to keep people from voting for candidates who are not favorable to the organization. The National Rifle Association backed John McCain in the 2008 presidential election, just as the Sierra Club pushed Barack Obama. These were positive endorsements of candidates with name recognition. When a notorious candidate is better known than his rival, negative endorsements are used. You may have heard of white supremacist David Duke, likely because of the amount of bad press and negative endorsements he received. But you and I both probably can't name the last person he ran against, even though that person was the election's winner! In another example, Richard Pombo, Republican Representative from California and Chair of the House Resources Committee, who worked to disarm the Endangered Species Act, was ousted in 2006 by a Sierra Club-led negative endorsement and $1 million in campaign funds to back his opponent Jerry McNerney.

Public Meetings

Public meetings, similar to the hearing process, are important venues for citizen organizations. These groups may send a single representative, a group, or even "pack" the meeting with supporters in order to demonstrate solidarity. In the past, public meetings have run the gamut from sedate to wild. Caravans of logging trucks have been used to show the commitment and protest of loggers over threats to the timber industry. Animal protectionists have dressed up as mountain lions, salmon, owls, or other creatures to gain attention. But most public meetings are rather plain gatherings organized for the exchange of information and exposure of points of view.

Citizen Initiative and Referendum

Citizen initiative and referendum are becoming more frequent strategies among policy-influencing groups. Many states allow for the passage of "citizen legislation" that carries the same power of law as legislation passed by the legislative branch. These proposed "statutes" appear on the ballot as "propositions," and, in California, we vote on them all the time. The main differences between initiatives and legislation are that the proposed ballot measure must be backed by a petition including the signatures of 5% of the number of voters in the most recent governor's election. This amounts to roughly 600,000 signatures to qualify an initiative for the ballot in California. Unlike legislators, voters have little political stake in their exercise of the ballot. Their votes are even anonymous and secret. Legislators claim no such anonymity. Their votes are public information and are part of their political capital. This is one of the reasons why citizen initiatives are being used more often these days. The process allows the introduction of legislation that might indeed be too controversial for the tastes of legislators. Witness the outcome of California's Proposition 209 (the nondiscrimination initiative, also called the anti-affirmative action initiative) in the 1996 statewide election. California's legislature would never have passed this measure by the same margin it was passed by the electorate. Too risky for legislators, the question was put to the voters and passed. Another lesson about political strategies has been learned.

Oversight Monitoring

Oversight monitoring is the strategy in which organizations play a watchdog role in seeing that policies and regulations are administered to their liking. Oversight is an official function of the legislative branch, but certain citizen organizations believe that agencies are not being closely monitored. Being alert to activities that may threaten the causes of the organization, some groups employ large numbers of paid and volunteer staff to see that regulations are being appropriately enforced, or to conduct scientific research to investigate changes in conditions. Oversight can be very touchy, as it requires some amount of cooperation on the part of an agency or governmental body. When oversight turns up violations or improprieties, such discoveries are newsworthy and may raise an alarm. Revelation of such news does not endear organizations to agencies. If cooperation is not an issue, that's no big deal. But an organization cannot expect a continued relationship of tolerance from an agency on which it has blown the whistle.

Boycotting

Boycotting can be a powerful tool used by organizations to protest and bring about change by making economic pain a reality for a company or companies that are not practicing business in a manner approved by the organization. Some classic examples include the boycott of Gallo by the United Farmworkers Federation, and the boycott of tuna products sold by companies that killed dolphins in the process of catching tuna. In the Gallo case, Gallo eventually agreed to hire union labor. As to tuna, Star-Kist and Chicken of the Sea began labeling their cans "dolphin safe." Boycotting can work with products that have substitutions. Changing tuna brands or choosing chicken instead is a fairly easy choice for consumers. Going without electricity to protest policies of the regional energy company, however, is probably not going to succeed.

The future will witness continued experimentation in methods to gain the political upper hand. Appeals for support will employ strategies ranging from scientific analyses to heart tugging emotionalism and everything in between. The task faced by the involved citizen is to sort through the strategies, the hype, the spin employed by diverse interest groups and to gain a personal understanding of issues through conscientious reasoning and careful consideration.

Suggested Readings

Beierle, T. C., & Cayford, J. (2002). *Democracy in practice: Public participation in environmental decisions.* Washington, DC: Resources for the Future.

Creighton, J. L. (2005). *The public participation handbook: Making better decisions through citizen involvement.* San Francisco, CA: Jossey-Bass.

Dunlap, R. E., & Mertig, A. G. (Eds.). (1992). *American environmentalism: The U.S. environmental movement, 1970–1990.* New York: Taylor & Francis.

Milbrath, L., & Goel, M. L. (1982). *Political participation: How and why do people get involved in politics?* (2nd ed.). Washington, DC: University Press of America.

Smith, P. D., McDonough, M. H., & Mang, M. T. (1999, October). Ecosystem management and public participation: Lessons from the field. *Journal of Forestry, 97*(10), 32–38.

chapter eighteen

Forestland and Timber Management Controversies

Forests for All: Conflicts in Values for Biodiversity and Wood Products

Wilderness Preservation and Roadless Area Management

New World colonists thought the forests of America were so endless that they said a squirrel could travel from coast to coast without ever hitting the ground. This notion persisted until the treeless Great Plains was discovered to the west of the Mississippi. Forests began again at the foothills of the Rockies, and a region of incredible trees was found in the Pacific Northwest. The wealth of the timber resource helped build the economic foundation of large sections of the West. Strong beliefs in the silvicultural appropriateness of converting old-growth forests to productive new stands were the rationale behind timber operations on a massive scale. Development of new forms of heavy equipment increased productivity and economic efficiency of lumbering and milling operations. As the demand for wood products grew, so did the need to open up new areas to logging. Eventually, timber uses would come into conflict with other forest resource values.

The doctrine of "multiple use" held that federal forestlands would be managed to provide timber, grazing, minerals, water, wildlife, and outdoor recreation. Set forth in the Multiple Use and Sustained Yield Act of 1960, multiple use was a response to a new generation of forest users who wanted forested places to recreate. Multiple use was supposed to deliver all the forest values, mixing timber operations with wildlife productivity, recreation with grazing, and mineral extraction with water development. It was as if the era of abundance was being reinvented. The forests were going to provide something for everybody! But no forested area could possibly meet the demands of multiple use. It was a doctrine that satisficed. It was particularly unacceptable to the growing legions of preservationists, those who believed in leaving wildlands alone. Four years after the Multiple Use Act, the **Wilderness Act of 1964** was passed, establishing the **National Wilderness Preservation System**, to the cheers of preservationists.

Many wilderness areas in the U.S are in high mountain regions of the West.
(Photo by Steve Dennis)

Setting aside wilderness became a titanic struggle. Wilderness areas could only be established from **roadless areas** of a minimum of 5,000 acres. While some areas of national parks, high mountains, or relative inaccessibility were rather easily declared wilderness, other federal areas were multiple use lands, and there were stakeholders interested in uses besides wilderness preservation. On national forest lands, individual "wilderness study areas" were drawn up for analysis, pushed by preservationist publics wielding wilderness as a method to lock up areas where "nature" would be the dominant influence on the landscape. Timber, grazing, and mining interests would object to these proposals, protesting that wilderness squelched economic development. In case after case, the Forest Service found itself mired in battles over wilderness on national forests across the country. Twice the agency attempted to solve the wilderness questions by taking a nationwide approach to wilderness designations. The **Roadless Area**

Review and Evaluation (RARE) study was developed in the early 1970s to inventory roadless areas nationwide and make recommendations as to which areas should be designated as wilderness. Of 56 million acres studied, the USFS estimated that 12 million should undergo further consideration for wilderness potential. Dissatisfied, the Sierra Club sued the USFS on the grounds that the agency had failed to prepare a satisfactory environmental impact statement under NEPA. The court decision on RARE left 56 million acres in limbo, neither wilderness nor open for development. Scrambling for designations one way or the other, both the timber industry and preservationists pressed for some resolution to the nationwide conflict over which lands would be wilderness and which would be multiple use. In 1977, the Carter Administration instituted **RARE II**, another massive planning effort intended to resolve the wilderness allocation issue. Holding 227 public meetings in 1977, RARE II was an enormous exercise in public involvement. The new study and environmental impact statement considered 66 million acres but, like RARE I, once again was unable to satisfy preservationists and industry. Legal maneuverings continued to tie up the wilderness designation process by the time Ronald Reagan moved into the White House in 1981. Reagan the federalist canned the RARE II process and handed the wilderness designations issue back to the state congressional delegations. For the next 30 years, wilderness would be studied within each state, and each state's congressional representatives could carry wilderness bills to the legislature for consideration. After all, the reasoning held, wilderness establishment was a congressional matter. During this period, another 25 million acres were added to the National Wilderness Preservation System.

Initiating an end-run around the wilderness designation process, in January 2001, just days before Clinton left office, the USFS adopted a new Roadless Area Conservation Rule. This rule effectively blocked road building and logging on 58 million acres, more than 25 percent of USFS lands. Targeted by the Bush administration, the regulations were altered to bring states' governors into the process of designating roadless areas, similar to Reagan's state congressional delegations approach to wilderness proposals a generation earlier. The Bush "State Petitions" regulations were challenged in federal court by four western states and a collection of environmental groups, citing violation of NEPA and the ESA, leading to reinstatement of the Clinton-era roadless rule in 2006. Subsequent litigation for and against the roadless rule has kept its implementation uncertain, swaying with maneuvers of presidential administrations and the press of changes in power in the House of Representatives in 2007 (Democratic majority) and 2011 (Republican majority). A testament to citizen involvement, ten years after its original adoption, the Roadless Area Conservation Rule had protected almost all of the 58 million acres covered under its regulations. The future of the roadless rule, however, is anything but certain.

Species to the Rescue

Preservationists felt stymied by the wilderness preservation method. Though more than 80 million acres were designated as wilderness by the 1980s, there remained lands of "questionable" value for wilderness that preservationists felt needed protection. Notable among these lands were the remaining stands of old growth, or virgin, timber in the Pacific Northwest. The richest timber region in the world didn't get that way by avoiding old-growth stands. As a result, old growth was converted (harvested) and replaced with young forests. By 1990, the USFS estimated that roughly 20 percent of its land base in the Pacific Northwest was old growth. National and state parklands accounted for 3.8 million acres of old growth, including the redwood parks of coastal California. Private lands also held limited reserves of old growth, but their protection seemed beyond the scope of preservationists' legal remedies. Or was it?

Sensing an old-growth crisis that threatened **biodiversity**, preservationists sought other tactics when the wilderness process didn't satisfy them. They didn't have to look hard. In 1973, Congress had passed the Endangered Species Act whose primary purpose was "to provide a means whereby the ecosystems upon which endangered species and threatened species depend may be conserved." The ESA, unbeknownst to the politicians who drafted it and saw it through Congress, would become the strongest piece of environmental legislation yet passed. Originally intended to save grizzly bears, bald eagles, whooping cranes, black-footed ferrets, and other well-known or cuddly species, the ESA was subsequently interpreted to apply not only to **megafauna**, but to other species as well, including plant species. At first consideration, ESA would attempt to save endangered species through preservation techniques. But the law was inferred to mean that preservation required the maintenance of habitat sufficient to protect a species' condition in the wild. Protecting habitat thus became the agreed-upon solution to keeping species alive. And preservation became the method of choice. Thus the reduction of human activity was seen as the preferred means for providing habitat for endangered, threatened, and rare species. Reduction of activities such as logging would help protect species that required old-growth forest habitat. Enter the Northern Spotted Owl.

The Northern Spotted Owl was a little-understood bird that made it onto the cover of *Time* magazine by 1990. Eric Forsman, a graduate student at Oregon State University, had studied the numbers and distribution of the owl for his master's thesis. He had found that its numbers were declining. In his doctoral dissertation, Forsman found that old growth and mature forests were the "preferred habitat" of the owl. In 1973, during congressional consideration of the proposed Endangered Species Act, the U.S. Fish and Wildlife Service had begun to prepare a list of species that might be considered endangered. Hearing of Forsman's work, the service placed the Northern Spotted Owl on the list. That summer, the Oregon Game Commission set up an Endangered Species Task Force and recommended that old-growth forests and spotted owls should be given special attention. The first "buffer zones" of 300 acres around identified spotted owl nests were proposed. Subsequent studies would claim that spotted owls needed far more than 300 acres, and that the habitat needed to be mature or old growth forest. For more than two decades since, the spotted owl has become the poster child for the debate between preservation and development of the Pacific Northwest forests. Protecting the owl under the ESA has become the mechanism by which preservationists have sought to set aside old-growth forests.

Even before the owl's listing as **threatened** in 1990 under the federal ESA, the state of Washington listed the owl as endangered, and Oregon listed the owl as threatened in 1988. In the years leading up to that, the "need for further study" was frequently claimed in litigation to tie up timber harvest plans proposed on USFS and BLM lands. Until the population health of the owl was known, litigants said, it would be potentially disastrous to threaten their habitat with logging. Similarly, because protection under the ESA would permanently tie up huge acreages of old growth, the timber industry claimed more studies were needed. In the undecided interim, timber harvesting continued as preservationists sued in a sparring match that used the USFS, the BLM, and the USF&WS as referees. More studies, more litigation, more task forces, more protests, more polarization have marked the spotted owl issue. Science has been abused by both sides, in arguments to expand or reduce the quantity, and range of the owl. Litigants actually have made money from taxpayers by recovering court costs for representing "public interest" plaintiffs. Protesters became media stars as antics were elevated to newsworthy levels. And the timber industry, in many areas went into decline. In Oregon, timber harvests in the 1990s and 2000s averaged less than half what they had been in the 1980s. Mills closed because of a lack of trees and the modernization of milling equipment that required fewer workers. Layoffs in the timber region brought about increases in spousal and child abuse, divorce, alcoholism, foreclosures, and suicide.

The century-old debate between preservation and use had once again come to a head, and the compromises reachable by prior generations seemed to evade the new players. Even a Clinton-organized "Forests Summit" held amid great media attention in 1993 failed to achieve an answer. The **Forest Ecosystems Management Assessment Team (FEMAT)**, organized to provide a regional "ecosystems solution," came up with a middle-of-the-road approach and selected the infamous "**Option 9**," which assured only more satisficing and continued polarization and claims of capture. Headlines tell the story: "Report Outrages Environmentalists" (*Portland Oregonian*), "Outraged Loggers Reject Plan" (*Seattle Post-Intelligencer*). Distrust and extremism reign in the new debate. Somewhere in the middle lies the answer, but no one seems prepared to go there. Why is this controversy so thorny?

Forest Practices and Their Susceptibility to Criticism

Forestry as imported into the U.S. by Pinchot and others, centered on the practice of growing trees for economic values. Timber for lumber and protection of watersheds were the two main objectives of early forest management. Secondary benefits, such as outdoor recreation, grazing, and wildlife, were nice extras, but not the focus of management until the post-World War II era. Timber production was the center of forestry education. "Managed" stands of trees were considered more productive than "natural" stands, so a convenient starting point for timber management was to remove old-growth trees and replace them with young, vigorously growing trees. Because many of the forests in the country were old growth, a lot of harvesting could be done to achieve managed conditions.

Pinchot sold government management of forests to the U.S., and the response was the establishment of the forest reserves (later, national forests). The timber industry had little use for these public forests, as long as there was an abundant supply of private timber. But eventually, private timber supplies could not keep up with demand for wood products, and the national forests became the source of timber to make up the difference. Gradually increasing harvest levels on national forests became controversial because people felt that national forests belonged to everyone, that forests should be preserved for future generations. People couldn't buy into the foresters' vision that cutting trees down was good for the forest anymore than they were likely to believe a wildlife manager telling them that a bullet to the heart of a buck is good for a herd of deer. Foresters failed to make their case, and when controversies such as Bitterroot and Monongahela broke out, it was too late to recapture public confidence.

Silviculture

Forest management practices are, of course, more complex than simply cutting trees. Cutting is simply the most noticeable aspect of timberlands management. In as brief a form as possible, the following will attempt to summarize the basics of one aspect of forest management known as silviculture.

The concepts of sustained yield and non-declining even flow form a basis for connecting silvicultural management to social objectives. Sustained yield simply means to grow as much as is cut, replacing removed trees with new ones. Non-declining even flow adds an extra dimension, with the objective that the yield be relatively steady and sustainable. The idea behind non-declining even flow is to elevate timber management beyond the "**boom and bust**" cycles so common to resource exploitation. Even flow would provide a steady supply of forest products to regional economies dependent on forest resources.

Silviculture is essentially the management of the ecological process of succession. Succession is the gradual replacement of plants, animals, and soil following occasional disturbances such as fires, floods, volcanic eruptions, and other acts of "nature." Gradually, seeds drift into the disturbed area, critters explore, small shade-intolerant plants grow in the full sun, new plants move in as the environment slowly changes, plants die and regenerate soils that support again other forms of plant life, shrubs move in over grasses and forbs, trees begin to take root, and eventually, the disturbed area starts to look more and more like the environment that was there before the disturbance took place. Silviculture uses a man-caused disturbance to kick-start new successional processes. Most people call this harvest. Silviculturalists call it regeneration. The removal of trees from an area is similar to natural disturbances, though silviculturalists are able to control the extent and form of man-caused disturbances through choices of regeneration methods.

Regeneration methods are based on the type of replacement stand desired. A stand is an area of forest delineated by similar characteristics such as age, species, elevation, and topographic location. A stand is typically the unit of management in silvicultural practice.

The unsightly aspect of timber clearcutting. (Courtesy of the Weyerhaeuser Archives)

The selection of a regeneration method is based on four primary factors: (a) desired age class and species composition of the replacement stand, (b) the supply of seeds for the new stand, (c) the necessary seedbed structure, and (d) growing conditions. Silviculture, as a practice, is not bound by social considerations, but forestry is. Therefore it should be noted that an important fifth factor involved in the choice of regeneration methods is the social component (i.e., aesthetics, legal constraints, public input, managerial objectives). Once these factors are considered, choices are made from the following common, "natural" regeneration methods:

Even-aged Replacement Stands
- Clear-cutting
- Seedtree
- Shelterwood

Uneven-aged Replacement Stands
- Selection
- Coppice

Clear-cutting, the most controversial of methods, is used to regenerate even-aged stands of trees that are able to grow in areas exposed to the sun and weather. These species are classified by silviculturalists as **shade intolerant. Seed tree** regeneration is similar to clear-cutting, though five to twenty trees per acre are left in the harvested area to provide a source for seeding the site. After new growth is established, the seed trees can be removed. Shelterwood is a method whereby rough "strips" of trees are completely removed, but neighboring strips of trees are left standing, providing seeds, and shelter from wind and sun. Strips are removed and re-grown alternately over time so the protective capacity is maintained. **Selection** is a regeneration method used to maintain uneven-aged stands and to meet objectives for fire hazard reduction, pest management, and aesthetic qualities. Coppice regeneration is used in species that reproduce through sprouting, where the original tree creates the foundation for new trees after harvest—in effect, much like pruning.

A shelterwood timber harvest removes trees in rows, leaving adjacent trees standing. (Courtesy of the Weyerhaeuser Archives)

These regeneration methods provide disturbances that lead to "natural" stand replacement through the process of succession. Additionally, artificial means are sometimes used to enhance regeneration of a stand. Seeding may be used to quickly return seeds to the disturbed site. Seeds are selected for genetic quality from vigorous trees. Transplanting of seedlings specially grown for reforestation is also used to quickly return growing trees to the harvested area. The seedlings are grown from quality genetic seeds as bare-root or container stock in nurseries and transported to the site for planting. Site preparation methods are used to modify the seedbed and growing conditions in a harvested area. The treatment of leftover slash by removal, prescribed burning, or scattering is determined by site factors and growth considerations. Slash may either be tractor disked into soils to hasten decomposition, or left on the surface to provide microclimates for seedlings. Extensive site preparation, such as the terracing methods that fueled the Bitterroot Controversy can be objectionable on aesthetic and economic grounds.

Selection is a harvest method that picks and chooses trees, rather than removing all of them in a specific area.
(Photo by Steve Dennis)

After a site is harvested, silviculture relies on succession with an occasional tweak to grow new trees on the site. Growing trees are classified in stages called seedling (<3' tall), sapling (<4" diameter at breast height, or dbh), pole (4"–12" dbh), standard (12"–24" dbh), and veteran (>24" dbh). Trees' positions relative to other trees in the stand's canopy are called dominant (biggest guys), co-dominant (next-biggest guys), intermediate (medium-sized, or average), and suppressed (small, shaded, and suffering from competition). Managing a stand for timber productivity involves reaching a level of **stocking** where the **density** of trees per acre allows maximum growth. Overstocked, or high-density, stands will be full of trees competing with one another, reducing their growth. Under-stocked, or low-density stands may have rapidly growing trees, but there aren't many of them, so total timber volume is low. Proper stand density to maximize production is considered fully stocked.

Maintaining a fully stocked condition requires an intervention in the successional process every once in a while. Foresters refer to these as silvicultural treatments. These treatments include liberation (removing overstory to "release" understory), cleaning (removing all but the desired species), improvement (adjusting species composition), thinning (removing poles for a financial return and to fatten up residual trees in the stand), salvage (recovering damaged trees as timber), and a host of others, including pruning, weeding, and sanitation. Additionally, silviculturalists are concerned with **fire protection and suppression**, and they must use methods such as **integrated pest management** to control deadly forest pests such as spruce bud worm, pine bark beetle, and pine blister rust. All this reproduction and management from harvest to harvest is called a rotation. The processes of growing trees and silviculturally treating stands are less controversial than harvesting, but they are not without debate. Use of pesticides and herbicides in certain silvicultural treatments has raised objections primarily over water contamination by toxic chemicals. The use of prescribed fire remains controversial due to safety and air quality concerns, and also because of Smokey's long-heard message that forest fires are bad news. But none of the techniques employed in the growing process raises blood pressures more than the practices of harvesting.

Harvesting, or harvest engineering, is the means by which timber is removed "from the stump" to the mill. These methods also play a role in the selection of regeneration methods.

The four main procedures of harvest engineering are

- Cutting

- Primary Transport

- Loading

- Hauling

Years of fire suppression have caused dangerous fuel loads to build up in many forests.
(Courtesy of the Weyerhaeuser Archives)

Fire prevention and suppression are major roles of the USFS and State Forestry agencies.
(Courtesy of the Weyerhaeuser Archives)

Modern machinery such as this delimber processor has reduced the workforce needs of timber operations.
(Courtesy of the Weyerhaeuser Archives)

Cutting is the method employed to get a tree from a standing to a downed position. Tree fallers are skilled in their ability to drop trees without breaking them up and in causing minimal damage to surrounding vegetation. Once dropped, the fallen tree is bucked to remove branches and cut into sections approximately 33 feet in length. Now referred to as logs, the sections must be removed from the site by primary transport. Primary transport falls into two categories: (a) skidding and (b) yarding. Skidding is the dragging of logs from the stump to a landing where they can be loaded onto trucks. A big-wheeled machine called a skidder is used on level or moderate slopes, and a bulldozer or "Cat" is used on steeper slopes. On slopes too steep for ground equipment, or on sensitive sites, yarding is used to move timber to a landing. Cable yarding systems employ a cable suspended from two trees at the bottom and top of a slope, or between towers built for yarding. Trees or towers are braced by guy cables to stabilize them for heavy loads. A pulling cable is then threaded through a pulley that moves up and down the main cable. From this, another cable called a choker drops to the ground and is used to grab the logs. Yarding, or pulling logs up the cable, is the job of a large machine called a yarder. In high-lead yarding, logs ride with one end suspended by the choker and the other just off, or dragging on the ground. Skyline yarding may use two chokers to fully suspend the log above the ground and reduce soil impacts. Yarding for particularly sensitive sites is done entirely by helicopter. Logs are then piled at the landing for loading by a separate crane, or a crane integrated into some logging trucks. Timber is then transported by logging-trucks over roads that may be engineered and constructed specifically for that purpose, eventually to connector roads and highways to nearby mills.

The massive tower of a cable yarding system, used to haul logs uphill where they can be loaded onto trucks.
(Courtesy of the Weyerhaeuser Archives)

Helicopters are used to remove timber from steep or sensitive terrain.
(Courtesy of the Weyerhaeuser Archives)

In reading the previous descriptions, you may have found yourself visualizing massive old trees groaning and crashing to the ground, logs cabled and yanked across the forest floor, and treeless slopes littered with stumps and severed limbs. Many aspects of harvest, or the successional disturbance that silviculturalists call regeneration, are ugly and potentially damaging to the environment. **Second growth** stands of even-aged single-species trees are biologically non-diverse and potentially susceptible to fire and pest infestation. Logging roads remove potential wilderness from the prerequisite "roadless" status, mar views of hillsides, and have the potential for encouraging erosion. Skid trails can become drainage paths that increase erosion. High-lead yarding leaves fan-like grooves that move up and gather at the tops of slopes. Wildlife habitat is altered. Quickened runoff accelerates erosion and changes streams and aquatic habitats. And the harvested area may not only lose some aesthetic appeal, it may also become downright ugly.

Silviculture faces these challenges in managing timber operations. It may be technically feasible to harvest trees by methods that are known as *"light on the land"* but demand for wood products and the economics of getting raw logs to mills nearly prohibits their use. Logs are big and heavy. The equipment used to move them is also big and heavy and expensive to purchase and operate. The expense of building a road to a stand of timber, setting up a yarder or moving in skidding equipment, and employing crews to cut, skid, yard, load and haul, is sizable. Short-term economic efficiency demands that all these costs must be matched and exceeded by the value of the timber to be removed. Thus cutting just a few trees and moving on to a new locale usually doesn't work. The need to create "**economies of scale**" in timber operations works against the need for strict environmental protection.

Tree plantation in southeastern U.S. (Courtesy of the Weyerhaeuser Archives)

The U.S. is a timber-exporting nation, only needing to import special woods that cannot be grown domestically. (Courtesy of the Weyerhaeuser Archives)

Back in the bad old days economies of scale were the only factor considered in harvesting timber. Loggers went after the nearest, biggest trees, clear-cut, dropped, hauled or rolled them down slopes to the nearest waterway, and then floated them in massive "log drives" to the nearest mill pond. The waste and environmental damage were extensive and also major reasons why government got into the forestry business. Today, harvest practices are governed by a formidable array of federal and state laws intended to prevent a reoccurrence of the immense damages caused in the past. California's Forest Practices Act is one of the most environmentally sensitive in the nation. But these laws do not guarantee that logging operations will have no environmental impacts. The logging industry could not economically survive if it could only conduct logging that would not affect the environment. The industry frequently opposes regulations that it considers overly protective and economically unfeasible. And regulations do not go far enough to satisfy preservationists who are opposed to logging. For those areas that they want protected the only good logging is no logging.

Crosscut saws, used before development of the chain saw, were efficient enough to work in big timber.
(Courtesy of the Weyerhaeuser Archives)

Crosscut saws were a two-man operation.
(Courtesy of the Weyerhaeuser Archives)

Early motor-powered saws also required two operators. (Courtesy of the Weyerhaeuser Archives)

Even one person could handle large trees such as this one with the modern chain saw. (Courtesy of the Weyerhaeuser Archives)

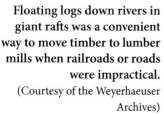

Floating logs down rivers in giant rafts was a convenient way to move timber to lumber mills when railroads or roads were impractical. (Courtesy of the Weyerhaeuser Archives)

The Struggle Will Continue

Society uses wood products. Society grows and harvests trees to produce wood products. Society likes forests. Society protects forests. The battle over old-growth forests in the United States will carry on until they are defined as either protected (as in wilderness and parks) or are cut down. Until then, old-growth forests outside of specifically protected areas will be a stage for controversy. The debate of future generations will be over the best ways to treat second and third growth stands. Forested acreage in the U.S. is actually expanding. Much of this expansion is in younger trees not yet ready for harvest. We have worked ourselves into a corner by overharvesting and not regenerating soon enough. Consequently, there is a "timber gap," where supplies are expected to diminish for a couple of decades. Fortunately, it is expected that the gap will be filled in after this generation by trees that are already growing. Until the gap is filled, pressure to harvest old-growth trees will continue. In response, preservationists will draw the line in the sand.

This chapter has only scratched the surface of forestry and the old-growth debate. Hopefully you now know more than you did. But more hopefully you'll be interested enough to follow this issue and approach it sensibly as a "somewhat more informed citizen!"

Our demand for wood products keeps logs rolling our way.
(Courtesy of the Weyerhaeuser Archives)

Suggested Readings

Adams, D. A. (1993). *Renewable resource policy: The legal-institutional foundations.* Washington, DC: Island Press.

Amacher, G. S., Ollikainen, M., & Koskela, E. (2009). *Economics of forest resources.* Cambridge, MA: MIT Press.

Chase, A. (1995). *In a dark wood: The fight over forests and the rising tyranny of ecology.* New York: Houghton Mifflin.

Clary, D. A. (1986). *Timber and the forest service.* Lawrence, KS: University Press of Kansas.

Dana, S. T., & Fairfax, S. K. (1980). *Forest and range policy* (2nd ed.). New York: McGraw-Hill.

Daniel, T. W., Helms, J. A., & Baker, F. S. (1979). *Principles of silviculture* (2nd ed.). New York: McGraw-Hill.

Floyd, D. W. (Ed.). (1999). *Forest of discord: Options for governing our national forests and federal public lands.* Bethesda, MD: Society of American Foresters.

Hays, S. P. (2009). *The American people and the national forests: The first century of the U.S. Forest Service.* Pittsburgh, PA: University of Pittsburgh Press.

Loomis, J. B. (2002). *Integrated public lands management: Principles and applications to national forests, parks, wildlife refuges, and BLM lands* (2nd ed.). New York: Columbia University Press.

O'Toole, R. (1988). *Reforming the forest service.* Washington, DC: Island Press.

Tappeiner, J. C., Maguire, D. A., & Harrington, T. B. (2007). *Silviculture and ecology of western U.S. forests.* Corvallis, OR: Oregon State University Press.

Turner, T. (2009). *Roadless rules: The struggle for the last wild forests.* Washington, DC: Island Press.

Wilkinson, C. F. (1992). *Crossing the next meridian: Land, water, and the future of the west.* Washington, DC: Island Press.

Wilkinson, C. F., & Anderson, M. A. (1987). *Land and resource planning in the national forests.* Washington, DC: Island Press.

chapter nineteen

Wildlife Management and Controversies

Of all the conflicts in resource management, wildlife tends to be the most heated. Protection of wildlife has become an American tradition. The arguments over other resources, such as forestlands, oil reserves, grazing, outdoor recreation, and water, are often couched in their relationship to wildlife and wildlife habitat. The battle over old-growth forests pits the spotted owl and marbled murrelet against the timber industry. In addition, drilling oil on Alaska's Arctic National Wildlife Refuge is a battle with the protection of caribou; wild horses are in competition with domestic livestock on western rangelands; desert tortoises enjoy the same spaces as off-road vehicle recreationists and solar energy development; and water management is in some places harnessed by the habitat requirements of anadromous fish such as salmon and steelhead trout. The wildlife resource is important to Americans, and it lies at the heart of many of our struggles over resource management.

Chapter 10 introduced the Bambi Syndrome and anthropomorphism. These concepts lie close to our reasons for feeling as strongly as we do about wildlife. In this chapter we'll look at some of the basics of wildlife management and discuss why these practices can be controversial. Additionally, we'll take a brief look at several wildlife management issues and see how they unfolded.

Basic Concepts of Wildlife Management

When wildlife survives, it is a renewable natural resource. Habitat is the key to wildlife survival. Habitat is where wildlife lives; it is the resource base upon which wildlife depends. The crucial elements of wildlife habitat are food, cover, water, space, and the arrangement of these resources. Food is obviously crucial to all organisms, and all organisms have different dietary needs. General categories of diet are herbivorous (plant eaters such as deer), carnivorous (meat eaters such as cheetahs), and omnivorous (plant and meat eaters such as bears). The more limited the breadth of a species' diet, the more susceptible that species is to population fluctuation based on the availability of its food source. Cover is the resource that we refer to as shelter. Cover consists of the soil, shrubs, trees, grasses, water, and landforms that offer refuge for rest, eating, playing, traveling, breeding, and rearing. Cover also includes the materials some species use to build nests or other structures such as beaver dams. Water is essential to some species at all times and to others only on occasion. Fish, of course, constantly use water as cover, for oxygen, and as a transport for food. Species such as the gila monster need water only once in a while, and can obtain it from plants and animals. Space is to wildlife what elbowroom is to us. Habitats are limited in space and can only support certain levels of wildlife populations. Connected with space is the concept of territory, an area that an organism will attempt to defend, and range, the distances over which wildlife might travel. Finally, arrangement is the manner in which food, cover, water, and space are organized in an area. Arrangement can be influenced primarily by natural factors, such as those in a wilderness area, or it can be intentionally managed to produce optimal habitat conditions, as in some wildlife refuges. Arrangement that allows spaces for organisms to find food, water, and cover will be better for survival than arrangement that limits access to these essential habitat ingredients. One aspect of arrangement, known as edge is particularly useful, for it provides contact zones between areas for foraging and hunting (prospect) and areas for cover (refuge). Imagine a new 20-acre patch clear-cut in an area that's 80 percent forested and 20% open meadow. What successional species will first move into the clear-cut site? Do deer like to eat these plant species while able to run to the cover of the nearby forest? An increased edge in habitat arrangement generally provides certain wildlife with better opportunities for prospect and refuge.

The limits of habitat for a species in a given locale are referred to as its carrying capacity. Carrying capacity is the level of populations that can be supported over time by a habitat without damage occurring to the habitat resources or to the wildlife populations. Carrying capacity is a limit where, once exceeded, habitat resources decline and wildlife suffers ill health, displacement, or mortality. Because habitat is limited, carrying capacity exists for all species in all habitats. Carrying capacity can be exceeded either by natural causes or through change caused by people. Wildlife management requires methods to keep populations within the carrying capacity of their available habitat.

Valuable waterfowl habitat in Yukon Delta National Wildlife Refuge, Alaska. (John Cowan Collection)

Succession was explained in the previous chapter. This natural continuous change affects habitat over time. As habitat changes, so too does an area's carrying capacity for different organisms. Different food sources, new cover arrangements of soils and plants meet the needs of different animals over time. Because successional cycles are punctuated back to a starting point through disturbances such as fire or flood, many species have evolved to thrive during "mid-successional" stages. Others are adapted to recently disturbed areas, and some inhabit areas where disturbance was so long ago that it reached a late successional stage or "climax condition." Late successional stages are not necessarily optimal habitat for all species.

Wildlife Manager John Cowan with a young Black-crowned Night Heron. (John Cowan Collection)

Population dynamics (change) is the up-and-down fluctuation of a species' population in a given area (habitat) over time. The two principal factors of population dynamics are natality (birth rate) and mortality (death rate). Natality is strongly related to a species' reproductive nature including (a) the number of young per birth, (b) the number of births per year, and (c) the age at which breeding begins. Generally speaking, smaller animals give birth to more young, more often, and at a younger age than most large animals. They therefore have comparably higher natality rates. The rate of mortality is influenced by (a) starvation from lack of food or water, (b) severe climatic conditions, (c) levels of predation, (d) parasites and diseases, and (e) harvest through hunting, fishing, and trapping predation by humans. As smaller animals tend to have higher natality rates, so too do they have higher rates of mortality. Wildlife populations demonstrate widely variable rates of population growth and decline. Some of this variability is the result of human activity, but people do not cause all changes in habitat, nor are we the sole cause of wildlife mortality. Wildlife populations have been dynamic throughout evolutionary time, which mostly took place in the absence of humanity.

Given all these changing factors that affect wildlife populations, how easy do you suppose it is to manage wildlife? It's about as easy as herding cats or teaching table manners to a marmot. Though not an easy task, managing wildlife within some parameters is doable. We ask managers to do this because we like wildlife. Managers have to rely on a set of management tools, some of which are readily at their disposal, and others which are proffered or withheld depending on institutional circumstances or the status of the controversy over their use. The tool kits of wildlife managers include:

- Laws

- Predator Control

- Refuges

- Stocking

- Extirpation

- Introduction of Exotics

- Habitat Management

- Harvest

- Public Education

Laws

Society has established numerous laws and regulations regarding the treatment of wildlife and wildlife habitat. Laws and regulations vary from conditions of blanket protection (no harvest, harassment, or detriment to habitat) to conditions of regulated protection (certain levels of harvest and habitat alteration are acceptable), to conditions of no protection (the species needs no protective measures), to conditions of control (populations of the species are intentionally reduced). Laws and regulations can be flexible, allowing managers the discretionary authority to manage populations and habitats. Or they can be inflexible, forcing managers to protect species by every means within their power. Flexibility is of course, preferred by wildlife managers, as wildlife populations are inherently flexible and their habitats are not static. Blanket protection laws are usually forced on wildlife managers through legislative actions forged in the political arena. These types of laws include certain regulations under the Endangered Species Act, and a host of other laws with names such as the **Marine Mammal Protection Act (1972)**, the **Bald Eagle Protection Act (1940)**, and the Wild and Free-Roaming Horses and Burros Act (1971). Managerial flexibility varies within the language of these laws and as the result of amendments and new regulations passed over time. The examples above are federal laws. Remember that wildlife management is primarily a state responsibility. Some states (e.g., California) have their own endangered species acts, or other blanket protection laws (e.g., California's moratorium on the hunting of *Felis concolor*, the mountain lion).

Predator Control

Predator control is a little-used method that has a history of failure that calls for caution in its application. Bounty hunting for wolves, coyotes and mountain lions, once believed to be the answer to larger herds of deer, wound up killing predators and deer, as herd populations escalated above carrying capacity in the absence of population limits through predation. The classic case of the wasting of the deer herds of the Kaibab Plateau north of the Grand Canyon in the early 1900s is often cited, if not substantiated, as a good reason to frown on predator control. Under some limited circumstances, predator control might be instituted to protect small populations of rare, threatened, or endangered species.

Pintail ducks in a courtship flight over a waterfowl wildlife refuge.
(John Cowan Collection)

Wildlife Refuges

Wildlife refuges are areas of habitat that have been set aside by law to protect species and increase their numbers. Four general types of refuges include those for (a) big game, (b) small game, (c) waterfowl, and (d) nongame species. Big game and small-game refuges are dedicated to the protection of species that are popular with hunters (thus the term "game"). To propagate numbers, hunting may be extensively limited or used only when carrying capacity is threatened. Waterfowl refuges are managed so as to provide sanctuary to migratory birds, as well as opportunities for hunting. Refuges for nongame species are established specifically to protect species that are regionally or globally rare, threatened, or endangered or to protect some other species of interest. Refuges can be intensively managed to provide optimal habitat conditions, or they may be essentially left alone when natural conditions provide high-quality habitat without human intervention.

Stocking

Stocking is used to release wildlife into under-populated habitat. The stocked wildlife originates from either artificial rearing or from transplantation. Stocking is used to "re-introduce" wildlife to habitats from which it may have become regionally extinct, such as attempts to stock desert bighorn sheep or the California condor. Stocking is used to move "problem" bears away from recreation areas or as a means to cull overstocked habitat areas. Stocking is also used to increase harvest opportunities, as seen in the practice of releasing fish into waters for "put-and-take" fishing.

Fish hatcheries are a wildlife management strategy called stocking.
(Photo by Steve Dennis)

Extirpation

Extirpation is used only to control pest species in limited areas when the local annihilation will not threaten the species' existence elsewhere. Not usually a wildlife management tool, extirpation has been problematic when species have been hunted to extinction, as was the case with the passenger pigeon or the great auk.

Introduction of Exotics

The introduction of exotic species has been both successful and tragic. A form of stocking, it is used to populate habitat with a desired species, or to use an exotic species in an attempt to control a "problem" species. The introduction of ring-necked pheasant and chukar has been successful (and popular with hunters) in the U.S., as has been the introduction of trout and salmon to waters where they were not indigenous (native). Exotics have also been disasters in some areas. In New Zealand, rabbits were introduced by Scottish immigrants, thinking bunnies would make for good hunting. Without predators, and being rabbits, they shortly became a menace to the grazing industry. Unable to control their numbers, New Zealanders introduced weasels and stoats to prey on the rabbits. But rabbits were faster than many of New Zealand's species of flight-challenged birds, so the weasels, stoats, and rabbits all flourished to the decline of a unique assemblage of flightless birds. Constant vigilance in extirpation efforts and the transplanting of some birds to safe islands have been the only strategies capable of warding off complete extinction of several species.

Habitat Management

Habitat management outside of wildlife refuges is key to the success of many species of wildlife. Habitat on lands managed by government agencies and private lands all play a role in providing homes for wildlife. No one could have predicted the nesting of peregrine falcons on the ledges of high-rise office buildings in Los Angeles, but habitat management consisted mostly of curtailing some window washing. Wildlife cohabits with humans in urban, suburban, and rural settings, at times so successfully that the local population can become a nuisance. Agricultural, forestry, mining, livestock, and water management activities all affect wildlife for better and for worse. The key to wildlife management is to maintain a quality habitat and ruin as little as possible.

This wastewater treatment facility also serves as valuable waterfowl habitat.
(Photo by Steve Dennis)

Harvest

Most wildlife harvest is, to be blunt, to kill. Some harvest is the live collection of animals for the pet industry or for stocking aquariums and zoos. Harvest is simply predation by humans. Legal harvest is usually called hunting, fishing, or trapping. Illegal harvest is invariably called poaching. Wildlife managers rely on harvest to keep populations within the carrying capacity of their habitat. If habitat is limited or if "natural" predators are absent from the habitat, harvest is one means to keep populations in check. Harvest is potentially very controversial. Anti-hunting activists have stopped hunts on numerous occasions, much to the chagrin of hunters who support wildlife through excise taxes, licenses, and permits. Wildlife managers are in the unenviable position of trying to explain why a bullet to the middle of an animal is good for the animal's family. Anthropomorphism leads people to surmise that this same logic would approve of us blowing away the handsomest member of each other's family. There is no convincing some people that harvest is a viable or humane management tool. Though efficient and relatively inexpensive, harvest methods can be politically unacceptable and also provide fertile ground for controversy.

Public Education

All of this leads us to the tool of **public education**. Wildlife managers have not been particularly adroit at getting across the message that harvest is a humane and reasonable method for handling excessive population growth. Hunting made a bad name for itself through market hunting of years past, as well as the extinction and near extinction of species that were shot for "sport." Overcoming anthropomorphism and convincing publics and politicians that they are expert at wildlife needs presents wildlife managers with a daunting task. As public scrutiny bears down on the management of the wildlife resource, managers are often caught in the middle of controversy. In the next section, we'll take a look at a select few wildlife controversies to demonstrate how all these factors and influences play out.

Angel Island Deer

Angel Island is a California state park scenically situated near the middle of San Francisco Bay. As an island, it has a readily definable quantity of habitat. In the late 1970s, the resident black-tailed deer herd on the island had grown to more than 200. Browse species had been significantly reduced through overgrazing, and the **habituated** deer made a living by working over tourists for snacks. The herd began to show signs of malnourishment and disease. California's Department of Fish and Game, as the agency responsible for wildlife, studied the herd and determined that the best course of action would be to shoot the excess animals and bring the herd's population down to a manageable size within its carrying capacity.

When the hunting plans were made public, animal protectionists went ballistic and dragged the San Francisco press along with them. Headlines proclaimed that the hunt amounted to government-sponsored slaughter. Publics were solicited to join in the fray as resident "owners" of the herd. The DFG was accused of ignoring other options so that its own biologists could enjoy the "sport" of shooting deer. They were asked how killing could possibly "save" deer. Next, protectionists brought suit against the DFG, and a court order blocked the hunt. Unable to gain any ground in explaining why the shooting was humane and economical, the DFG succumbed to public outcry and went back to the drawing board, as the deer grew weaker. The introduction of predators was suggested, as was sterilization, but the only politically correct option became transplantation. So at a cost of approximately $3,000 per animal, 203 deer were captured and transplanted to the Myacamas Mountains 140 miles to the north. The site had recently been burned over and was selected because good forage recovers in the first rainy season following fires in that area.

The animal protectionists had succeeded, and all was well again in the city by the bay. The press moved on to other issues, and it was left to the DFG to sort out the management of the newly relocated herd. After having fitted 15 deer with radio transmitters, biologists found half of them dead within three months. Within a year, two were left and one was missing. Malnutrition, predation, poaching, and vehicle collisions were the causes of death. The success rate of the transplantation was abysmal. More than $600,000 of public money had been spent to ensure the death of a couple hundred deer in a manner that most people would consider less humane than a bullet. Fish and Game's perspective on this issue warranted a couple of small mid-section articles in the San Francisco papers that earlier had been so willing to give the topic front-page coverage over the shooting controversy. The protectionists may have won, and the wildlife managers may have lost, but the biggest losers were the deer.

Feral Horses and Burros

Feral is a term used to describe animals that were once domesticated (or their ancestors were) and are now wild. Species that were exotic to the Americas, horses and burros were brought to the West by Europeans and were used extensively as the beasts of burden for transportation, logging, and mining. Many tribes of Native Americans adopted horses and adapted to new hunting lifestyles that centered on the use of the horse. By 1804, the Lewis and Clark expedition was buying horses from Native Americans! As Native Americans were decimated, horses escaped from dwindling tribes. Horses and burros used for hauling were often turned loose as they gradually became obsolete, their labor replaced by steam and gasoline engines. Freed horses and burros adapted well to the arid landscapes of the West and began to swell into sizable herds of "wild" animals.

For roughly half a century, horse and burro populations were kept in check by ranchers, hunters, and resource managers who shot them or rounded them up for sale as pet food and hides. National parks and monuments intentionally destroyed feral horses and burros, under the agency's mandate to control exotic species. **"Mustangers"** would lasso horses from horse or vehicle, attach a tire or two to drag, and wear the horse to a stop. The horses were then trucked off to slaughterhouses. One day in the 1950s, Nevada rancher Velma Johnston pulled up behind a truck loaded with panicked and bloody horses. Soon to become known as **"Wild Horse Annie,"** Mrs. Johnston initiated a campaign to save wild horses that went all the way to blanket federal protection passed by Congress. Marshaling forces such as the **Humane Society of the United States**, **Wild Horse Organized Assistance (WHOA),** and a host of other grassroots groups, Annie saw legislation passed in California as early as 1959; with widespread public support also came passage of the Wild and Free Roaming Horses and Burros Act in 1971. Fury, Black Beauty, and National Velvet had obviously struck a chord, as did the popular movie Billy Jack, which depicted the slaughter of wild horses.

Feral, or wild burros are the descendants of work animals used in the pre-automobile days.

John Cowan Collection

Courtesy of the Library of Congress

Wildlife managers reacted with skepticism to the Horses and Burros Act. They predicted that feral horse and burro populations would double every six or seven years, that the increased numbers would become problematic for the livestock industry and to the habitat for native wildlife. Studies, of course, ensued. Though most wildlife biologists agreed that feral horses and burros caused habitat deterioration, at least one found impacts from burros in Death Valley National Monument to be benign, and her "preliminary" results were published in *National Geographic*. As predicted, populations doubled on schedule, and wildlife managers began to ask for legislative remedies to the overpowered 1971 Horses and Burros Act. In 1977, the National Park Service proposed "direct reduction" (aka shooting) of approximately 2,000 burros overpopulating the Grand Canyon. Though the NPS was correct in planning to control exotic species, public outcry (including thousands of letters from fourth graders) forced the agency to postpone the action and prepare an environmental impact statement. The NPS removed a statue of **"Brighty of Grand Canyon"** from the park's south rim and replaced it with an interpretive exhibit explaining how the exotic burros damaged the environment.

Congress responded to the management issue by passing the Public Rangelands Improvement Act in 1978. Easing blanket protection somewhat, PRIA allowed for limited removal of feral horses and burros and gave impetus to the start-up "adopt-a-horse" and "adopt-a-burro" programs conducted by the BLM. It was now legal to confer ownership to people who would care for wild horses and burros as pets. But the door was also open for commercial processors to gain title to horses and burros after a year of humane ownership, and the animals were once again heading to slaughterhouses. When adoption programs were unable to keep pace with government roundups, excess horses and burros were incarcerated in expensive feedlot arrangements.Unknown assailants in Nevada shot several herds of wild horses, and the Earth Liberation Front claimed credit for firebombing a BLM wild horse corral near the California – Nevada border, as the controversy grew more heated.

But a small success story unfolded at Grand Canyon. Following two years of environmental impact statement preparation, the NPS concluded that the feral burro population in the park was closer to 300 animals. After weighing the alternatives, however, the NPS recommended "direct reduction." Galloping to the rescue, a citizen group known as The Fund for Animals, boasting media stars and famous author Cleveland Amory at the helm, offered to foot the bill for transplantation of the burros. The NPS, cognizant of its public relations, granted Amory's group the opportunity to round them up. The results were a success. The Fund for Animals captured all of the burros and carted them off to the fund's "ranch" in Texas to the tune of a little more than $600,000. The NPS could breathe easier for a moment, and the Fund for Animals made a media splash with their "rescue."

Still unresolved, the controversy over feral horses and burros continues. The livestock industry is willing to manage only a limited quantity of wild horses because they compete for forage with cattle and sheep. Protectionists view every feral horse and burro as near-sacred symbols of the American West, and they question the right of ranchers to practice dominant use of federal rangelands. Managers are stuck in the middle, receiving conflicting directions from Washington that don't allow for implementation of wildlife management strategies. By 2011, BLM Director Bob Abbey, in the face of strong pro-wild horse public opinion, called for a scientific program review and the use of fertility control measures as the primary method to maintain healthy wild horse and burro populations. He further called for BLM to meet this goal working in cooperation with the Humane Society of the United States. While BLM struggles with another directive, the costs of managing these two exotic species grows higher, and the opposing groups continue to have their boot heels dug in deep.

Cougar

The mountain lion (*Felis concolor*) is one of only a few species left in North America that has the ability to prey on humans. Fortunately, they rarely exercise that option. Mountain lions were extensively hunted for bounties during the days of market hunting and predator reduction programs intended to protect deer, elk, and livestock. Remarkably elusive, avoiding humans and mostly one another, mountain lion populations are extremely difficult to estimate. Concerned that their numbers had dropped too low and that the species was in decline, California banned the hunting of mountain lions in 1971. Since then, mountain lions can be taken only under a "depredation permit," where a specific lion is known to have taken livestock or pets, and in cases where a lion poses an immediate threat to safety. In effect, California is the world's largest mountain lion refuge.

When populations were roughly estimated above 5,000, and mountain lion sightings had tripled from their 1982 levels, the Department of Fish and Game suggested opening a limited lion hunt in 1987 and again in 1988. Their recommendation was to hold a revenue-generating lottery for 190 permits that could be used during a 79-day lion-hunting season. Considering the proposal, the **Fish and Game Commission** was overwhelmed by protests and threatened legal action. Another flurry of media excitement brought nationwide attention to the issue. Hunters backed groups such as the **California Sportsmen's Task Force**, and protectors created organizations such as the **Mountain Lion Foundation**. Sportsmen claimed that the lion population was exceeding its carrying capacity and needed to be culled before the species became a danger. Protectionists ridiculed the method of treeing cats with hunting dogs and then taking a dead-on shot for the kill. They also debated the unverifiable figures for population levels and pointed out that sightings were on the rise due to the increase of human population in cougar habitat. The commission and the DFG backed off the proposal, while signatures were collected that put a citizen initiative before voters on the 1990 ballot. Known as the mountain lion initiative, Proposition 117 passed that June, maintaining the hunting ban and earmarking funds for wildlife habitat acquisition and improvement.

A treed cougar being hunted under a depredation permit.
(Jon Hooper Collection)

Barbara Schoener liked to rise early and start her day with a jog on the equestrian path in the Auburn State Recreation Area. On Saturday, April 23, 1994, the 40-year-old mother of two set out on her morning run on a beautiful spring day. When she failed to return by late in the day, El Dorado County sheriffs launched an intense search. Her body was found the next morning a few feet off the trail, covered by some leaves and mauled. As tests would later prove, Schoener had the dubious distinction of being the first person since 1909 to die by mountain lion attack in California. A week after she was killed, the culprit was treed and shot—an 80-pound female and new mother. Three days after that, her seven-week-old cub was caught.

In the ensuing weeks, media from local papers to Rush Limbaugh would join in a debate over numerous aspects of the death, the mountain lion controversy, and the handling of the trial and execution of the perpetrator. As if mountain lion attacks were a public menace, television and newspapers warned people how to avoid encounters and survive attacks. Animal rights activists claimed that in killing the mother lion, trackers had ignored "due process and the presumption of innocence." Retorts asked if the lion's Miranda warnings should have been read. Statistics on mountain lion attacks in the West and in British Columbia paraded through the media, noting impressive increases since the 1970s. Rush Limbaugh inaccurately reported to the nation that, as of May 22, a trust fund in memory of Barbara Schoener had accumulated $9,000 in donations, while a trust for the mountain lion cub had collected $21,000. Mistaken as to the amount the Folsom Zoo had received for the cub (The zoo had not created a trust but still ended up with about $5,000 donated for the cub's care), Limbaugh helped propel the trust for Schoener's family to well over $100,000. The Schoener family filed a claim for damages against both the state and the DFG, but then withdrew it, recognizing precedents that the state is not responsible for the actions of wild animals.

The buzz over mountain lions swelled in 1994, when Iris Kenna of San Diego was also killed by a cougar in Southern California. A subsequent attack in 1995, three in 2004 (including a fatality), and another in 2007, have kept the mountain lion question in the news. Legislation amending Proposition 117 and returning it to the ballot has been proposed. The Mountain Lion Foundation offered as a fund raiser an "adopt-a-lion" gift package, complete with adoption papers and photo of an "adoptee" mountain lion. Like many issues involving wildlife, the controversy over mountain lions dances on an uneasy perch manipulated by publics and politicians. The professional wildlife managers of the Department of Fish and Game are again governed by blanket protection laws, that emanate from the will of the people. The critical element of wildlife management is clearly exemplified through this case study. It is politics.

The Endangered Species Act

It has previously been stated that the Endangered Species Act of 1973 (and its subsequent amendments) ... has become the strongest piece of federal resource protection legislation yet passed by Congress. Let's try to reduce the complexity of this law's enactment to a few key principles. The fundamental basis for the ESA consists of (a) endangered species, (b) threatened species, and (c) critical habitats. Endangered species include "any species which is in danger of extinction throughout all or a significant portion of its range." Threatened species include "any species which is likely to become an endangered species within the foreseeable future throughout all or a significant portion of its range." The threatened category was created to help conserve species *before* they came close to extinction, as well as to provide a designation for formerly endangered but recovering species that no longer required the highest level of protective regulations. Critical habitat is loosely defined in the act as areas that are "essential to the conservation of the species." Application of the law has gone beyond existing ranges of the threatened or endangered species to include areas that would become necessary for the continued survival of a recovering population of that species. This further extended the act's considerations to include populations of threatened and endangered species in given geographical locations, where endangerment of the population might be of regional significance, but only potentially threatening to the species as a whole.

The Grizzly Bear has been classified as "threatened" under the Endangered Species Act since 1975.
(John Cowan Collection)

The **listing process** is another key element of the ESA. The Secretary of the Interior is the administrator with sole authority to list a species as threatened or endangered. A listing, delisting, or change can be initiated by "the appropriate Secretary or pursuant to petition from any interested person." (Note the power of an individual citizen to petition for a species' listing!) After a 90-day review, the merits of the petitioned listing are evaluated, and a decision is made whether to go forward with the listing process. If it is a go, the Secretary of Interior has one year to make a final listing determination, but can take an extra six months if substantial disagreement exists (and it frequently does). Listing is a complex mix of scientific data, definition of critical habitat, and extensive involvement by interested publics. Altering the regulations that govern the listing process has had a profound effect on the numbers of listings. The Reagan administration added complexity to the listing process, slowing listings. In a lame duck move in 2008, the Bush administration altered ESA regulations to eliminate requirements for consultation with federal biologists regarding "actions" that could negatively affect at-risk species. Shortly after entering office in 2009, President Obama issued a presidential memorandum directing departments to once again consult the U.S. Fish and Wildlife Service or National Oceanic and Atmospheric Administration on "actions" potentially detrimental to vulnerable animals and plants. Political manipulation of elements of the ESA should by now be clear.

When a species is listed as endangered, it becomes subject to strict **protective measures**. First, it becomes illegal to "**take**" the species anywhere in the U.S. or on the high seas. To take "means to harass, harm, pursue, hunt, shoot, wound, kill, trap, capture, or collect, or to attempt to engage in any such conduct." **Harm** became the disputable term in the definition of "take," as habitat degradation could be considered harmful. **Section 7** of the ESA sets forth the responsibilities of agencies under the act. The seemingly innocuous order that "federal agencies refrain from any action that might jeopardize the continued existence of any endangered species or threatened species or result in the destruction or adverse modification of habitat of such species" has become the teeth of the law's protective measures. Section 7 of the ESA has been called "the conscience of contemporary environmental law." It is Section 7 that forces agencies to protect endangered species.

The once-endangered American Bald Eagle was removed from the Endangered Species List in 1999.
(John Jackson, Montague, CA.)

The ESA, like most environmentally related legislation, contains provisions for exceptions and exemptions. Best known among these is the exemption process, created in 1978, which ends up under review of the seven-member **Endangered Species Committee** popularly referred to as the "**God Squad**." An exemption, which reduces species protections under the act, can be made when a minimum of five members of the Endangered Species Committee find that a federal action is of greater importance than the protection of a species, and that there are no reasonable alternatives available. Even though it's a seldom-used provision, the committee's authority to rule on the survival or extinction of a species has been likened to the power of God.

Michael Bean's *The Evolution of National Wildlife Law* is an excellent reference on the ESA and other wildlife-related laws. It is strongly recommended reading for those who are interested in this topic.

This chapter has only scratched the surface of the subject of wildlife management and wildlife controversies. From the reintroduction of gray wolves into Yellowstone to the relocation of California condors to northern Arizona—in a desperate attempt to save them—wildlife issues have a tight grip on our society's environmental psyche. Wildlife is probably the barometer by which we measure the environmental effects of humanity, as these animals are our neighbors, and are therefore dependent on our actions. Changes in wildlife habitat are changes in human habitat. Wildlife is the canary in the mine that is home to us all.

Suggested Readings

Adams, D. A. (1993). *Renewable resource policy: The legal-institutional foundations.* Washington, DC: Island Press.

Bauer, D. C., & Irvin, W. R. (Eds.). (2010). *Endangered Species Act: Law, policy, and perspectives* (2nd ed.). Chicago: American Bar Association, Section of Environment, Energy, and Resources.

Bean, M. J., & Rowland, M. J. (1997). *The evolution of national wildlife law* (3rd ed.). Westport, CT: Praeger.

Bojorquez, J. (1994, May 12). On the prowl. *The Sacramento Bee*, pp. F1, F5.

Bolen, E. G., & Robinson, W. L. (2003). *Wildlife ecology and management* (5th ed.). Upper Saddle River, NJ: Prentice-Hall.

Chase, A. (1987). *Playing God in Yellowstone: The destruction of America's first national park.* New York: Harcourt Brace Jovanovich.

Coggins, G. C., Wilkinson, C., & Leshy, J. (2007). *Federal public land and resources law* (6th ed.). New York, NY: Foundation Press.

Cruise, D., & Griffiths, A. (2010). *Wild Horse Annie and the last of the mustangs: The life of Velma Johnston.* New York: Scribner.

Dennis, S. R. (1979). *The feral burro controversy.* Unpublished manuscript, California State University, Chico.

Goble, D. D., Scott, J. M., & Davis, F. W. (Eds.). (2006). The Endangered Species Act at thirty. Washington, DC: Island Press.

Harrington, W., & Fisher, A. C. (1982). Endangered species. In P. R. Portney (Ed.), *Current issues in natural resource policy* (pp. 117–148). Washington, DC: Resources for the Future.

Moehlman, P. D. R. (1972). Getting to know the wild burros of Death Valley. *National Geographic, 141*(4), 502–517.

"Rescued" deer die. (1982). *Outdoor News Bulletin, 37*(3), 2.

Satchell, M. (1980, April 27). Can we save the burros? *Parade.*

Vega, E. T. (Ed.). (2007). *Endangered Species Act update and impact.* New York, NY: Nova Science Publishers.

chapter twenty

Range Management and Grazing

Home on the Range

Livestock grazing is a sanctioned activity within the doctrine of multiple use. Though most livestock production in the U.S. comes from private lands in the East and the South, the 17% that comes from the western states, and the mere two percent that is produced on public lands kicks up a storm of controversy. Grazing, like mining, timbering, and water development, has its roots well established in the pioneering era of the West. Unfortunately, like those other pioneer activities, grazing also followed a pattern of boom and bust, of resource exploitation and depletion. Today, if grazing is to survive on western rangelands, it will do so through a blend of better stewardship practices and the continued strength of its political ties.

Cows and Cowboys

Devoid of domesticated livestock, the plains and large sections of the western states were home for huge numbers of grazing animals, including bison, elk, deer, and antelope. Even with large herds of wild animals, the prairies and rangelands supported vast quantities of quality forage, enticing to settlers who came west for the mining but stayed on for the ranching and farming. For several reasons, grasses and forbs managed to exist symbiotically with the herbivores that munched them. First, herds were migratory and prowled about in patterns that followed the better forage, leaving grazed areas time to recover and thrive. Second, predators including Native Americans provided a limiting but not destructive check on populations. Third, animals' hooves would cut up and aerate soils to actually improve water retention, while feces returned fertilizer. As long as animals moved about, the effects of grazing were scattered enough to allow plant life and soils to stabilize each other. Thanks to stable soils and plants, grazing by native herbivores actually worked more like pruning. Coupled with automatic fertilizer delivery, grazing indeed improved plant growth.

Cattle on lands typical of those managed by the BLM.
(Courtesy of U.S. Bureau of Land Management)

Impressed by grazing potential, Spanish missionaries introduced cattle into Texas, New Mexico, Arizona, and California in the eighteenth century. Later to be called Texas longhorns, these cattle proliferated on the open range, supplying the economic base of the mission economy. British settlement brought cattle to the Willamette Valley in the future State of Oregon, and demand from the California gold rush brought herds south, starting a ranching industry to feed the boomtowns of western gold and silver miners. Grazing on a massive scale took hold after the Civil War with the legendary drives of Texas longhorns toward settlements in the north and to the west. The advent of railroads by the 1870s opened up huge markets to ranchers who could use grass to grow walking steaks and then take them on a hike to distant cattle cars. Decimation of the bison; bounty hunting for predators; market hunting for deer, elk, and antelope, and the driving of Native Americans onto reservations paved the way for ranchers to lay claim to lands and a lucrative industry.

The "wild west," by today's standards, was not a misnomer. Regulation of land use practices was virtually nonexistent, and the rules that limited settlement under the Homestead Acts and other statutes could legally be manipulated to pull together the resources necessary for the establishment and operation of cattle ranches. In the arid parts of the West, ranching required a base ranch on which living quarters, barns, corrals, and hay farming could be situated. The base ranch needed water, timber, and arable soils, so it was established on the alluvial outflow of creeks descending from nearby mountains. The Homestead Act limitation to 160 acres per homesteader was easily circumvented by acquiring title to adjacent homesteads for each family member, ranch hand, and the occasional drifter. These titles were then bought by the base ranch owners, consolidating a foundation from where ranching operations could occur over huge stretches of unclaimed public domain lands.

A "base ranch" adjacent to BLM land and Eagle Lake, California.
(Courtesy of U.S. Bureau of Land Management)

Of course, there were other claimants to public lands. The Homestead Act of 1862 envisioned Jefferson's "yeoman farmers" occupying 160-acre farms, raising crops, and forming the backbone of an agricultural economy. Conditions in the West, however, were such that many 160-acre squares did not possess the soil, water, and timber resources necessary to build a viable farm. As ranchers, early on, grabbed up the fertile drainages and limited arable bottomlands of the basin and range region, the leftover lands available for farm homesteading were barren, poorly soiled, and without adequate water sources. Once a base ranch was established, "dummy" homesteaders could buy lands to add to the base operation and increase the size of the single consolidated ranch. But so many acres were inadequate for homesteading that ranchers would not even need to purchase them fraudulently. In the absence of federal laws opposing such actions, ranchers were able to run herds on unclaimed public domain land. Thus, a relatively small base ranch was able to run large herds of cattle across huge portions of public domain lands. The base ranch might occupy only 1% or 2% of the total land used by the ranch.

Competition for the land resource came only from sheepherders and farmers, and ranchers weren't shy in their intimidation of these "squatters." The storyline of many old Hollywood Westerns depicts the suffering farmer standing tall against the hired guns of the cattle baron. The hired guns inflict pain and suffering until a lanky stranger rides in with a clouded gunslinger's past. After most of the hired guns "bite the dust," the lonesome hero rides into the sunset, and the farmers are saved when the curtain goes down. Except for the ending favoring the farmer, these Westerns are based on the historical "range wars" of the turn of the century. Threats, property destruction, and an occasional murder kept farmers and sheepherders from insisting on their federal rights. With the invention of barbed wire, ranchers could fence off huge sections of the public domain. Congress passed the **Unlawful Inclosures Act of 1885** to demonstrate federal commitment to homesteading, but enforcement was lacking and most fences stayed up. Western states dropped ranchers' liability for damage caused by their cattle on other property, forcing farmers to fence to keep cattle out! Considering that the difficulty in eking out an existence from rough land and the fear of being burned out or shot at kept farming to a minimum, ranchers were left virtually free to run the land as they saw fit. Through intimidation, legal possession of water rights and key arable lands, fencing, and a void in federal laws that mandated other land uses, ranchers established a "**code of the West**," through which a viable industry developed. Legendary in proportions, the ranching industry claims itself the economic backbone of many sparsely populated regions throughout the West. But pressures from other interests are growing, and the traditions of the rancher's code are eroding across a changing western landscape.

Regulation Rides In (or Tries To)

By the time ranching had consolidated its power in the West, public sentiment was beginning to favor the concepts of greater federal control in resource management. Land withdrawals for national parks and forest reserves resulted from the growing political influence of preservationists and conservationists. Pinchot introduced a grazing regulation program on the national forests in 1906, charging a nickel per animal unit month (AUM). But Forest Service control did not extend to the public domain lands, and ranchers rode herd over federal controls until the Taylor Grazing Act of 1934. But, as noted in chapter 9, even the grazing advisory boards established through the act, were manned by ranchers, effectively thwarting federal interest in controlling the range. The establishment of the Grazing Service, along with grazing districts, provided an opening for regulation of ranching on the public domain. The recording of range allotments permitted to each ranch, as well as the quantity of allowable

AUMs, brought a form of control over the never-legalized "range rights" claimed by the ranchers. The newly established BLM took over management of the public domain in 1946, and over the next three decades, grazing fees inched up to $1.35 per AUM, and a type of standoff evolved between the ranching industry and its federal regulators. Western congressmen were effective at keeping regulatory legislation at bay and grazing fees at a minimum. The 1970s, however, saw the beginning of a series of changes that have altered the old freedoms enjoyed by western ranchers. The passage of NEPA opened the door for examination of the BLM's grazing policies and produced a turning point in range management. A 1974 suit by the **Natural Resources Defense Council** challenged BLM's Environmental Impact Statement, which described the grazing program from a national perspective. The court ruled that NEPA calls for "detailed analysis" specific to local conditions (*NRDC, Inc. v. Morton*, 388 F. Supp. 829, D.D.C. 1974). Citing a BLM report, the judge noted that only 16 percent of BLM-managed grazing land was considered to be in excellent or good condition, while the other 84% ranged from fair to bad. Going back to the drawing board, the BLM was ordered to eventually produce 144 EISs on grazing. Passage of the Wild and Free Roaming Horses and Burros Act of 1971 presaged the coming of other wildlife protection laws that would limit grazing—most importantly, the Endangered Species Act that followed two years later. The Federal Land Policy and Management Act (FLPMA) in 1976 and the Public Rangelands Improvement Act (PRIA) of 1978 structured the BLM's planning and management processes and elevated range improvements to the agency's highest priority.

All this regulatory fervor did not sit well with a century-old ranching industry accustomed to calling its own shots. In the early 1980s, ranchers staged the **Sagebrush Rebellion**, aided by Ronald Reagan's appointment of **James Watt** to head the Department of the Interior. Like Reagan, a self-proclaimed "rebel," Watt fed the hopes of the ranchers, maintaining that federal lands (particularly the BLM's) should be relinquished to private hands. Running into a dead end on that concept, the rebellion backed the transfer of western rangelands to state control. This move spawned several unsuccessful bills and a lawsuit by Nevada that succeeded only in killing the "rebellion" when a federal judge in that state ruled that Congress, not the states, owns the public lands. The one achievement of the Sagebrush Rebellion was to secure a hands-off attitude toward grazing through the Reagan-Bush years. Grazing fees remained $1.35 per AUM, compared with a fair market value estimated at $6.35, fueling criticisms that ranching is over-subsidized by the federal government. Clinton's interior secretary Bruce Babbitt pushed for grazing reform in the 1990s, but through his term, and Bush's secretaries Gale Norton and Dirk Kempthorne, grazing fees stayed at $1.35 per AUM, and dramatic change on the range remained mired in the machinations of western politics and the BLM bureaucracy.

Ranchers aren't hicks. They could sense the mood of change in the 1970s, just as they can smell the approach of a summer thunderstorm. They knew that their generations-old way of life needed to accommodate changes in values for the range, or they would soon collectively ride off into the sunset for the last time. Both the ranchers and the BLM have begun to recognize that they need to work cooperatively rather than contentiously. Ignored for years by most of the nation, grazing on the public lands is now under the magnifying glass of the environmental movement. The problems have been identified. Solutions are harder to come by, but progress is being made.

Grazing Problems

It is **overgrazing**, not grazing, that is hard on the land. Patterns of overgrazing were established from the boom days of the Texas longhorn herds. The common resource—grass and the soils that supported it—was severely decimated by an industry that freely ran over it. More cattle meant more money, and grass, the most important unit of investment, was free. If one rancher didn't use it, another one would, so incentive to run more animals was high, as well as disastrously exploitative. Some areas of the West have never recovered the tall grasses that brought ranchers there originally. Other areas have recovered, either through reduction of grazing levels or elimination of grazing altogether.

These two photos show a riparian area damaged by overgrazing, and one year later, following restoration conducted by the BLM. (Courtesy of U.S. Bureau of Land Management)

Vital to arid lands grazing are the riparian areas along streams that flow down from the uplands. Riparian areas are a resource rich with water, grasses, forbs, sedges, willows, cottonwoods, sycamores, and other plant and tree species. Their survival is symbiotic with the development of soils that are washed down along streams to be caught up in root systems and decaying vegetative matter from surrounding plants. This buildup of soils also acts as a huge sponge, collecting and filtering water, and recharging a localized aquifer that feeds the roots of plants and trees that are farther from the stream. This filtration of water also slows its flow, minimizing erosion to periods of heavy rainstorms and spring runoff. Streams **meander**, cutting snakelike patterns across a fertile bottomland built up by years of slow erosion and plant growth and decomposition. Plants growing along the banks of streams protect soils and provide cooling shade that further diversifies available habitat. Wildlife such as beaver are drawn to such streams, finding appropriate plant growth for their toothy palate and building dams that further slow the water, improving aquifer recharge and providing pond habitat for insects, fish, amphibians, birds, and other mammals. These streams act as oases, permanent homes for many species, a piece in the habitat mix, for others, and stopping-over points for migratory animals. Such streams also provided the life-sustaining resources that allowed for human settlement and, eventually, the locations that were used as the base for western ranching operations.

Previously overgrazed riparian area undergoing restoration work by the BLM. Note return of creekside vegetation. (Courtesy of U.S. Bureau of Land Management)

Riparian areas were not devoid of grazing animals. Bison, antelope, bighorn sheep, deer, moose, and elk would all take their turns at grazing these fertile areas. They would come and go, pruning plants to actually improve growth, opening up soils with their hooves, and leaving behind fertilizer. The healthy range of the mid-nineteenth century was enormously attractive to people who could recognize the economic potential of ranching in these regions. In managing the range resource, economic gain held priority, while stewardship of sustaining systems went by the wayside. Cattle, when raised in large numbers, can turn a balanced riparian area into a canyon-like desert. The overgrazing of upland areas and stream banks mangles vegetation that holds top-soils in place, allowing sheet erosion to carry off tons of sediment, reducing water percolation, and increasing stream flows. Runoff, filled with sediment, pebbles, rocks, and boulders, cuts gullies that accelerate erosion, forcing water into channels that carry once-rich soils away, knifing and undercutting roots to break up and whisk away ever more soil. Loss of the lowlands soil sponge lowers the local water table, starving plants and trees away from the stream channel and further exposing now-unprotected soils to the elements. Wildlife species dependent on the stable riparian system are lost, removing their role from the stream environment's web, and accelerating the system's decline. Once-placid stream meadows were turned into desert arroyos, meandering streams replaced by eroded cut-bank channels prone to flash flooding and drought. The massive sediment loads from this erosion carried downstream to fill the small reservoirs built for irrigation, rendering them useless. In a generation or two of ranching, riparian areas all over the West suffered this fate. This process, known as desertification, is the downside to unregulated grazing on the western landscape. The problem was an epidemic by the 1920s, but no laws were enacted to reverse the tide until the Taylor Grazing Act of 1934. Effective regulation would not be enacted for another four decades, until the NRDC NEPA ruling in 1974.

Grazing Solutions

Bringing back the rangelands of the West is no small task. Expecting a return to the tall-grass prairies and riparian wealth described in the days of Lewis and Clark, Fremont, Bridger, Ogden, and others is beyond reason. That West isn't coming back. What is at stake, though, is the long-term sustainability of a regional livelihood, plus the protection of resource qualities on which that livelihood and other activities can thrive. Range managers consider their objectives to include the following:

- Production of Commercial Livestock

- Soil Protection

- Water Conservation

- Wildlife Conservation

- Protection of Aesthetic and Recreational Values

On many parts of the western range, meeting these objectives is a challenge of recovery rather than passive monitoring. Overgrazing was key to the decline of rangelands, but reduction of cattle and sheep numbers is not the only solution. **Moving livestock** is critical to managing the range. Back in the (good?) old days, ranchers would simply turn herds loose in the spring to graze on the open range and then move them to the lowlands and supplement their feed in the winter. Livestock were prone to denuding and trampling areas before moving on to "greener pastures," if left to their own limited mentality. This was not characteristic of native herbivores that also faced the threat of predators. Fencing, too, prevented cattle from moving about, forcing them in their quantity to over-munch the browse to which they had access. Cutting up the range into grazing allotments provided a means to count cattle on tracts of permittees' lands. But it also put a check on opportunities to simulate migration. Moving livestock around, keeping their impacts minimal in any single locale, is vital to the recovery and sustainability of the range. This type of management requires planning and close, hard-working attention. But it is a critical component of a coordinated range recovery program.

Riparian-area improvement is also crucial to range resource health. Immediately linked to the viability of riparian areas are erosion reduction and aquifer recharge. Fencing (or other means) to exclude cattle during recovery periods is a first step in restoring stream ecosystems. Installing boulders and/ or logs and gabions to slow stream flows, force meandering, and increase pooling, helps aquifers to recharge, soils to accumulate, and riparian vegetation to take hold. Programs where such measures have been implemented have shown dramatic improvement not in decades, but in years. Not only are riparian communities coming back to flourishing conditions, but a grazing, wildlife, and recreational resource is returning to sustainable proportions.

Ranchers, many of whom are descendants of the early exploiters of the range, are learning that such stewardship measures bring the range back to health and indeed make for better ranching. But, much like loggers, ranchers believe they are under siege. It has been more popular in the media of the environmental era to bash examples of grazing problems than it has been to tout demonstrations of effective stewardship. Opponents of public-lands grazing find it simple to price the gap between grazing fees and estimated fair market value in order to back their argument that the industry is over-subsidized by the federal government. In a tax-cutting, deficit-fearing political environment, such an argument carries a lot of weight. Ranchers counter that forage quality on public lands, plus the costs of managing cattle over large tracts of land, put current grazing fees closer to economic reality than what one might expect to pay for an AUM of pasturage in Arkansas. Simplistic solutions, such as reducing livestock levels and raising fees, can back ranchers into a financial corner, bringing them out fighting with a political clout that is surprisingly powerful. Wielding the federal regulatory cudgel against public-lands grazing only encourages polarization and escalates a political range war.

Over the long haul, citizens need to ask themselves whether they see public-lands grazing in the West as a valuable component of American culture. Certainly, the quantity of livestock produced on public lands is not crucial to the sustainability of McDonald's, Burger King, and the Safeway meat counter. What is at stake is a way of life that supports a small number of Americans spread over a broad section of the nation that went ignored for a century. If the livelihood and indeed the cultural mystique of the "cowboy" should remain more than another memory of America's past, then cooperative change is more appropriate than inflammatory warfare. The answers to effective range management are not necessarily simple. Finding them and putting them to work is a challenge for informed citizens.

Lush forage in improved grazing area, Tanque Verde, Arizona. (David E. Simcox Collection)

Suggested Readings

Butterfield, J., Bingham, S., & Savory, A. (2006). *Holistic management handbook: Healthy land, healthy profits*. Washington, DC: Island Press.

Coggins, G. C., Wilkinson, C., Leshy, J., & Fischman, R. (2007). *Federal public land and resources law* (6th ed.). New York, NY: Foundation Press.

Culhane, P. J. (1981). *Public lands politics: Interest group influence in the Forest Service and the Bureau of Land Management*. Baltimore: Johns Hopkins University Press for Resources for the Future.

Dana, S. T., & Fairfax, S. K. (1980). *Forest and range policy* (2nd ed.). New York: McGraw-Hill.

Dasmann, R. F. (1984). *Environmental conservation* (5th ed.). New York: John Wiley & Sons.

Donn, V. V. (Ed.). (2003). *Public lands: Current issues and perspectives*. New York, NY: Nova Science Publishers.

Foss, P. D. (1960). *Politics and grass: The administration of grazing on the public domain*. Seattle: University of Washington Press.

Holechek, J. L., Pieper, R. D., & Herbel, C. H. (1998). *Range management: Principles and practices* (3rd ed.). Upper Saddle River, NJ: Prentice Hall.

Nelson, R. H. (1984). Ideology and public land policy: The current crisis. In S. Brubaker (Ed.), *Rethinking the federal lands* (pp. 275–298). Washington, DC: Resources for the Future.

Owen, O. S., & Chiras, D. D. (1990). *Natural resource conservation: An ecological approach* (5th ed.). New York: MacMillan.

Savory, A., & Butterfield, J. (1999). *Holistic management: A new framework for decision making* (2nd ed.). Washington, DC: Island Press.

U.S. Department of the Interior, Bureau of Land Management. (1988). *Opportunity and challenge: The story of BLM*. Washington, DC: U.S. Government Printing Office.

Vallentine, J. F. (2001). *Grazing management*. San Diego, CA: Academic Press.

Wilkinson, C. F. (1992). *Crossing the next meridian: Land, water, and the future of the West*. Washington, DC: Island Press.

chapter twenty-one

Water Management and Controversies

Water: The Vital Resource

Some Basics

Water is crucial to life. Among natural resources, water and air are invaluable to us. Wildlife, outdoor recreation, grazing, minerals, timber, and soils are all important resources, but in the absence of these natural resources, we'd find ourselves looking first for water. We have quite a thirst to slake.

Water is an interesting natural resource. It appears on earth in fluid, gaseous, and solid states. As a fluid, its weight is drawn to low-lying areas by gravity's inexorable pull. As a gas, it rises to decorate our atmosphere in a process that purifies it for consumption of terrestrial organisms. As a solid, it packs the seasonally and near-permanently cool regions of the planet under snow and ice. We humans are 80% water. If we dehydrate to 75%, we die. We are creatures of water and users of water.

Most of the earth's water lies in the oceans and seas. Seventy percent of our planet's surface is covered with saltwater. Less than 1% of all water on earth is fresh, fit for use by terrestrial plants and animals. Fortunately, freshwater is a renewable resource. The Earth's system called the **water cycle** purifies water evaporated from oceans, lakes, reservoirs, irrigated lands, and even swimming pools, as vapor climbs into the skies. On its return to the earth's surface as precipitation, most water (except that tainted as **acid precipitation**) is pure and drinkable. But, of course, accumulated precipitation doesn't fall straight into water bottles, canteens, and sprinkler systems. It falls in widely varying amounts all over the earth, including straight back into the ocean.

As I write this in midwinter, rising moisture from across the Pacific has mixed with easterly moving polar air from Siberia and whirled its way toward my home in the Sierra foothills of Northern California. Pushed against hills and mountains, the saturated air has risen, cooled, and condensed to form rain. Overnight the rain gauge has picked up an inch. That means that across the 43,560 square feet (one acre) comprising the parcel deeded in my name, enough rain has fallen to cover it an inch deep. On each square foot, one-twelfth of a cubic foot has fallen. A cubic foot of water is roughly seven and half gallons. One gallon of water weighs about eight pounds, so a cubic foot weighs in at about sixty pounds. That means about five pounds of water fell last night on each of the 43,560 square feet of this acre, that's about 217,800 pounds. One hundred and nine tons! Over the surrounding square mile, almost 70,000 tons of water has come down. In the next 12 hours, another inch will fall, and 70,000 more tons of water will alter its gravitational course on this square mile.

Those tons of water will choose a variety of paths. Some will be caught in shallow pools and later evaporate; birds and other organisms will drink some of it; some will be taken up in the roots of forest vegetation; while other water will make its way through pore spaces in the soil to percolate downward and accumulate as **groundwater** in **aquifers**. That water may eventually be pulled out by wells, or it may continue seeping to lower elevations to make its way again to the surface at springs. But most of the water now falling will move across the surface, forced by gravity to seek the shortest continuously descending route it can find. It will flow in rivulets and channels, ditches and ruts, into brooks, streams, creeks, and rivers toward the sea. Along the way, the water from this square mile will be joined by water from many other square miles, swelling the creeks and rivers to levels measured by hydrologists as cubic feet per second (cfs)—the number of cubic feet of water passing a stationary point on a waterway in a one-second period. A good portion of the water that falls on this acre will make its way to the Sacramento River, the final channel that transports water from these hills to the Pacific under the Golden Gate Bridge. From here to the river, the water will descend 2,000 feet over 25 miles along Little Chico Creek. When these waters enter the Sacramento at an elevation of 190 feet, they will course 200 more miles before reaching the sea. As the Sacramento River is swelled by numerous similar tributaries, it is not unusual for it to reach a flow of 150,000 cfs once it's 25 miles from here. In these conditions nine million pounds of water, or 4,500 tons, passes by an observer every second. Every second, enough water to more than cover the annual needs of four to five average American households flows by. (The average annual household consumption in the U.S. is a little less than an acre-foot, which equals 43,560 cubic feet, or 326,700 gallons.) Two hundred and seventy thousand tons go by in one minute, enough to meet the needs of more than 250 families. Most of this flood-level flow will meet its salty sibling at San Francisco Bay, but not all of the water in the Sacramento's watershed has yet made it to the river. Some of it has been trapped by lakes and man-made reservoirs; and at higher elevations, the water has fallen as snow to peacefully rest until melted in spring. Much of this water is going to be put to work, manipulated by humans to perform a variety of tasks.

Flood control is a critical function of water-managing agencies.
(Photo by Steve Dennis)

Water Uses

Water serves a variety of useful and necessary functions. One of its great merits is that water cannot be destroyed. It can, however, be fouled or rendered unusable. The toilet that you flushed this morning probably contained water that came from the same source as the water you used to brush your teeth. Exiting your home, the water from the toilet and tooth-brushing sink merge into a wastewater transport system that may end in a septic tank and leach field, or be carried to a wastewater treatment plant for purification. Water from a properly designed leach field will recycle as groundwater, and the output of the treatment plant is recycled for agriculture or taken up through the grand recycling process of evaporation. Water is used and reused. It is measured and transported from place to place (usually downhill) to meet a constantly increasing set of demands that we place on it. Because it can be measured and transported, we have some ideas about what water is worth. It is obviously scarce in some areas and abundant in others. Among the more interesting aspects of human water management are the efforts that are made to make water abundant in regions where it would naturally be scarce.

Government regulations and funding have greatly improved our treatment of wastewater. (Photo by Steve Dennis)

We are most familiar with the domestic use of water. Domestic use includes our consumption of water for drinking, cooking, watering urban landscapes, washing clothes and our bodies, and carrying away sewage. In much of the U.S., we use water safe enough to drink for all of these purposes. Delivering **potable** water to residences requires careful water management and treatment. When the sprinklers go on in suburbia, it looks like a lot of water is being used. True as that is, agricultural uses far exceed domestic water use. Approximately 85% of California's water consumption goes to irrigate crops. In Arizona, 90% goes to irrigation. Other consumptive uses for water include numerous industrial applications, where water is used in processing of foods, minerals, wood products, and myriad other functions. Water is used as a cleaning solvent, a coolant, a transportation device, and for energy.

In its fluid state, water weighs in pretty heavy. It responds unquestioningly to the force of gravity and moves from higher to lower elevations. Harnessing this phenomenon, people have stuck waterwheels in streams to push millstones, and have built huge tubes that force tons of water to descend hundreds of feet into the drive flanges of giant hydroelectric turbines. Hydroelectric power is called "clean" power because the generation of electrical energy does not require the burning of fossil or radioactive fuels.

Water serves us as a medium for transportation. The oceans of the world provide the main trade routes for raw materials and commodities. Rivers and canals branch far inland to bring cities into arterial attachment with the seas. Called waterways, their construction, operation, and maintenance is the major concern of the U.S. Army Corps of Engineers.

Not only is water crucial to humans, it is also indispensable to wildlife. The water needs of wildlife range from those of trout and ducks to the water-miserly kangaroo rat and desert tortoise. Wildlife requires varying quantities and types of water. Fish and many marine mammals need total immersion in saltwater or freshwater; waterfowl need wetlands; ungulates need an occasional drink from a brook, lake, or pothole. Our changing attitudes about the importance of wildlife have changed our thinking about managing water for wildlife purposes.

Whitewater rafting takes place on both "wild" and managed rivers.
(Photo by Steve Dennis)

Many forms of outdoor recreation are dependent on water. Fishing, sailing, whitewater rafting, swimming, sighteeing, and skiing are among hundreds of activities that use water for recreational purposes. Recreationists seek beaches and surf, flowing streams and rivers, reefs and tidepools, swamps and estuaries, bays and oceans, lakes and reservoirs, ice and snow, mirroring ponds and tumbling waterfalls—all to provide interactive and aesthetic experiences that generate recreational benefits.

Water Management

Water is an unpredictable resource. It does not always come and go at a rhythm that exactly meets all of our needs and the many uses to which it is put. We would like it if water were always available when we crank the faucet or hook up the irrigation system. We'd like to see plenty of water in our reservoirs for boating and fishing. Steady flows would keep fishers and white-water rafting guides happy, and inundated marshes would be good for wildlife. We want our water unpolluted so we can drink it, gaze upon its beauty, and swim and play in it. We want a place to deposit our sewage and agricultural drainage, and water provides that mechanism. We want to live in warm desert environments and grow lawns and nonnative landscape vegetation. We want to be able to build our homes and businesses near it without fear of flooding; but at the same time, we never want to run out of it. In other words, we ask too much of water. Climate and geographical patterns do not provide a steady and consistent supply of freshwater to the terrestrial portions of the earth. Precipitation in some parts of the world is measured annually in meters, while in some deserts it has not rained in decades. Rain and snow can fall during brief "wet seasons" and then be absent the rest of the year. It can fall so fast and furious that it can't be controlled or stored. Water is a blessing that can also be a beast.

Development in floodplains is an invitation to disaster.
(Courtesy of the U.S. Army Corps of Engineers)

We manage water because, to a certain extent, we can. We're at least a little more proficient at managing water than we are at controlling the weather. Bending water to our will, we have moved it to places where agriculture and human settlement would be impossible without it. We have controlled floods and produced energy. We have created artificial lakes and channels for shipping. We have triumphed over water, but not always, and not without cost. In changing the flow of water we have solved some problems but created others. We have learned from our successes, and we try to repeat them. We have also learned from our mistakes, though inevitably, we repeat them. Water management, its conservation, will be paramount among resource issues in the future. Our technological, ethical, socioeconomic, and political institutions constantly grapple with the management of this resource that affects us all. The stakes involved in overcoming water issues are high.

A home in Kentucky losing sale value after the Salt River flood in 1997. (U.S. Army Corps of Engineers)

Issues

Simply stated, water issues boil down to supply and demand. When supply exceeds demand, we may face flooding and pollution problems. When demand exceeds supply, we face drought and its problems, such as crop failure and water rationing. Let's revisit the list of water uses mentioned earlier, and reconsider those uses in light of some of the problems they may cause.

Domestic water use in the U.S. runs about 225,000 gallons per household per year, roughly two-thirds of an acre-foot. In Europe, the average household consumption is about 60,000 gallons per year. In many Third World countries, the average annual household use is 30,000 gallons or less. As for people living in a desert, consider the average annual use of the 3 million or so households in the greater Los Angeles area. These folks use roughly 2 million acre-feet annually. A little of that water is obtained locally from surface runoff, and some from wells. But most of L.A.'s water supply comes from hundreds of miles away, from the Colorado, Owens, and Feather rivers. Moving this water required the development of the most massive plumbing system in the world—the water projects of California and the Colorado River basin. The dams, reservoirs, canals and aqueducts, pumping stations, and delivery systems have left their mark on the environment. But, as mentioned earlier, domestic uses account for only about 10% of the water used in California. The water projects' primary beneficiary is agriculture.

Groundwater

The problems with domestic water use relate mostly to water purity and supply. Residential water users expect their water to be drinkable and tasteless. Considering the variety of toxic minerals, compounds, and bacteria that can enter water along transportation corridors that stretch for miles, this expectation is a bit unrealistic. Keeping drinking water clean is no small undertaking. **Water quality** is based on water's (a) clarity, (b) pH, (c) turbidity,

(d) dissolved solids, (d) dissolved oxygen, (e) pathogen (bacterial) content, and (f) temperature. Even small changes in some of these factors can render water useless for drinking without some form of treatment. Domestic water supplies come from underground aquifers (groundwater) and from surface water. Each of these supplies has its advantages and disadvantages. Some of the hazards to groundwater include

- Nitrate pollution from antiquated and inadequate septic systems;

- Leaching of contaminants from landfills containing toxic materials;

- Leakage from underground storage tanks and pipelines (gas station tanks are an example);

- De-icing salts used on roadways in wintertime;

- Pesticides and fertilizers from agricultural, landscape and garden applications;

- Accidental spills of toxic materials;

- Careless past practices (perhaps decades ago) of dumping toxic materials

Groundwater is extremely hard to purify once it has become polluted. Often the only corrective action is to remove the source of the pollution, if it can be identified, and then wait and monitor water quality to see if it can filter itself back to purity over time. This strategy obviously removes that source of water from the supply side of the equation for some period, thus exacerbating the problem of shortage. Protection of groundwater resources is addressed through federal legislation, notably the Safe Drinking Water Act (1974), the Resource Conservation and Recovery Act (1976), and the Comprehensive Environmental Response, Compensation, and Liability Act of 1980 (a.k.a. Superfund).

Surface Water

Surface water transported by rivers, aqueducts, canals, tunnels, and pipes must be protected from similar forms of pollution. Generally referred to as **point source and nonpoint source pollution**, surface water is exposed to runoff injected directly into the waterway (point source) and from widespread accumulations of toxic materials that enter a waterway from all over (non-point source). The classic early environmental movement image of a drainpipe disgorging frothy muck into a river is a great example of point source pollution. The runoff of salts, brake linings, and oils from roadways to numerous spots along a creek is one example of non-point source pollution. Acid precipitation, caused by emissions from fossil fuels combustion, is another example of non-point source pollution. The most notorious example of a national water pollution problem occurred on Cleveland's **Cuyahoga River** in the 1960s. So laden with flammable chemicals, the river actually caught fire and destroyed seven bridges before it burned itself out. The containment of runoff or its sanitation can be costly and resisted by polluters. However, federal regulations promulgated under the **Clean Water Act of 1972** have forced industry, agriculture, and waste treatment to dramatically reduce their levels of toxic discharge into the nation's surface waters. The improvement has been substantial, but the task remains incomplete.

Water Can Be Owned

The supply of domestic water sources presents another thorny problem. In many cases, the culprit is geographic. When people settle near water, they likely will have a bountiful supply. Those who congregate in areas where there is little water will have a shortage. But it isn't that simple. And that's because water flows toward money. We'll get into the legal aspects of water policy in a bit. For now, recognize that water can be owned. Therefore it can be bought, or swindled, bilked, extorted, and sold, much the way other "dollarable" resources can be transferred between buyer and seller. When the expanding L.A. metropolitan area needed water at the start of the twentieth century, people looked to the waters of the Owens Valley some 250 miles to the northeast. The newly formed L.A. Department of Water and Power bought the rights to most of the water that flowed in the Owens River, and proceeded to build an aqueduct to move it to L.A. The folks who lived in the Owens Valley had settled near water, but money and engineering moved it to a desert close to the Pacific. During the 1976–1977 drought in California, lawns in the L.A. basin were gleefully green, fed by water from the Rocky Mountains via the Colorado River. San Francisco Bay area communities drawing water from the Sierras were forced to ration, and lawns turned brown. In Marin County, north of San Francisco, the drought crisis forced the purchase of water from Contra Costa County supplies, and emergency monies were brought in to build a pipeline attached to the Richmond San-Rafael Bridge across San Francisco Bay. The Marin Municipal Water District did not have the storage capacity necessary to meet the needs of county residents through a drought period. Water-supply issues plague a nation rich with water resources. Las Vegas, located in southern Nevada, is greedily eyeing the waters in the northeast part of the state to feed a residential population that continues to swell in one of the fastest-growing metropolitan areas in the country. Fountains, water parks, swimming pools, and lawns adorn Las Vegas, but the water supply is not close by. Desert cities in the Middle East have for years relied on **desalinized seawater** to supply urban needs. The process remains prohibitively uneconomical in the U.S., except for a few examples, such as the Tampa Bay Seawater Desalination facility on Florida's west coast. It is still cheaper to buy water from somebody else. The supply, so to speak, is somewhat fluid.

Agricultural Use

Agricultural use of water is extensive in crop-growing regions. Humans have used irrigation for thousands of years to reduce their reliance on rainfall.

The Hohokam of the Gila, Verde, and Salt rivers basin (modern-day Phoenix, Arizona) built irrigation canals and thrived from A.D. 400 to A.D. 1400. Farmers, ranchers, and miners built small irrigation works to move water from its source to where it was needed. Aquifers were tapped by wells with buckets or small pumps driven by the wind. Generally, the lands east of the Mississippi have a far more reliable pattern of precipitation than the lands to the west. In the East, rain also falls during summer months and early autumn, aquifers are relatively shallow, and streams and rivers often run across flatlands or in valleys rather than canyons. West of the Mississippi, or the famed "100th meridian" that slices through the stacked plains states and forms the eastern border of the Texas panhandle, water plays to different weather patterns and topography. The only part of this region that can be counted on for abundant rainfall is the Pacific Northwest (Northern California, Oregon, Washington), on the west side of the Cascades mountain range, and southern Alaska. The rest of the area is considered semiarid or arid. Precipitation also tends to concentrate seasonally in the West, falling predominantly in winter months. Except for the desert southwest, which enjoys a "monsoon season" in late summer; the occasional thunderstorms in the Rockies and the ranges of the Great Basin; and the ocean rains on the coasts of Oregon and Washington, much of the west doesn't see or smell rain for half the year. Precipitation in the West also falls on a landscape unlike that of the eastern U.S. Many creeks and rivers in the west run at the bottom of inconvenient or downright humongous canyons with little arable land close by the water. Potential farmlands perch on plateaus, enjoying good crop-growing temperatures, but the water to irrigate crops tumbles seaward thousands of feet below. California's agriculturally rich central valley suffered a double whammy: too wet for agriculture in the winter and spring, and too dry in the summer and autumn. Agriculture in California required the draining of massive wetlands, marshes and lakes, followed by the reinfusion of controlled irrigation. Agriculture in the West is a story of the engineering of water.

The round green agricultural plots created by center-pivot aerial irrigation are easily noticed from the air. (Courtesy of the Army Corps of Engineers)

Managing water for agriculture includes a few basic practices:

- For aquifers, conservation and recharge to avoid depletion

- Flood control—dams, dikes, levees

- Storage—lakes, reservoirs, and other impoundments

- Transport—"natural" stream channels, canals, aqueducts

- Pumping—moving water up in elevation from aquifers, over hills and mountain ranges, or onto fields

- Crop application—flooding, furrow, sprinkler, drip

- Drainage—percolation of irrigation water into soils, soil conservation, and agricultural runoff

All of these necessary practices present problems to agriculture, to engineers, and to the un-engineered environment. Overcoming one problem can lead to negative side effects, also known as **externalities**.

Tehama County, California, has taken steps to limit the export of groundwater to Central Valley users to the south. (Photo by Steve Dennis)

Getting water out of aquifers and onto the surface to irrigate crops presented a problem. The answer was to build wells. But hoisting a bucket up a well shaft was not an adequate solution for irrigation. Wind-powered pumps could drive more water, but it wasn't until the invention of the **centrifugal pump** and its extensive deployment in the 1920s that groundwater made a massive impact on agricultural practice. These pumps could draw hundreds of gallons per minute out of the ground, putting thousands of new acres into production. Construction and maintenance of canals and ditches for surface water transport could be avoided because all the water needed was right under the farm. However, the problem was soon revealed. Withdrawals from aquifers quickly exceeded the rate at which the aquifers' waters were replenished, or **recharged**. Groundwater supplies in some areas dried up completely, putting farms out of production. In many other agricultural areas, it became evident that groundwater supplies were limited, perhaps to only a few more years or a couple of decades. The overdraft of the world's largest aquifer, the Ogallala beneath Colorado, Kansas, Nebraska, New Mexico, Oklahoma, South Dakota, Texas, and Wyoming is also the largest depletion of an aquifer on earth, losing the equivalent of a year's flow down the Colorado River annually. Because of the recharge limitations of groundwater supplies, wells are not a solution to agriculture's dependence on water. Only recently have some states and counties begun to consider regulation of groundwater use. In Tehama County, California, the first step has been to attempt to limit the export of groundwater, not necessarily to reduce the amount of water withdrawn. Solutions to agriculture's thirst are limited. We can conserve water, and we can develop surface water supplies. Like most resource problems, the solutions are never particularly simple.

Managing surface waters is, at first glance, a simple task. One has only to build structures to impound it or direct its flow. But recall that water is rather heavy, and it can fall from the sky in great abundance at times. Dropping a dam across a creek or a river is no small task. The water of a reservoir exerts enormous pressure on the dam that blocks its travel downstream. It was not until the twentieth century that engineers sorted out methods to build dams on a scale to which we're now accustomed. Until **reinforced concrete** and **earth-filled** methods became sophisticated, the bigger the dam, the more likely was its failure. The dam that failed in the Johnstown Flood was once the largest of its type in the world. The deep canyons of the West afforded numerous potential dam sites, but the rivers were also fairly big, and damming them required marvels of modern engineering.

Individual farmers did not have the ability to control water, much beyond cutting ditches to sluice water from nearby streams to their farms, and to shovel up small dikes to improve drainage and beat back minor flooding. The construction of dams, flumes, canals, levees, and other structures required the pooling of financial resources and the involvement of government. Farmers formed water districts, municipalities managed corporations, and state and federal governments adopted agencies to work on water development. Controlling floods, providing water for irrigation, and answering the needs of growing urban areas was viewed as a noble cause. Water development became synonymous with the growth and strength of the nation. And with typical bravado, America began the largest program of water development ever seen.

By 1935, engineering and $49 million worth of construction had parked the 726-foot **Hoover Dam** in the ancient path of the Colorado River, creating the largest man-made reservoir in the world. It was named after Elwood C. Mead, head of the Bureau of Reclamation. Engineering technology had proven that it was able to triumph over water. During the next four decades, virtually all of the major rivers of the West were dammed, diverted through hydroelectric plants and controlled channels to power and irrigate farms and cities. Although gloriously beneficial to the economic development of the West, water engineering was not free of environmental costs.

Blocking the flow of a river meant flooding a reservoir into a valley or a canyon. Reservoirs destroyed diverse and valuable riparian habitat, small farms, archaeological and historic sites, and river-based recreation opportunities and replaced them with sterile, fluctuating shorelines, flat-water recreation opportunities, and a lot of stored water. Dams themselves blocked the migratory routes of anadromous fish, requiring the construction of fish ladders over low dams and hatcheries below dams that were too tall to be surmounted by ladders. And though they could stop floods, dams also blocked the flow of river-borne silts over downstream **floodplains**, the very silts that had made the West's valleys ripe for agriculture. Silts now backed up behind dams, inexorably filling reservoirs in a slow form of destruction that could not be prevented. Engineers could create massive structures that were safe from earthquakes and floods, but dams are mortal. The silting in of reservoirs behind them will be a problem for future generations. It is a legacy that will not go away.

Reservoir impoundments carry one set of environmental drawbacks. Downstream channelization—and irrigation itself—created other problems. Dams provide a false sense of security and encourage development within floodplains that may not be as safe as they appear. Of course, the worst-case scenario is a dam's failure. The Johnstown Flood, St. Francis, and Teton dams give testimony to the immensity of such preventable disasters. But a dam doesn't have to fail for flooding to occur. It only requires precipitation that exceeds the experts' calculated predictions. Hydrologists measure floods according to the expectation that a certain-sized event will occur, on average, once during a period of years. Flood sizes are referred to as "10-year flood," "25-year flood," and "100-year flood." Floodplains on lowlands are also marked topographically according to the same scale. A 10-year flood will spread water beyond a river's banks for some distance, until the elevation exceeds the level sought by the floodwaters. The odds of flooding once every ten years or so isn't a huge crisis for farms raising annual crops. A 25-year floodplain is a tempting place for people to build houses and towns. And how often is a 100-year flood going to happen, anyway? Sometimes they can happen two years in a row, as was seen in California in 1996 and 1997. Building in floodplains is a risky enterprise, because we can't be sure when the odds will come up. Measurements of precipitation and water flows in the West have been accumulated for only a little more than a century and a half, but the readings have been accurate for less time than that. We don't really know how often a 100-year flood will occur. The data on which flood predictions are based are quite limited. So, when we develop on floodplains, we take a calculated risk. The only problem is that the calculations aren't certain.

Moving water to desired locations brings another set of problems. The first of these problems is keeping the water from going where we don't want it. Dams are not the only structures used in flood-control. Downstream, we have built huge systems of levees, dikes, weirs, and flood control channels called bypasses and catchment basins to tame water into cooperating with us. We have reconstructed rivers to flow in concrete channels, or **rip-rapped** their banks in attempts to halt stream bank erosion. These structures may keep us from getting our toes wet, but they also build a false sense of security. Channeling water consolidates its weight and power, increasing its force on structures designed to contain it. Over time, flood control structures weaken and fail, sometimes catastrophically. Silts, too, are channelized with the water, and become unavailable to the soil-building process. Wetlands and riparian habitat are lost when water is forced into flood denial.

As if these issues surrounding our management of water weren't daunting enough, the very practice of irrigating farmlands carries with it risks of increasing the **salinity** of soils to a point where lands are lost for productive use. Geologically, much of the West has been at times, covered by shallow oceans. The bedrock underlying soils in California's San Joaquin Valley was laid down as sea floor sediments laden with levels of salt that were toxic to terrestrial plants. Heavy application of irrigation water leaches salts from this shallow bedrock and brings salt in solution into the soil. Tomatoes attempting to grow in such soil don't appreciate this.

Draining irrigated lands poses another difficult problem. Salinity could be reduced if irrigation water could be drained off before it encounters bedrock, but the cost of building such a system is prohibitive. Water drained from irrigated lands also can carry toxic concentrations of fertilizers, pesticides, herbicides, and minerals leached from soils. Drainage systems that move water off of farmlands and prevent flooding and buildup of toxic concentrations are few and far between. Improperly disposing of agricultural wastewater has caused environmental disasters such as the one at **Kesterson National Wildlife Refuge** in California. Built as a shallow reservoir to trap the drainage from agricultural lands of the Westlands Water District, Kesterson enjoyed a brief stint as a refuge that was attractive to migratory waterfowl. Unknown to wildlife managers, the waters of Kesterson were tainted with a trace element called selenium, which began to accumulate as drained waters moved in, evaporated, and moved in again. Selenium was relatively abundant in the coast range foothills that had eroded in geologic time to form the soils of the San Joaquin Valley. Irrigation of those soils brought the selenium into solution and carried it away when fields were drained, right into the San Luis Drain and Kesterson, where it became concentrated to a level that proved toxic to thousands of waterfowl. Biologists resorted to firing blank-loaded cannons to scare the birds away from the attractive but deadly waters of the refuge. But it was to no avail. Kesterson had become a death trap.

Hydroelectric Power

Hydroelectric power, the "clean" way to produce energy, also carries with it some environmental nuisances. Essentially controlled waterfalls, hydroelectric plants rely on the damming of streams to obtain the amount of fall needed to drive electric-generating turbines. Originally built as small structures that produced local power, hydroelectric plants grew larger as dam-building technology rose to new heights. Eventually, power generation became concentrated in about 300 large dams located mostly in the northwestern and southeastern U.S. These dams now produce about seven percent of the country's electrical energy. Most of the "good" dam sites in the country have been used. By the mid-1970s, public opinion on the continued development of dams and hydroelectric power had shifted to skepticism and powerful opposition. The environmental costs of huge reservoirs and the rerouting and manipulation of water resources were seen to outweigh the benefits of further dam and hydroelectric developments. U.S. citizens did not want to lose any more Hetch Hetchys, Glen Canyons, or Little Tennessee Rivers. The trend has been to revisit opportunities for small hydroelectric developments on lesser streams. Many small hydro plants have been abandoned in favor of the large facilities. The output potential from developing small hydroelectric plants is considerable. Bringing such facilities on line, however, will undergo far more environmental scrutiny than could have been imagined by the builders of similar plants in generations past.

Wildlife

Wildlife is another water customer, usually the recipient of leftovers (recycled) and unconsumed surface water supplies. In California, a little more than 40% of the surface water total is not consumed, so it is therefore counted as water that's available to wildlife. Protection of wildlife habitat is becoming more important as an objective of water management. Unfortunately, many aspects of water management run counter to the maintenance of high-quality wildlife habitat. Species of wildlife evolved to survive under conditions where humans were not tinkering with water. The draining of wetlands and the channeling of streams, blockage of rivers by dams, flow regulation to the tune of electrical power demand rather than climate, and the discharge of wastes into waterways have all impacted wildlife habitat. Species that have been able to adapt have survived, and in some cases thrived. Other species have been driven to the brink of extinction. Managing water for wildlife habitat requires a certain amount of undoing or, at minimum, the mitigation of the impacts of developing water for human purposes. Undoing includes new practices such as allowing wetlands to return to their natural state rather than continue their draining. Mitigation includes practices such as providing minimum flow levels downstream of dams to protect fish populations. As we learn more about the impacts our water development methods have caused, we attempt to return to wildlife what has been taken. But providing water for habitat is controversial. Increasing wildlife's wedge from the water-supply pie chart means cutting a smaller wedge of waters for other purposes. As our demand for water exceeds our supply, struggles over water allocation grow intensely political.

The Politics of Water

The uses of water by humans are governed by a wide variety of laws, ranging from simple to complex and conflicting. Federal, state, and local laws, international treaties, court decisions, and local customs all play a part in regulating our use of water and ownership of the resources under, within, and on top of it. Water can be considered a common as well as an appropriated resource. As a common resource, it is available to be used and enjoyed by all. As an appropriated resource, water can be owned by an individual or corporation, and its use limited to that of the owner(s). Ever since Roman times, running water was something that could not be owned. Owners of adjacent lands, however, have long enjoyed the right to use water for certain purposes. Called a **usufructuary** right, it basically means that landowners adjacent to streams (riparians) have the right to use water, as long as their use does not hinder the use of the water by other people. The water is not owned; it is a common resource that carries an obligation to users not to ruin it.

In the eastern U.S., the common-law **riparian doctrine** has held precedent from the time of settlement. With relatively abundant water resources, it was possible in the East to use water without substantially decreasing its downstream flow. As settlement has expanded, however, increasing urban and agricultural uses have compromised the ability to maintain downstream flows and water quality. Not everyone lives adjacent to a stream, so cities are allowed to divert water to non-riparian users and to dump wastewater into different watersheds. State laws and permit systems provide the means to alter strict interpretation of the riparian doctrine, allowing movement of water to locations where it is needed.

The need to move water from one place to another was the driving force behind the establishment of water laws in the western U.S. It became apparent to settlers of western lands that control of water was essential to economic survival. In order to provide for water's ownership, the **prior appropriation doctrine** has become the standard in the states of Alaska, Arizona, Colorado, Idaho, Montana, Nevada, New Mexico, Utah, and Wyoming. A blend of riparian and prior appropriation doctrines is used in the other less-arid western states of California, Kansas, Nebraska, North Dakota, South Dakota, Oklahoma, Oregon, Texas, and Washington. These states attempted to foster the riparian doctrine, while recognizing the need for appropriations to be made by state and federal governments for water development projects.

The prior appropriation doctrine functions essentially as a first-come, first-served method of determining rights to water. As an example, let's follow a forty-niner who finds gold in a California streambed. He stakes a claim to mine the area, and after the "easy" placer gold is scooped up, he moves upstream and uphill, following the ore bearing vein that was the source of the gold found in the stream. This gold, however, is hard to get. The miner stakes a block of claims, forms a company, and hires men to perform the hard labor of tearing up the mountainside. But now they're mining well up above the water, and water is needed to process the ore through sluice boxes. The mining operation is dependent on water, so water must be brought to the mine. Since water doesn't readily move uphill, the only source of water for the mine is upstream, at an elevation high enough to allow water to flow down to the mine via a flume. That source is five miles upstream, and the mine needs virtually all of the water that flows in the drier summer months. So the miner claims (appropriates) the rights to the stream five miles away from the mine and diverts enough of it to fill the flume with water year round. Now, water flows in the old stream channel only during the rainy season and spring snowmelt. The mine is a success, but downstream uses are now changed. A five-mile stretch of the stream is virtually dry four months out of the year, and the stream that moves below the mine is polluted by the mine's runoff. Until after the turn of the century, no one worries much about the impacts of the mine. After the gold runs out, in fact, a new electrical company buys the water rights, refurbishes the flume, and builds a generating plant near the spot where the original placer gold was found. Now, the water, less polluted, produces power instead of gold. In a similar manner, water was diverted to irrigate crops, feed livestock, or to carry logs to mills throughout the West. When economic enterprise needed water, the developer was given (or purchased) rights to it. Water ownership was one of the most expedient means to promote the development and exploitation of the West's natural resources.

Water law not only covers ownership of volumes of water, but it also attempts to describe who owns access to lands adjacent to, under, and on the surface of waters. On a global scale, the seas are primarily an international common resource for transportation and fishing. Transportation is regulated along established **shipping lanes** and by individual nations within their territorial jurisdictions. The fishing and harvesting of other marine organisms is regulated by individual states and nations, and through treaties (or conventions) between nations. As with the regulation of any common resource, lines of authority over the seas of the world are neither simple nor absolute.

Regulation of **seaward resources** begins at the coastal tidal boundary measured as the mean low waterline (the location of the waterline at the average of low tides). From this line to the mean high waterline are shore-lands that usually fall under state jurisdiction. From the mean low waterline seaward, several maritime zones are recognized. Within three nautical miles, coastal states have regulatory authority over seabed resources. Western Florida and Texas enjoy this right to a distance of nine nautical miles because of the importance of oil reserves in those areas. Twelve nautical miles marks the boundary of nations' territorial sea, within which nations have exclusive jurisdiction and can exercise their laws of customs, immigration, and sanitation. Beyond 12 nautical miles lies the area considered the high seas, where all nations have the right to most freedoms of transportation, flying, fishing, and setting of undersea cables and pipelines. Exceptions to the high-seas jurisdiction include **outer continental shelf (OCS)** areas, which are measured by depth rather than by distance. The OCS resources are those seabed areas up to 200 meters in depth, adjacent to nations' coastlines. Additionally, most coastal nations have agreed to a 200-mile-wide exclusive economic zone, where countries can claim rights to natural resources while committing to environmental protection. Marine fisheries are thus regulated to a 200-mile limit by the adjacent country. There is, of course, overlap, and marine resources farther than 200 miles at sea can be regulated. On the high seas, different nations may enter into treaty arrangements with one another to protect specific fishery resources. Treaties to protect marine mammals, such as the International Convention for the Regulation of Whaling, are but one example whereby certain nations have agreed to regulate the taking of marine resources.

Estuarine and wetlands. Estuarine and **wetlands** have long been a target of "progress." Estuaries were dredged for navigation, filled for development, and made into a prime location for the dumping of industrial, agricultural, and residential wastes. Wetlands were systematically drained and protected from future inundation by levees and dikes. Conversion to agriculture or development was viewed as a benefit providing higher economic use of land and removing a source of pestilence, notably the breeding grounds of mosquitoes. No federal legislation attempted to protect estuaries and wetlands until the **Federal Water Pollution Control Act of 1948**. Prior to 1948, estuaries and navigable waterways had been regulated solely by provisions of the **Rivers and Harbors Act of 1899**. This century-old piece of legislation empowered the U.S. Army Corps of Engineers to rule on permit applications made by persons or agencies seeking to alter tidelands, estuaries, and navigable waterways for varying purposes. The intent was to protect waterways for navigation purposes, a responsibility assumed by the federal government under the Constitution's **Commerce Clause** (Art. 1, Sec. 8). Viewing its mission as navigation, the Corps would consider permit applications solely with regard to their impacts on navigability. Pollution, habitat loss, and other resource concerns were ignored. With passage of the Federal Water Pollution Control Act of 1948, the first steps toward pollution control were taken. Enforcement of the FWPCA, however, was sadly lacking. The **Water Quality Act of 1965** was an effort to strengthen pollution controls, establishing a Federal Water Pollution Control Administration and allowing the federal government to set water quality standards in states that did not set their own. Leaving control and enforcement in state hands, the WQA left room for improvement. In 1970, functions of the Water Pollution Control Administration were transferred to the newly created Environmental Protection

Planting seagrasses in a wetland area
along the Galveston Navigation Channel.
(Courtesy of the U.S. Corps of Engineers)

Agency (EPA), and in 1972, Congress passed the **Federal Water Pollution Control Act Amendments**. Virtually every year since then amendments to this act have passed, creating a complex web of statutory and regulatory authority over water quality. The goals of the 1972 amendments remain the guidepost, if yet unreached, stating that (a) discharge of pollutants into navigable waterways should be eliminated (by 1983!), (b) fish, wildlife, and recreation values shall be protected, and (c) wastewater treatment plants shall be planned and developed in each state and backed by federal financial assistance.

Legislation. Wildlife management legislation opened other avenues for regulatory authority over waters. Beginning with the **Fish and Wildlife Coordination Act Amendments of 1958**, federal permit considerations required consultation with the U.S. Fish and Wildlife Service. The National Environmental Policy Act of 1970 required broader scrutiny of project proposals. Today, the definitions of "navigable waterway" and "wetland" have become important distinctions in the determination of authority over surface waters of the nation. The ecological importance of wetlands has brought environmentalists to their protection. Congress and the courts have attempted to define wetlands, but definition and regulatory authority are divided among agencies including the U.S. Fish and Wildlife Service, the Corps of Engineers, and the **Natural Resource Conservation Service.** Just what constitutes "navigable"—and to what extent a chunk of land must be inundated, from what type of water source, and what type of plants grow on it before it is labeled a "wetland" —is as yet not clearly defined. Thus regulatory authority is somewhat ambiguous, contentious, and constantly subjected to the tinkering of the judiciary and Congress. Feeding the uncertainty, of course, are the "takings" concerns of the Constitution's due process clause under the fifth and fourteenth amendments. Government regulation of a farmer's private land could be considered a taking if the farmer wants to drain land for watermelons and the government wants wetland inundation for frogs and ducks. Lacking a watertight definition of wetlands, the government tests muddy waters when it brings its power to bear over private lands use. The controversy over wetlands regulation will continue to plow forward, as do controversies over other natural resources.

Controlling the Valves

Ownership of water is not quite as simple as surveying lines and recording their positions the way we define ownership of land. The combination of riparian and appropriated rights can sometimes leave the question of determination of ownership as fluid as the water. "Owners" include international, federal, state, special district and local governments, Native Americans, corporations, and private parties. These entities may seldom find themselves in agreement over the distribution of water resources. Treaties, compacts, and contracts are among the legal devices used to determine ownership and water supply entitlements. But the water supply is never consistent, and minimum allotments may not always be available.

Questions of entitlement to water generally fall to adjudication, and court rulings rather specifically identify ownership and quantities. Water managers, in effect, become the enforcers of the legislature and courts when they fiddle with valves that control the flow of small to massive volumes of water. When you hear of "contracted water" under dispute, it is usually a question of where water owners contest a reduction in what they consider to be their entitled supply. There is little incentive for an owner to willingly agree to a reduction in supply. Water has value, and owners will naturally try to hang onto it. Agencies that operate large water impoundments and conveyance systems such as the Bureau of Reclamation, the Corps of Engineers, the Tennessee Valley Authority, and California's Department of Water Resources, control flows to numerous contracted owners, often agricultural, municipal, and public utility districts and corporations. The distribution of smaller quantities of water must also be deliberately handled, and this function is often taken care of by a watermaster service such as that maintained by the DWR in California. Watermasters operate the valves that divert water to individual owners. They are, in effect, the officers of the courts assigned to make sure that owners receive the amounts of water to which they are entitled.

Of course, water does not always flow in shortage; and at times, nature's capriciousness offers more bounty than we know what to do with, thrusting managers into the role of minimizing flood damage. California maintains what is called the **Joint Operations Center (JOC)** in Sacramento, where hydrologists, climatologists, engineers, and other water experts from the Bureau of Reclamation, Corps of Engineers, Department of Water Resources, National Weather Service, National Oceanographic and Atmospheric Administration, and others work to control the state's water diversions network to provide appropriate supplies and to stave off flooding. During storm emergencies such as the 1996 and 1997 floods, the JOC resembled the headquarters of a military campaign, making very real life-and-death decisions.

Only the Beginning

This chapter has attempted to provide a basic introduction to one of the most complex areas of renewable resources management. Numerous references can provide a far more thorough treatment of this topic than is possible in the confines of this text. Some suggested works include Reisner, *Cadillac Desert*; and Wilkinson, *Crossing the Next Meridian*. Additionally, case studies such as those of Hetch Hetchy, **Echo Park**, Tellico Dam, Mono Lake, and the proposed Auburn Dam will provide insight into the workings of water in the U.S. This is not merely a domestic issue. Nations worldwide are embroiled in questions over the development of water resources. From the long-term effects of the Aswan High Dam on the Nile to the construction of the massive Three Gorges Dam on the Yangtze in the People's Republic of China, water development continues to strain relations between supporters and opponents. The outcomes of our scientific, philosophical and political debates hold ecological implications for the future of whole regions—and indeed for the planet.

Suggested Readings

Adams, D. A. (1993). *Renewable resource policy: The legal-institutional foundations*. Washington, DC: Island Press.

Barcott, B. (1999, February). Blow up. *Outside*, 70–79, 102–104.

Brooks, D. B., Brandes, O. M., & Gurman, S. (Eds.). (2011). *Making the most of the water we have: The soft path approach to water management*. Sterling, VA: Earthscan.

Dasmann, R. F. (1984). *Environmental conservation* (5th ed.). New York: John Wiley & Sons.

Dunbar, R. G. (1983). *Forging new rights in western waters*. Lincoln, NE: University of Nebraska Press.

Fradkin, P. L. (1996). *A river no more: The Colorado River and the West*. Berkeley, CA: University of California Press.

Frederick, K. D. (1982). Water supplies. In P. R. Portney (Ed.), *Current issues in natural resource policy*. Washington, DC: Resources for the Future.

Nebel, B. J., & Wright, R. T. (2000). *Environmental science: The way the world works* (7th ed.). Upper Saddle River, NJ: Prentice-Hall.

Owen, O. S., & Chiras, D. D. (1990). *Natural resource conservation: An ecological approach* (5th ed.). New York: MacMillan.

Powell, J. W. (2003). *The exploration of the Colorado River and its canyons*. New York: Penguin Books.

Reisner, M. (1988). *Cadillac desert: The American West and its disappearing water*. New York: Penguin Books.

Sipes, J. L. (2010). *Sustainable solutions for water resources: Policies, planning, design, and implementation*. Hoboken, NJ: John Wiley.

Water Education Foundation. (2005). *Layperson's guide to water rights law*. Sacramento, CA: Water Education Foundation.

Wilkinson, C. F. (1992). *Crossing the next meridian: Land, water, and the future of the west*. Washington, DC: Island Press.

chapter twenty-two

Mineral Resources, Mining, and Management Issues

The resources addressed in previous chapters are generally considered renewable. Mineral resources are considered nonrenewable, because it takes so long for nature to create them. Freshwater, wildlife, timber, forage, and recreation resources can recover from use mostly through natural processes. Human management may provide a nudge of assistance to these processes, but nature really provides the mechanisms for replenishment and recovery. Mineral resources are also renewed through natural processes, but renewal occurs in the immense scale of geologic time, rather than within a season, a few years, or a generation or two. The replenishing of diminished supplies of oil and coal will take tens of millions of years, which is about 9,999,999 years too long to do us any good. By then, humans will have evolved into something not yet dreamed up by science fiction. Some mineral resources can be reused, or **recycled**, providing a means to reduce the need to constantly mine for supply. But recycling is energy intensive and cannot keep pace with the demand for mineral resources that are recyclable. So, even with the advent of recycling, we're really diminishing a nonrenewable resource when we consume minerals.

Dependence on Minerals

We consume vast quantities of minerals. The U.S. alone consumes about 20% of the world's annual production of hard rock minerals. Each U.S. citizen will consume 43,000 pounds of minerals each year. The cars we drive and depend on require huge amounts of minerals such as iron, steel hardeners (e.g., tungsten and molybdenum), and copper and aluminum. The roads under the cars consume gravel, concrete, and asphalt. Buildings, bridges, and innumerable construction materials are composed of minerals. Our high-tech computer, photo, and printing industries use gold in circuitry and silver in photo processing. We rely on the sands of crushed gravel for bottles and jars, aluminum and steel for cans, gypsum for the sheetrock in our homes, and petroleum products for huge industries in plastics and the production of energy. Minerals development occupies a significant niche in the global economic portfolio, and we have grown dependent on a continuous supply of nonrenewable mineral resources.

Mineral Classifications and Supply

Minerals can play hard to get. Mineral resources are tied up in the earth's crust and are accessible only on land and on the shallow continental shelf margins of the oceans. Many mineral deposits are unobtainable because of their depth beneath the surface. The accessible, mineable minerals are referred to as mineral reserves. Globally, reserves are not equally distributed. The U.S. has the world's richest coal reserves, while the Middle East holds the largest supplies of oil. Australia, the states of the former Soviet Union, the U.S., and Canada are the largest hard-rock mineral-producing nations. Even though direct and indirect economic impact of the mining industry is $1.9 trillion annually, or roughly 12% of the nation's **gross domestic product (GDP)**, we still greatly depend on imports of minerals such as chromium and manganese, importing close to $60 billion worth each year. These resources, as well as energy resources such as oil, are considered strategic minerals, in that their continued supply is inextricably linked to economic stability and national security.

About 80 hard-rock minerals are considered to be economically important, including gold, lead, mercury, silver, sulphur, tin, tungsten, and zinc. When the word "shortage" comes up, we, of course, think "oil," as the importance of that resource is felt at the gas pump and in the significant aspects of U.S. foreign policy. But many minerals are present only in limited quantities; in known reserves that will be exhausted within decades at current levels of consumption. Mineral supply presents a problem without ready solutions, and the potential for shortages is knocking on the world's door.

In the most general sense, minerals are classified as hard rock and energy. There is some room for confusion, though, because uranium is classified as a hard-rock mineral, while its use is reserved primarily for energy. Coal is classified among energy minerals, but it is still a hard rock that is mined rather than pumped. Ignoring these problem rocks, most minerals are effectively described by the hard-rock energy distinction. The most common hardrock minerals with which we're concerned include gold, silver, uranium, copper, molybdenum, iron, lead, aluminum, and the varied gemstones. Others (in by no means an exhaustive list) include cobalt, potash, chromium, bauxite, barite, manganese, salt, asbestos, arsenic, strontium, tungsten, nickel, tin, sulphur, zinc, gypsum, and gravel. These minerals are located in geologic deposits where they have accumulated over enormous amounts of time. Salt and gravel may be replenished in shorter time periods through farming of tidal salt ponds and the power of rivers and creeks to wash gravel downstream. A mineral deposit that can be mined at a profit is called an ore deposit. Ores are considered along a range from high grade to low grade, depending on the percentage of the mineral that is present in the surrounding rock or lode. For example, copper ore is considered high grade when it is about 3% copper (60 pounds per ton). Low-grade copper ore is about three-tenths of 1% copper (six pounds per ton). Gold ores can be economically mined with as little as eight-hundredths of an ounce per ton, though fluctuating gold prices can have a dramatic impact on the viability of mining operations that are dependent on such low-grade gold ore.

Energy minerals include oil, coal, natural gas, oil shale, and tar sands. These minerals are also present in deposits, and accessible reserves are scattered about the globe sometimes in such friendly places as Alaska's North Slope or Europe's North Sea. Oil and natural gas are pumped from wells. Coal is mined, as are oil shale and tar sands, though the energy potential of oil shale and tar sands must be extracted through heating processes that remove the oily substance from parent rock. Significant reserves of oil shale exist in southwestern Wyoming, eastern Utah, and western Colorado. Viable tar sands are found in Alberta, Canada, and account for 47% of all oil produced in that country. However, the high cost of production in addition to environmental impacts, have thus far prevented the exploitation of oil shale. As oil prices continue to rise, the likelihood of future oil shale and increased tar sands production grows stronger.

The U.S. has the largest coal reserves of any nation on earth (23%), followed by Russia (14%) and China (13%). Coal-fired generating plants produce about 50% of the energy consumed in the U.S. Common classes of coal are lignite (brown coal), bituminous (soft coal), subbituminous (a combination of brown and soft coal), and anthracite (hard coal). Most coal in the U.S. is bituminous, which is of medium value when compared with the energy values of the other coals. World coal supplies, according to some estimates, may last another 1,500 years. Natural gas is basically methane given off by the decomposition of plants and organisms that turned into oil and coal through eons of being compacted and heated by accumulating layers of overlying sedimentary rock. This is why natural gas is often found with coal and oil deposits. Not as plentiful as coal, natural gas may last us another century at our current levels of consumption. Significant discoveries of natural gas have recently been made in Appalachia and Louisiana. Oil, the heart of our transportation systems and petrochemical industries, has the potential to dwindle quickly. Certain estimates, which include expectations for as-yet-undiscovered reserves, maintain that we will exhaust the world's oil supply within 100 years. Worldwide peak oil is expected sometime in the first two decades of this new millennium. And these estimates are from the optimists.

Mining Methods

Extracting minerals from parent rock involves the many processes of modern mining and the subsequent processing of ores. Mining is commonly distinguished as surface mining and subsurface (or underground) mining. Most non-energy minerals come from surface mines (90%). These mines can be open-pit, contour, strip mines, placer mines, or quarries, depending on how the ore is removed. They all share the common denominator that they produce a hole in the ground, as deep as hundreds of feet, or even a thousand feet, and as broad as a mile or two across.

"Pick and shovel" mining prior to the advent of large machinery.
(Courtesy of the Library of Congress)

In order to get to **mineral bearing ores**, surface mines are started by removing the overburden, which is the rock and topsoil that lie on top of the ore. In an open-pit mine operation, ores are removed by first blasting to loosen them, then scooping the rock into a transportation device such as a conveyor, massive trucks, or even hopper cars of a train running on a railroad built within the mine. Spiraling downward to provide a negotiable gradient for trucks and/ or trains, the pit burrows deeper into the surface of the earth. The Kennecott Copper Mine, near Salt Lake City, at .75 miles deep and 2.5 miles in width, is the largest open-pit mine in the world. Contour mines are similar, though they progressively chew away at the sides of hills and mountains, following contours, again, for purposes of transporting ore and machinery. Strip mines are generally associated with coal mining on reasonably flat lands. Huge shovels called draglines remove the overburden, then the coal is blasted and hauled away. The dragline is moved to adjacent strips, and the overburden and topsoil are replaced to "reclaim" the mined area. Placer mines involve the sluicing or dredging of gravel that has washed down from ore-rich lodes. Placer mining was the dominant method used during the California gold rush, as gold was first found among the gravel in creek and river bottoms. Once stream gravel played out, hydraulic mining was invented to break up whole mountainsides and wash ores down into sluices. Hydraulic mining was eventually outlawed because of its massive impacts on water resources. Placer mining, however, still occurs in some parts of the world, usually through dredging. Today's "recreational" gold miners are placer miners using suction dredges to draw gravel from streambeds. Quarrying is one of the most ancient of mining practices, and it is used to remove rock that is useful in blocks (like granite, marble, and limestone), or crushed to produce gravel and concrete mixes. The rock or ore itself is the product sought in a quarry. Quarries look much like small, open-pit mines.

Subsurface mining, or underground mining, involves the construction of shafts or adits that tunnel into areas where mineral-rich veins, or seams, occur in the lode. Underground mining is used when it is impractical to move the massive quantities of rock relocated in open-pit mining, or when the deposit is relatively small but economically viable to mine. Subsurface mining is also used to penetrate to depths that would be impossible to reach by open-pit mining. Some underground mines go as deep as two miles into the earth's crust, such as the 2.4 mile deep TauTona gold mine in South Africa. Subsurface mining has seen numerous disasters ever since miners began tunneling into the earth for minerals. There is substantial risk of cave-ins, and numerous coal mines have been swept by explosions and fires. Health risks to miners, such as black lung disease, create other dangers. Mine-safety and worker protection regulations have improved these conditions, but for decades prior to these changes, underground mining was among the most dangerous and abbreviated careers in the country.

Solution mining, also called in-situ leaching or in-situ recovery, is a relatively new innovation that involves pumping water, or acids, sometimes heated, into ore deposits to dissolve minerals. These dissolved minerals, in solution with the water, are then pumped back to the surface for processing. Salt and potash are readily mined through solution processes. Coal slurry techniques mix water with crushed coal for transportation from the mine site to a processing plant, a railroad, or a power-generating station. Both the solution and slurry methods have economic and practical advantages under certain circumstances. The reliance on massive quantities of water and the potential for pollution of aquifers still create unresolved drawbacks to these two methods.

Drilling wells is the means used to tap oil and natural gas resources. Wells are also used to capture geothermal energy. Well-drilling technology has come a long way from the first 70-foot-deep oil well constructed in Titusville, Pennsylvania, in 1859. Wells are now drilled from massive platforms at sea, through arctic tundra, and on "slant" angles when a vertical approach is unworkable. Oil fields were once notoriously polluted by small spills and "gushers" that occurred when drills pierced oil deposits that were pressurized by trapped natural gas. Oil's value and environmental and safety regulations have combined to reduce greatly the localized hazards of oil drilling, though the blowout of British Petroleum's Deepwater Horizon platform and well in the Gulf of Mexico in 2010 underscored the dangers of drilling. The transport of oil and natural gas, generally, presents the greater hazard. The issue surrounding oil and natural gas development boils down to a question of the environmental risks we are willing to take to bring new oil reserves into production. Lingering images of limp, oil-soaked birds on the coast at Santa Barbara, Prince William Sound, and along the U.S. Gulf Coast graphically portray one possible outcome of the risks of oil development. But it is also these images that have galvanized our efforts to reduce the environmental impacts of oil development.

Mineral Processing

Extracting minerals is only the beginning of a series of processes used in turning them into consumable products. Hard-rock mineral ores are often crushed in huge **ball** or **rod mills** and then heated in ovens called smelters to separate the valuable minerals from the ore. Gold is extracted through a method called heap leaching, where cyanide is sprinkled over the top of ore piles as tall as 200 feet. The gold bonds with the cyanide as it percolates through the "heap" and is then pumped to a processing plant to remove the gold from the solution. The unimplemented **synfuels** projects would heat oil shale in **retorts** to melt oil out of the surrounding shale or sandstone, requiring huge amounts of water and energy. Energy minerals are transported to power plants or refineries where they are processed into a variety of fuels and synthetics to meet needs from combustion and lubrication to the cleaning and manufacture of petrochemical materials.

The Barrick Goldstrike Mine in Nevada, owned by a Canadian corporation, processes more than 1.5 million ounces of gold annually. Of the $2 billion invested in the mine to date, a tiny fraction has been paid to the federal government for mineral rights and title.
(Courtesy of Mike Dennis)

Environmental Issues

Minerals production and consumption cause a number of environmental problems. As with our use of other resources, there are significant costs to be borne for the pleasure of use. Also similar to the environmental problems associated with other resources, much of the environmental damage has resulted from the exploitative practices of the past. Mineral development in the U.S. proceeded virtually unfettered until the 1960s. For a century and a quarter before that, the mining industry carried on without any environmental protections, exacting a toll that has left scars to this day. Mining had been an extremely labor-intensive, pick-and-shovel undertaking in the old days, keeping impacts to a minimum, along with supplies. The inventions of dynamite, steam, and internal-combustion engines; hydraulic cannons; pneumatic drills; and a host of other industrial trappings allowed for a massive escalation in our ability to produce mineral goods. The scale of mining operations grew to enormous proportions, and the impacts were sure to fall under the intensifying scrutiny of the environmental movement that rose in the 1960s and 1970s.

Hydraulic mining for gold in California was outlawed early in the 20th century because of environmental degradation caused by massive siltation. (Courtesy J. Lenhoff Collection, Cherokee Museum)

Mining impacts accrue to soils, air, water, wildlife, and aesthetics. Surface mining produces considerable impacts in the vicinity of the mine. The holes in the ground created by surface mines displace wildlife, vegetation, and topsoils. Open-pit mines often fill with water, creating toxic lakes that are hazardous to waterfowl. Settling ponds used for the leaching of minerals present a similar hazard. The material removed and discarded (overburden or tailings) has to be put somewhere, usually nearby. These unconsolidated **tailings** consist of particles from the size of gravel to the size of dust. Composed of formerly solid rock, tailings expose potentially toxic minerals to winds and precipitation. In the past, tailings piles were ignored. Water seeped through and produced toxic compounds such as sulphuric acid, which became severe polluters of streams and creeks, killing aquatic organisms for miles downstream. This **acid mine drainage** (AMD) also could seep into aquifers, ruining water supplies. Small tailings particles could be carried off by winds, producing severe local air pollution.

These problems could not continue unabated as the scale of mining operations grew. Public sentiment and governmental regulation forced industry to improve the technologies of mining. To mitigate the impacts of tailings, piles are constantly compacted and sprayed with water to minimize particulate air pollution. Liners of nonporous clays and plastic placed beneath tailings, coupled with dam barriers, reduce AMD seepage into surface waters and groundwaters. Surface coalmines replace overburden and topsoils and then replant vegetation to initiate the reclamation process. These procedures mitigate environmental impacts, but they do not reduce them completely. Liners do leak, dams have broken, and particulates escape into the air. The key to risk reduction in mining operations is effective planning. Modern mining methods are far less damaging than the careless practices of the recent and distant past. This is true in developed nations and when conducted by enlightened mining companies operating in foreign countries. But exploitative and environmentally dangerous practices continue to occur in underdeveloped countries where environmental regulations are either nonexistent or unenforced.

Air pollution is another serious by-product of minerals production. Beyond the impacts on air quality in the vicinity of mining operations, air quality is also harmed over broad regions. Smelting emits particulates and compounds such as sulphur, carbon, and nitrogen dioxides. Because the time-honored "solution to pollution is dilution," smokestacks from smelters are propped hundreds of feet high—or even a thousand feet high—so that pollutants will catch higher elevation winds and be carried to greater distances. Similarly, the stacks of coal-burning and fuel-oil-burning power plants are monolithically massive enough to spread pollutants to the four winds. Unfortunately, winds trend from west to east across the U.S., so there is relative predictability as to where downwind air pollution will concentrate. The best known of the air-polluting impacts of smelting and fossil fuels electrical generation are **visible reduction** of air quality and acid precipitation. Coal-fired power generation in the Midwest is the culprit behind the acidification of lakes and damage to deciduous forests in New England and southeastern Canada. The loss of the legendary visibility in the Four Corners region of the Southwest is blamed on smelting and coal-burning operations. The increasing acidity of lakes and the reduction in air quality in the Sierra Nevada is the result of a potent cocktail of auto, industrial, and power generation emissions. To reduce these hazards, technologies have been applied to auto and industrial exhaust systems, such as **catalytic converters** and **smokestack scrubbers**. Such devices have reduced emissions of certain pollutants, but not the emission of others. Our consumption of vast supplies of hard rock and energy minerals is the driving force behind the pollution they cause. For all the safeguards we might invent, there is no pollution-free solution to the extraction, development, and consumption of mineral resources.

Policies and Laws

Very few laws and regulatory provisions governed mining and mineral development during mining's heyday in the hills of California and the Comstock Lode of Nevada. It was, however, these mining booms that precipitated the need for legal structures to bring order to a characteristically wildly western way of going about the business of mining. John Marshall's discovery of gold at Sutter's Mill on the American River in 1848 kicked off an unbelievable rush to California and ushered in statehood two years later. Land ownership in California consisted of former Mexican ranchos and a pile of public domain. Mining proceeded almost entirely on federal land, with no structural mechanism in place to provide for purchase, deeding, and ownership. "**Claims**" became the statement of possession, and possession, as they say, is nine-tenths of the law. Local rules and customs evolved out of a need to keep miners from murdering one another and to allow for some semblance of orderly economic activity. But local jurisdictions and the new state had no authority to control ownership, which belonged in federal hands. Recognizing the importance of western mining to national economic growth, along with the need for orderly development, Nevada Sen. William Stewart introduced "An Act Granting Right of Way to Ditch and Canal Owners Over the Public Lands, and Other Purposes," which became known as the **Mining Law of 1866**. This first among federal mining laws officially opened to exploration virtually all of the western U.S. Applied to lode deposits, and only claims for gold, silver, copper, and cinnabar, the act recognized miners' rights to existing claims, and licensed their exploration and occupation for mining purposes. Placer deposits were added to the law in 1870, setting the stage for the famed General Mining Law of 1872. Also known as the "**Hardrock Mining Act**," the 1872 law became the dominating rule over mining on the public lands.

The **General Mining Law** of 1872 is called the "miners' Magna Carta." Miners could now consider the public lands to be "free and open" to mineral entry, and on discovery and development, transferable to their private ownership. The Hardrock Act established a system by which miners could stake a claim over an area for the purposes of prospecting, therefore entitling them to search for minerals without interference from other miners. Staking a claim does not vest a property right, but that changes when a valuable hard-rock mineral is discovered. On discovery, the 1872 Law provides for the status of an unpatented mining claim of 20 acres in size, which gives the miner "the exclusive right of possession and enjoyment of all the surface included within the lines of their locations." In effect, the law grants to the miner exclusive use of the land for purposes that are "reasonably incident to mining." Groups of as many as eight individuals could form "association claims" of up to 160 acres, and no limit was placed on the number of claims an individual miner could make. Maintaining ownership status over an **unpatented mining claim** requires that "not less than $100 worth of labor shall be performed or improvements made during each year (per claim)." Taking the next step toward ownership, miners could obtain a patent (i.e., a deeded title) upon completing $500 worth of assessment and improvement work. A patented claim is the official transfer of title from federal to private ownership. The "purchase" of a patented claim is conducted at the rate of $5.00 per acre for lode claims and $2.50 per acre for placer claims. Roughly 3 million acres under 65,000 mining patents have been transferred to private ownership under the 1872 law. In recent years, patenting has slowed dramatically as a result of increased agency pressure. But because the right to mine and occupy is guaranteed under the status of unpatented claim, miners and mining companies have ultimately found it unnecessary to seek patent.

In many ways, the General Mining Law provided for the more orderly transfer of mineral rights to private miners and "associations." It was certainly good for miners and mining. Over time, exercise of the General Mining Law has been intriguing, and the source of a great deal of controversy. Nevertheless, the 1872 General Mining Law remains in effect today, on federal lands that have not been withdrawn from mineral entry. The arguments opposing and supporting the General Mining Law are discussed in the following section.

•   Opponents of the Hardrock Mining Law point out that prospecting and mining can take place on the federal lands as a dominant use subjugating other land uses. They argue that mining can occur over vast acreages of public lands, putting them at risk of mining impacts.

Proponents answer that exploration and mining are limited to public lands that have not yet been withdrawn for other purposes. National parks and monuments have precluded most mineral entry, as have the more recently withdrawn wilderness areas. Other withdrawals of federal land for Indian reservations, military bases, and water projects have removed millions of acres from the authority of the1872 law. Energy minerals were pulled from the 1872 **GML** in the **Mineral Leasing Act of 1920**, codifying their ownership by the U.S. and providing for their extraction only through leasing. Though an accurate accounting is almost impossible, both sides acknowledge that far fewer acres are accessible under the General Mining Law than were accessible at the time of the act's inception.

•   Opponents declare that the 1872 General Mining Law paves a path for speculators and squatters to lay claim to public property at a cost next to nothing. They point to cabins on unpatented "claims" astride quality trout streams where a bulldozer is rented once a year for an "assessment" party that meets the law's requirements (Assessment has been replaced by a $100 annual rental fee). Such claims are often called **inholdings**, and access to them across public land is guaranteed to the claimant. They note that this type of squatting is very difficult to prevent, because precise definitions of "discovery" and "assessment" work are not provided under the 1872 law.

Proponents counter that cases of speculation and squatting are overblown by both the press and environmental groups. They argue that the BLM and the USFS have the authority to evict squatters under the law's requirement that activities be "reasonably incident to mining." They add that court cases have upheld the **"prudent person test"** of whether a discovery is realistically **marketable**. The cutest example of this was the 1968 Coleman case, where the Supreme Court nullified Alfred Coleman's claim to 720 acres of the Angeles National Forest because of his discovery there of quartzite. Pointing out that quartzite is "one of the most common of all solid materials," the court ruled against Coleman, and the USFS proceeded to evict him from the home he'd built near the popular Big Bear Lake resort area above Los Angeles.

• Opponents point out that issuance of title through patenting allows the owners to use the land as they wish, and offer examples where speculators have purchased public land at $5 an acre and then turned around to sell it for $2,000 an acre.

Those in favor of the act again state that such events are rare. They add that it is appropriate that owners of patented claims should be able to continue to use and obtain value from their property either when mineral values drop or when a mine is played out.

• Opponents object to the fact the 1872 Mining Law established no means to obtain payments of royalties from miners to the federal government. They point to the royalty requirements of the 1920 Mineral Leasing Act as an example of a reasonable means to end a "government giveaway" of mineral riches. They hold that the $5 per acre price is the sole cost to a mining company to start mining.

Advocates of the GML argue that mineral resources are not being "given away." They point to the BLM's own estimate that the actual cost to bring a 20-acre claim to patent is, at minimum, $37,000. This money is intended to meet only administrative costs and to conduct enough assessment work to prove discovery. The cost of developing a mine (building roads, facilities, and purchasing equipment and covering payrolls), and the amount of time that passes before extraction of valuable minerals actually occurs (10 to 15 years), presents a far more genuine picture of what miners pay for minerals. Payment of royalties, they add, would increase the cost of production and cut into already marginal profits, potentially to the point where mining could only continue at a loss. Under such circumstances, domestic mining would be outcompeted by imports—in effect, exporting American jobs overseas.

• Finally, opponents of the GML point out that the 1872 law makes no provision for environmental protection. Certainly, it is clear to anyone that more than a century of relatively unregulated mining has exacted a heavy toll on the environment. Detractors blame the GML for encouraging boom-and-bust development, because miners had no incentive to use land for anything except to yank out the mineral value and head for the next dig.

Those who support the GML quote the act's provision that mining is to take place "under regulations prescribed by law." The GML itself was never intended to be an environmental law. These proponents point out that the GML essentially provides the opportunity for other federal, state, and local regulations to govern the environmental aspects of mining. The mining industry recognizes the innumerable regulations imposed on their activities under laws such as the Clean Air Act, the Clean Water Act, the National Environmental Policy Act, the Endangered Species Act, and the **Surface Mining Control and Reclamation Act of 1977**. GML supporters also point out that much of the technological advancement in environmentally improved mining techniques has been the result of strict environmental regulations.

The merits and troubles of the General Mining Law of 1872 must now seem as clear as the mud seeping from the bottom of a tailings pile. Just as important as the law, however, are the means by which different administrations have dealt with it through the federal administrative bureaucracy. Looking at recent history, it is instructive to follow the Reagan-Bush-Clinton-Bush-Obama chronology of relations with the General Mining Law. Reagan rode into Washington as a sagebrush rebel and a tax crusader. He believed that less government is the best government, and he supported states' rights to greater control over the public lands. Evidence of his resolve came with the appointment of James Watt, a lawyer with the conservative Mountain States Legal Foundation, as Secretary of the Interior. Watt proceeded to gut federal regulations that were not sympathetic to economic development, regulations that often happened to be measures enacted for environmental protection. He believed the General Mining Law was a fine piece of real estate legislation and opposed any attempts to alter it. Watt further engineered funding cuts to the Environmental Protection Agency that left the agency almost incapable of enforcing compliance with environmental laws. A victim of political incorrectness, Watt was forced to resign and was succeeded by secretaries less vocal than he, such as Donald Hodel and Manuel Lujan (under Bush). Lacking Watt's flamboyance, they more or less occupied a cabinet space without distinction until the Reagan-Bush era succumbed to the presidency of Bill Clinton.

Clinton appointed a westerner with environmental leanings, former Arizona governor Bruce Babbitt, to the Interior post. Caught up in the euphoria of a new administration, Babbitt went on record as favoring the overhaul of the General Mining Law of 1872. He called it an antiquated giveaway of the public lands. He made headlines but not headway. Babbitt underestimated both the minerals industry and the power of western legislators. The arguments mentioned earlier in this chapter were trundled out into the open again, with the media paying special attention to the more sensational claims from the environmentalist perspective. Having been bogged down in committee hearings, proposals to make substantial changes to the GML never made it to the floor of Congress.

Needing a pro-environmental splash, Clinton turned to another old law, using the Antiquities Act to withdraw more than a million acres of southern Utah as the Grand Staircase – Escalante National Monument. Mineral rights and claims were not clearly decided under this proclamation, but the new monument status served to withdraw some public lands from mineral entry. Also under the Clinton Administration, the USFS withdrew acreage in the Rocky Mountains from land previously available for mineral entry. Mike Dombeck, chief of the Forest Service, pointed to abuses of the General Mining Law of 1872 as one reason for the agency's withdrawals. Unable to make legislative alterations to the General Mining Law, the Clinton Administration sought administrative remedies through the regulatory process, and revised government code governing hardrock mining on federal lands, authorizing the BLM to deny harmful mining operations and to increase mining companies' responsibilities to reclaim mined lands. These new regulations went into effect only hours before Bush's inauguration on January 20, 2001. Two months later, the Bush administration proposed suspending the Clinton regulations, and Bush appointed James Watt's protégée Gale Norton to head the Department of the Interior. By November of 2001, Norton announced an end to the BLM's harmful mine veto authority. In 2003, the Bush administration further liberalized dumping of tailings and waste on mining claims. The Obama administration little changed the 1872 General Mining Law, but focused on the concept of adding royalty payments to the paltry sums mining companies pay to the federal government for their "right to mine."

The open-pit Genesis gold mine in Nevada.
(Courtesy of Mike Dennis)

The political battleground over minerals management is broad, and complex. The General Mining Law stands like a mast from which all other laws hang as rigging—interrelated, knotted, and frequently tangled. The political arena, though, is no more than the arena in which society's needs for minerals and environmental integrity are aired. Consumer demand for mineral products, the mineral industry's importance to the nation's economy, and the frightening issues of limits to supply and environmental protection produce a tug-of-war between societal values. If we're willing to look carefully, we might find ourselves on both ends of the rope.

Suggested Readings

Adams, D. A. (1993). *Renewable resource policy: The legal-institutional foundations.* Washington, DC: Island Press.

Appenzeller, T. (2006, March). The coal paradox. *National Geographic*, 98–103.

Arrandale, T. (1983). *The battle for natural resources.* Washington, DC: Congressional Quarterly.

Bakken, G. M. (2008). *The mining law of 1872: Past, politics, and prospects.* Albuquerque, NM: The University of New Mexico Press.

Coggins, G. C., Wilkinson, C., & Leshy, J. (2007). *Federal public land and resources law.* New York, NY: Foundation Press.

Dasmann, R. F. (1984). *Environmental conservation* (5th ed.). New York: John Wiley & Sons.

Doremus, H., Lin, A., Rosenberg, R., & Schoenbaum, T. (2008). *Environmental policy law: Problems, cases, and readings* (5th ed.). New York, NY: Foundation Press.

Hamilton, M. S. (2005). *Mining environmental policy: Comparing Indonesia and the U.S.A.* Burlington, VT: Ashgate.

Landsberg, H. H., Tilton, J. E., & Haas, R. B. (1982). Nonfuel minerals. In P. R. Portney (Ed.), *Current issues in natural resource policy.* Washington, DC: Resources for the Future.

Leshy, J. D. (1987). *The mining law: A study in perpetual motion.* Washington, DC: Resources for the Future.

Mitchell, J. G. (2006, March). When mountains move. *National Geographic*, 104–123.

Montrie, C. (2003). *To save the land and people: A history of surface coal mining in Appalachia.* Chapel Hill, NC: University of North Carolina Press.

Nebel, B. J. (2000). *Environmental science: The way the world works* (7th ed.). Upper Saddle River, NJ: Prentice-Hall.

Owen, O. S., & Chiras, D. D. (1990). *Natural resource conservation: An ecological approach* (5th ed.). New York: MacMillan.

Smith, D. A. (1987). *Mining America: The industry and the environment, 1800–1980.* Lawrence, KS: University Press of Kansas.

U.S. Department of the Interior, Bureau of Land Management. (1988). *Opportunity and challenge: The story of BLM.* Washington, DC: U.S. Government Printing Office.

Watkins, T. H. (2000, March). Hard rock legacy. *National Geographic*, 74–95.

Wilkinson, C. F. (1992). *Crossing the next meridian: Land, water, and the future of the West.* Washington, DC: Island Press.

chapter twenty-three

Profiling an
Informed Citizen

The detectives in a crime story try to collect and develop information that will lead to a description of the criminal being sought. This information enables them to create a "profile" of the bad guy. The profile narrows the search for the perpetrator and improves the odds of bringing the bad guy to justice. The profile is an estimate, gathered from the available evidence. If we were to set up a profile for an "informed citizen," rather than a bad guy, what evidence would we expect to find? What would be the characteristics of a citizen who is informed about natural resources and the environment? How would someone go about becoming a more knowledgeable citizen and a more effective participant in the arena of resources stewardship?

If we were searching for informed citizens, the following ten bits of evidence would probably lead us to them. The profile for informed citizens would look like people who

- understand their values and have come to grips with the notion that their values might change over time;

- select a scope of interest regarding natural resources and the environment;

- are willing to gather information about a subject from several perspectives, recognizing that these perspectives might not agree;

- read, listen to broadcast media, and think about what they comprehend;

- understand the difference between science and pseudoscience;

- recognize the degree to which their opinions and judgments are based on facts, or faith, trust, and skepticism of the opinions of others;

- have developed a personal assessment of tolerable risk;

- are willing to listen more than to speak, to speak mostly to ask questions, and to speak at other times with knowledge and understanding;

- understand the complexities of environmental and natural resource systems; and

- understand the effectiveness of various types and levels of citizen involvement and choose to become involved by the most effective means possible.

Once we track down the person who possesses a good number of these traits, we will have found an informed citizen. We need informed citizens to help us learn and understand, and also to help us make good decisions about natural resource management and environmental stewardship. A closer look at each of these characteristics will provide a clearer description of what makes up an informed citizen.

Understand their values and have come to grips with the notion that their values might change over time. Informed citizens should ask themselves what they value, what is important to their lives and the lives of others, what they want to work toward, and what they want to pass forward to future generations. The answers to these questions form a basis for how one views the world. Similarly, informed citizens should work to establish their ethical and moral standards and learn to understand their spiritual nature. It is important to be honest in this assessment. It is also important to recognize that these values might change over time. Changes in our lives bring new information that can develop new understandings. As much as we might think we've got it all figured out, we need to recognize and come to grips with the likelihood that we're going to change as time marches on. In fact, the informed citizen should embrace open-mindedness and the willingness to change. Change is not a requirement. It is an opportunity. But it is an opportunity lost on the closed-minded.

Select a scope of interest regarding natural resources and the environment. Natural resource issues span the entire planet. They range from tiny questions, such as whether to buy recycled binder paper, to larger questions such as whether humans are causing global warming. There are so many issues that one person cannot possibly become knowledgeable on all of them, or even a fraction of them. Therefore it is necessary to make some choices. Informed citizens need to choose those issues that are most important to them and decide on their level of involvement. Involvement can range from awareness to activism, requiring different levels of study and commitment. Focusing on those issues of greatest importance helps people to study them effectively and to become effective participants.

Are willing to gather information about a subject from several perspectives, recognizing that these perspectives might not agree. Many natural resource issues are mistakenly portrayed as two-sided: tree-huggers versus loggers, individuals versus multinational corporations, saviors versus rapists. These good-guy, bad-guy dichotomies are simplistic and convenient, but dangerously misrepresent the situation. The issues—and the people embroiled in them—are not that simple. On issues of interest to them, informed citizens will seek information from more than one perspective. The informed citizen will read, listen to, and study different points of view from varied sources. Understanding the bases for different arguments over an issue helps one gain a broader view. It slows the rush to judgment and builds a foundation from which people can negotiate rather than fight over their differences.

Read, listen to broadcast media, and think about what they comprehend. We live in an age when bombardment by information occupies a large part of our waking hours. Once we get past reading the cereal box label at breakfast, we can read newspapers, books, magazines, websites, leaflets, brochures, signs, letters, papers, e-mails, and text messages. Click on the radio, television, or laptop, and words effortlessly enter our heads. These written and auditory tools of communication offer the means to convey an immense variety of messages. And there are far more messages than one could possibly digest in a single lifetime, or thousands of lifetimes, for that matter. As daunting as the variety is, an informed citizen needs to select a number of sources and obtain information from them. The sources selected should provide different points of view, not necessarily only those with which one agrees. Exposure to other points of view encourages us to spend some time thinking about them. Thinking about other points of view tests our convictions and may cause reconsideration. Even if the arguments are unconvincing, recognizing and understanding them better prepares the informed citizen to make a reasoned judgment. Additionally, knowing the arguments of an opposing point of view improves one's skill in negotiations.

Understand the difference between science and pseudoscience. The stakes of many natural resource and environmental issues are high. They have impacts on people's lives today and the lives of those who will be here in the future. Because the stakes are high, participants may employ means that justify their desired ends. Bending the truth or selectively representing reality are methods frequently used to shape perceptions and influence thinking. One of the least ethical of these warping processes involves the presentation of "findings" that are claimed to have been reached scientifically. This is not a condemnation of science, but a warning that science must be distinguished from pseudoscience. Scientific processes can lead to important discoveries, the development of new knowledge, and, at best, solutions to problems. We tend to believe in science and scientific methods. That is why claiming to have reached conclusions through scientific inquiry holds weight. And it is why the unscrupulous or the ignorant will start with the conclusions they want to reach, and then make the science fit. This is not science; it is pseudoscience dressed up to look like the real thing. Informed citizens should know something about the rigors of scientific research, statistical interpretations, and the degree to which conclusions can be definitively reached from findings. In other words, informed citizens need to be educated consumers of scientific reporting, able to dismiss pseudoscience and identify high-quality scientific inquiry.

Recognize the degree to which their opinions and judgments are based on facts, or faith, trust, and skepticism of the opinions of others. Knowledge is an imperfect thing. People once knew the earth was the center of the universe, that it was flat, and that you could fall off of it. Because they were afraid to test these suppositions, people believed what they were told. They believed the truth as presented to them by other people whom they trusted. We still develop some of our opinions on the perceived strength of the information we obtain from others. We trust and have faith in certain sources of information, and we are skeptical of others. We trust or distrust information according to our perception of the information source's credibility. Our perceptions of credibility, the reasons why we choose to believe or not believe, are worthy of examination. We tend to believe in things that agree with our own values and disbelieve things that conflict with them. Our perception of rightness and truth, therefore, is strongly influenced by our values. Values are a filter through which we sift information and define credibility. Because we can never have perfect information, we must acknowledge its limitations or take some portion of it on faith. Informed citizens need to recognize how they define credibility, and to what degree their opinions are composed of trust, faith, and skepticism. In effect, one needs to ask: "Do I really know what I think I know?"

Have developed a personal assessment of tolerable risk. Many natural resource and environmental issues are concerned with risks. We wonder if timber harvests are putting species at risk. We are concerned that grazing can harm riparian systems, thus putting wildlife habitat and water quality at risk. Some regulations on chemicals promulgated by the EPA were derived from quantifying the health risks attributable to the chemical's presence in the environment. The cars we drive obviously put our health at risk from accidents. But they also risk our health by polluting the air we breathe. We are willing to tolerate both of these risks in exchange for the mobility the automobile provides. To make these risks tolerable, however, we have improved auto-accident safety with seat belts, air bags, reinforced doors, crumple zones, and safety glass. And we have reduced pollution of autos by increasing engine efficiency, filtering exhaust through catalytic converters, and removing lead from gasoline. These improvements to autos have been made to protect health and reduce risk. Some people would argue that autos still pollute too much and that they are still unsafe in accidents. Others would contend that we've sacrificed performance for pollution control, and that some people are just as likely to get killed by an airbag as saved by one. These are different views of tolerable risk. Informed citizens need to be aware of their own tolerances for risk on a variety of fronts. Something as simple as deciding to buy a $150,000 home on a 25-year floodplain or a similar home for $200,000 on a 100-year floodplain involves the decision whether to pay $50,000 for a fourfold reduction in the likelihood of flooding. Because the floodplains were drawn with incomplete data, and because we can't predict the weather in the future, even our estimates of flood risk are inexact. We are forced to put trust and faith in what we think we know, and to set our tolerance for risk from those parameters. On natural resource and environmental issues with which they're concerned, informed citizens need to consider what the parameters of our understanding are, and to assess, accordingly, the levels of risk they are willing to tolerate.

Are willing to listen more than to speak, to speak mostly to ask questions, and to speak at other times with knowledge and understanding. It is just as important to understand the messages given by others, as it is to get your own message across. This is the crux of two-way and convergence communication. The principle is frequently lost, however, on those who rush to make sure they're being heard because they think their message is so important. We need to remember that our points of view are our own and that other people have a right to theirs. The benefit of asking questions to better understand the views of others is equal to or greater than what is gained from asserting our own points. Trying to understand is more valuable than trying to convince. It isn't easy, though. Issues get more confusing when one truly listens to the perspectives of others. Villains can turn out to be fairly normal people, and that new understanding might threaten our own sense of self-righteousness. But understanding others actually improves our ability to communicate with them. Our own willingness to listen might, in turn, increase their willingness to listen to us. Armed with shared understandings, there is greater opportunity to reach common ground, to achieve mutually agreeable solutions to problems.

Understand the complexities of environmental and natural resource systems. Environmental and natural resource systems are threaded through every aspect of our lives. We are consumers as well as stewards of natural resources. To illustrate this consumer/steward role, consider something as simple as caring for a front lawn. Caring for a lawn requires the consumption of water for irrigation, perhaps some fertilizer, a little space in a landfill for clippings, a little gas or electricity if a power mower is used, and tools such as the mower, sprinklers, a rake, an edger, or a weed-eater. Throw in your labor, and you and your neighbors will all have a nice lawn to gaze across. The consumption necessary to manage that front lawn also requires the stewardship of numerous resources, though these resources may be far removed from the front yard. The irrigation water needs to be pumped from an aquifer or stored in a reservoir and then delivered through systems to end up at the sprinkler heads. The water that drains from the lawn may carry fertilizers and pesticides into a storm drain that collects similar runoff from many other lawns and washes it into a creek, river, or bay downhill from your home. The fertilizer was mined in another state and processed at a chemical plant, then shipped by train and truck to arrive at your local garden center. The grass clippings will go to the sanitary landfill when the garbage is picked up this week, where they will mingle with the weekend's clippings from hundreds of other lawns. The gas or electricity for the power mower required the extraction of oil, the burning of fossil fuels, or a hydroelectric or nuclear power plant. The tools themselves are composed of metals mined from the earth, wood and rubber extracted from forests, and plastics synthesized from petroleum. These tools were manufactured, by workers in factories and assembly plants, in locations all over the world. Then they were shipped by sea and land to a nearby retailing center constructed on soils suitable for agricultural production. The production and manufacture of all the products consumed to maintain that lawn provide jobs integrated into society's economy. That patch of green grass is connected to a lot more than just your front yard. All of our natural resources are similarly linked to us, our environment, and our social structures, institutions, and cultures. An informed citizen recognizes this interconnectedness and also understands the complexity of dealing with natural resource issues.

Understand the effectiveness of various types and levels of citizen involvement and choose to become involved by the most effective means possible. Like it or not, we are all involved with natural resources and the environment. At minimum, we are consumers of natural resources and polluters of the environment. Our involvement with natural resource and environmental issues can range from apathy to activism. We may try to ignore them, or we may make them our life's work. We may participate by an occasional visit to the voting booth, or we may become a candidate in the election. It is up to individuals to decide their levels of involvement with natural resource

Exercising the right to vote is a good place for informed citizens to start making their selves heard. (Photo by Steve Dennis)

stewardship. Whether that involvement dominates your life or simply catches your attention from time to time, it is important to be aware of the mechanisms by which you can be most effective. Chapter 17 summarized a number of methods by which citizens are involved in debating, planning, and managing the stewardship of natural resources and the environment. These methods are variably effective, depending on how we use them, the nature of the issue, and the sociopolitical context within which the issue is being considered. Informed citizens will measure the efficacy of different forms of involvement, assess their own commitment to various issues, and decide to participate in a manner and at a level that works best for them. If their commitment grows, so will their level of participation. As their participation increases, so do their skills in the processes of gathering information, debate, discussion, and negotiation.

Informed citizens are people who are willing to become involved, to become better informed, to express their views, and to listen to and respect the views of others. No lesser set of credentials qualifies one for participation in the issues that mean so much to us all.

chapter twenty-four

Legacy

The earth's resources have cycled and created a foundation for life for millions of years. These processes will continue, even if they are rearranged by human activities. The questions we face involve not whether we're destroying the earth, but the degree to which we have an impact on the opportunities of organisms in the future. Our impacts, in the span of geologic perspective, are fleeting. All of human history may one day be summed up in an inch and a half of shale bedded thousands of feet beneath sedimentary rocks inexorably laid on top. In a retrospective at that scale, what we do today and in the near future won't do much to offset the environmental effects measured by the steady tick of an immeasurably patient clock.

For the duration of our lives, and those of several generations to come, we will have an impressive impact. We can look back only decades in time and bear witness to profound changes in our population, industrial development, technological advancement, and scientific understanding. Calculating the rate of change across our recent past and projecting that into the future portends sobering developments ahead. What will, for example, Los Angeles be like if it continues to grow for 60 more years at the rate it has grown since 1950? How will similar rates of growth affect Mexico City, Tokyo, Cairo, Chongquing, and the other thousands of our metropolitan settlements? What further pressures will we place on air, water, soils, minerals, parks, wilderness, and other species?

Perception of the future on a global scale may escape our imagination. We're more likely to be concerned on a local level and within a time frame of a few years or a generation. Our state and national policies toward the environment will affect the way we live, but these policies will be but a reflection of our social will and the realities of limits. In our daily lives, we are confronted with questions about using natural resources. We participate by espousing our point of view, staking claim to our values. We enter into discussions of whether timber harvests, new subdivisions, pesticide application, offshore oil drilling, nuclear energy, mining, dams, or new parklands should be allowed, accelerated, or minimized. These questions persist, and they are less resolved than they are approached, contested, and redrawn. We define our world by stating our values for it, and through using it to meet our needs.

Beyond the 25 to 30 thousand sunrises we're all likely to enjoy extend the dawns of our descendants The choices we make in this generation will affect their lives in much the same way as our great-great grandparents did when they decided that we should all drive around in automobiles. There is considerable truth in the adage that we are borrowing the earth from our children. The legacy that we bequeath to the next generations will emerge from the patterns of our lives and the expression of what we reserve for them.

A century and a half has passed since a former generation set aside the world's first national park as a "pleasuring ground for the benefit and enjoyment of the people." Their grandchildren, seeing the work unfinished, started the National Park Service to ensure that these places would remain "unimpaired for the enjoyment of future generations." These actions by our great, and great-great grandparents are part of the legacy we have inherited. They worked with one another to carve this monument to the future. They didn't all agree, and they didn't all get what they wanted. But their struggles and their efforts have helped to define what we are today.

The legacy that continues beyond our generation will evolve from our past, our lifetimes, and our visions for the future. We all, in large and small ways, are participants in that legacy. We owe it to ourselves, and those who will succeed us, to be informed and thoughtful over the choices we ponder and the decisions we make.

Selected Internet Sites Useful to the Informed Citizen

The Internet provides innumerable opportunities to gather information about natural resources, environmental issues, citizen organizations, government agencies, and the activities of national, state, and local governments. Individual sites are usually linked to related informational resources, truly creating a web of information. Directories function as tables of contents, allowing you to search for specific sites and then to access them with a click. Search engines will scan the internet for information you seek, offering another mechanism for access. On many web sites there are opportunities to find links to other related sites. Keep an eye open for links buttons. In an hour of surfing the web for natural resources information you'll be amazed at how much is available. The following list of useful internet sites will help you get started. In the scale of the internet, this list is the equivalent of one piece of straw in a barn full of hay. But it's a pretty good piece of straw, and hopefully it will come in handy.

Environmental Directories

The Environment Directory
http://www.webdirectory.com

Best Environmental Directories
http://www.ulb.ac.be/ceese/meta/cds.html

National Council for Science and the Environment
http://ncseonline.org

Envirolink: The Online Environmental Community
http://www.envirolink.org

United States Federal Government

U.S. Federal Agencies Directory
http://www.lib.lsu.edu/gov/index.html

The White House
http://www.whitehouse.gov.

The Federal Judiciary
http://www.uscourts.gov

The U.S. Senate
http://www.senate.gov

The U.S. House of Representatives
http://www.house.gov

Library of Congress
http://lcweb.loc.gov

Federal Natural Resource Agencies

Bureau of Indian Affairs
http://www.bia.gov

Bureau of Land Management
http://www.blm.gov

Bureau of Reclamation
http://www.usbr.gov

Environmental Protection Agency
http://www.epa.gov

National Marine Fisheries Service
http://www.nmfs.noaa.gov

National Oceanic and Atmospheric Administration
http://www.noaa.gov

National Park Service
http://www.nps.gov

Natural Resources Conservation Service (formerly Soil Conservation Service)
http://www.nrcs.usda.gov

U.S. Army Corps of Engineers
http://www.usace.army.mil

U.S.D.A. National Institute of Food and Agriculture
http://www.csrees.usda.gov

U.S. Fish and Wildlife Service
http://www.fws.gov

U.S. Forest Service
http://www.fs.fed.us

Property Rights, Individual Freedom and Responsible Government

Blue Ribbon Coalition
http://www.sharetrails.org

Frontiers of Freedom
http://www.ff.org

Mountain States Legal Foundation
http://www.mountainstateslegal.com

Northwest Legal Foundation
http://nwlegalonline.wordpress.com

Pacific Legal Foundation
http://www.pacificlegal.org

Environmental Organizations

The Audubon Society
http://www.audubon.org

Defenders of Wildlife
http://www.defenders.org

Earthjustice
http://earthjustice.org

Greenpeace
http://www.greenpeace.org

The Izaak Walton League of America
http://iwla.org

National Parks and Conservation Association
http://www.npca.org

National Wildlife Federation
http://www.nwf.org

Natural Resources Defense Council
http://www.nrdc.org

The Nature Conservancy
http://prod.nature.org

Rainforest Action Network
http://www.ran.org

The Sierra Club
http://www.sierraclub.org

The Trust for Public Land
http://www.tpl.org

The Wilderness Society
http://www.wilderness.org

Worldwide Fund for Nature
http://wwf.panda.org

Miscellaneous

Earth First!
http://www.earthfirst.org

Southern Utah Wilderness Alliance
http://www.suwa.org

Earthworks
http://www.earthworksaction.org

Mineral Information Institute
http://www.mii.org

Nevada Mining Association
http://www.nevadamining.org

Society for Conservation Biology
http://www.conbio.org

Society of American Foresters
http://www.safnet.org

The Wildlife Society
http://joomla.wildlife.org

Society for Range Management
http://www.rangelands.org

High Country News
http://www.hcn.org

Environmental News Network
http://enn.com

American Forests (formerly American Forestry Association)
http://www.americanforests.org

Wilderness Area Information (Multi-agency & University of Montana)
http://www.wilderness.net

The Ecological Footprint
http://myfootprint.org

The Story of Stuff
http://storyofstuff.com

Glossary

Acid mine drainage (AMD) The toxic drainage that occurs when water seeps through ore and tailings piles. Percolating water dissolves compounds from the tailings, such as sulphuric acid, which poses a threat to surface and groundwater. Lining the bottom of tailings piles with impermeable material is one method that has been used to mitigate AMD. (Ch.22)

Acid precipitation Any form of precipitation that has a pH less than 5.6. Acid precipitation comes from air pollutants such as sulphur dioxide and oxides of nitrogen. Acid rain, acid fog, and acid snow are all forms of acid precipitation. (Ch.21)

Administrative Bureaucracy A term used to refer to the federal administration. It includes the departments of the President's Cabinet, and all the agencies grouped within those departments. Additionally, the administrative bureaucracy includes the agencies and organizations set up to assist the Congress. This bureaucracy is enormous, ranging from the Federal Aviation Administration (FAA) to the National Oceanographic and Atmospheric Administration (NOAA), and from the Securities and Exchange Commission (SEC) to the Internal Revenue Service (IRS). (Ch.6)

Administrative Law That body of law dealing with governments and administrative agencies. (Ch.15)

Administrative Procedures Act of 1946 Congressional legislation creating many procedural guidelines for the operations of federal administrative agencies. Under Section 702, the APA described access to judicial review by parties "aggrieved by agency action." (Ch.15)

Adopt-a-Horse and Adopt-a-Burro Programs Established by BLM as a means to remove some feral horses and burros from the public lands. BLM would round up the animals and then offer them for adoption to private parties. (Ch.9)

Aggrieved Legal term for having been wronged, or in a position to potentially be wronged. (Ch.15)

Agricultural Water uses for cultivation of plants, and for livestock. Irrigation for crop production is accomplished through a variety of forms including flooding, furrow, aerial spraying, and drip methods. (Ch.21)

Alaska National Interest Lands Conservation Act of 1980 This Act settled claims to lands in Alaska between natives and federal agencies. It included designation of 44.7 million acres of parks, monuments, and preserves under the National Park Service, more than doubling the land area managed by the agency. (Ch.7)

Albright, Horace Second Director of the National Park Service. As a young man Albright went to Washington D.C. with Stephen Mather to work toward the establishment of the National Park Service. (Ch.7)

Alodial Property independently owned, without rent or mortgage. (Ch.4)

American Forestry Association A citizen organization created in 1875, and dedicated to the protection of America's forest resources. The AFA is still politically active today, supporting a balance between the interests of forest preservation and wise use. The organization's name was changed to American Forests in 1992. (Ch.4)

Anadromous A term used to refer to fish that spend part of their lives in fresh water, and migrate to sea for other parts of their lives. Salmon are an anadromous fish. They hatch and live as "fry" in fresh water streams, then migrate to the ocean where they live most of their lives. Late in life they return to the waters where they were born to spawn and die. (Ch.11)

Animal rights A cause for some citizen organizations opposed to hunting, trapping, or fishing, or use of animals for scientific research. (Ch.15)

Animal Unit Month (AUM) The amount of forage necessary to sustain one cow and her calf, one horse, or five sheep or goats for one month. AUMs are based on a formula in the Public Rangelands Improvement Act (PRIA, 1978) which uses a 1966 base of $1.23 per AUM, and makes adjustments for current private grazing land lease rates, beef cattle prices, and the cost of livestock production. AUMs are the basis for assessing fees for livestock grazing on the public lands. Originally set at five cents per AUM, the current rate is $1.35 per AUM, the minimum which must be charged under a presidential Executive Order issued in 1986. This rate is controversial. "Environmentalists" often argue that the rate is set too low, creating a federal subsidy for the livestock industry. Ranchers with livestock on public lands counter that the fees more than adequately reflect the grazing value of the lands permitted to them. (Ch.9)

Antiquities Act In passing the Antiquities Act of 1906, Congress gave the President the power to withdraw federal lands from entry and set them aside as national monuments. Intended to speed up the process of protecting archaeological resources being discovered and exploited in the southwest, the Antiquities Act was soon demonstrated to be a powerful tool for lands preservation used by Theodore Roosevelt. More recently, the Antiquities Act was used by Jimmy Carter to establish huge national monuments in Alaska, and by Bill Clinton who established several new monuments, including the Grand Staircase-Escalante National Monument in southern Utah. (Ch.4)

Appropriation The dedication of money for some purpose through the Congressional budget. (Ch.4)

Aquifer Porous rock, soils, or sands where groundwater accumulates beneath the surface. Aquifers are often "tapped" by wells, and are an important source of drinking and irrigation water. Aquifers are threatened by human activities when their pumping exceeds their rate of recharge, or when toxic pollutants seep into them from surface spills. (Ch.21)

Assistance Many resource agencies provide technical advice, financial assistance, and scientific research to improve the management of natural resources under their authority, and for other agencies and private parties. A well known example of this function is the Department of Agriculture's National Institute of Food and Agriculture which is tied to county farm bureaus throughout the country. (Ch.5)

Audubon, John James Naturalist painter of birds from the nineteenth century, for whom the environmental organization the Audubon Society was named. (Ch.4)

Babbitt, Bruce The Secretary of the Interior under President Bill Clinton, and former governor of Arizona. (Ch.7)

Bald Eagle Protection Act (1940) Federal law passed to protect the bird that had become America's symbol, making it a crime to kill or possess any parts of the animal. Bald Eagles were later protected under the Endangered Species Act. With populations re-established, the Bald Eagle was de-listed under the ESA in 1999. (Ch.19)

Ball or rod mills Machines used to crush rock, in large circulating drums. (Ch.22)

Bambi Syndrome A process described by wildlife managers, where people become emotionally attached to wildlife. Named for Disney's classic animated motion picture, the Bambi Syndrome is the anthropomorphism of wildlife. People influenced in this manner are not particularly satisfied by wildlife managers' claim that hunting is necessary to keep some species from exceeding their carrying capacity. The Bambi Syndrome begs the question "how can killing animals be good for them?" (Ch.10)

Bierstadt, Albert One of the Hudson River School landscape painters, Bierstadt is known for his paintings of western scenes. (Ch.4)

Biodiversity Complexity and quantity of the biota. High biodiversity is indicated by the presence of numerous and highly varied species of plants, animals, and micro-organisms. Biodiversity is considered essential to ecological well-being and the health of environments. (Ch.18)

Bison *Bison americanus.* The American bison, commonly referred to as the buffalo, was a once-abundant ungulate hunted to near extinction in the latter half of the nineteenth century. (Ch.4)

Bitterroot Controversy An issue that surfaced on the Bitterroot National Forest in Montana, and eventually gained nationwide attention. A University of Montana report on U.S. Forest Service timber operations on the forest found that the agency was engaging in uneconomical harvest practices. Use in the report of the term "timber mining" unleashed a media storm, considerable bad press for the U.S. Forest Service, and eventually new forest planning legislation by Congress. (Ch.14)

Bolle Report The name given to the report of the University of Montana School of Forestry on the timber management practices on the Bitterroot National Forest. Named for the Dean of the School of Forestry, Arnold Bolle. (Ch.14)

Boom and bust Phrase used to describe the pattern of resource exploitation where resources are greedily removed until they run out. Considerable economic gain is made in the boom period, but it is inevitably followed by economic hardship and ruin when the supply of resources is "played out." (Ch.18)

Boone and Crockett Club Citizen organization created in 1888 to protect big-game animals. Included future president Teddy Roosevelt among its founders. The group was influential in turn-of-the-century natural resource policy. (Ch.10)

Boston Common Considered to be the first municipal park in the nation, Boston Common was established in 1634 as a place where people could pasture their livestock. (Ch.13)

Brighty of Grand Canyon Fictional burro character of Marguerite Henry's children's book of the same name. (Ch.19)

Bundle of rights Ownership should be considered as a bundle of rights. Different types of ownership convey certain rights to the owner(s), while other rights are retained by others. For example, owning a house gives the owner the rights to sleep and eat there, paint the bathroom blue, choose the furniture, and to plant flowers or vegetables in the backyard. But the owner may not have the right to erect a 100 foot radio antennae in the backyard, or to plop an oil well in the front yard. The owner's bundle of rights is limited in order to protect neighbors' rights. Another example would be government ownership of a national park. The government has the rights to manage the park, but citizens possess a bundle of rights that allows them to use the park. The government's bundle of rights is actually created by the citizens in order to protect the park from themselves! (Ch.1)

Bureau of Biological Survey Originally established in the Department of Agriculture, this Bureau had most federal responsibility for wildlife, excluding fisheries. It was transferred to the Interior Department in 1939, consolidated with the Bureau of Fisheries, and renamed the U.S. Fish and Wildlife Service in 1940. (Ch.10)

Bureau of Land Management (BLM) Agency under the Department of the Interior responsible for management of the "public domain lands." Established in 1946 through a merger of the Grazing Service and the General Land Office. (Ch.9)

Bureau of Livestock and Mining A derogatory play on the acronym BLM, used by people who feel the Bureau of Land Management caters to (or is "captured" by) the livestock and mining industries. (Ch.9)

Cadastral Survey System From the term *cadastre*, which means the registration of the extent of landholdings for purposes of taxation. For purposes of lands disposition, the Federal government established a survey system of townships, a north-south east-west grid of 36 square miles, arranged in a square six miles on a side. Each square mile was referred to as a section, and given a number from one to 36. Sections measured 640 acres, and the "quarter section," or 160 acres, became the standard size for land transfers to individuals under the Homestead Act. (Ch.4)

California Desert Conservation Area Established under the FLPMA in 1976, this was a special management area of BLM lands in Southern California's Mojave Desert. (Ch.9)

California Environmental Quality Act (CEQA) California's state law, similar to NEPA, though CEQA also applies to private sector developments. (Ch.12)

California Sportsmen's Taskforce A California citizen organization established to protect and enhance legal opportunities for hunting and fishing. (Ch.19)

Captured The perception that a resources agency is overly influenced by a specific clientele group. For example, it has long been argued that the Bureau of Land Management is captured by the mining and livestock industries, and that the U.S. Forest Service is captured by the timber industry. Counter arguments have been made that these two agencies are captured by environmentalists. (Ch.14)

Carson, Rachel Scientist and author of *Silent Spring* (1962), a bestselling book that warned of the dangers of pesticide use to wildlife and humans. (Ch.4)

Catalytic converters Smog control devices that oxidize carbon monoxide and hydrocarbons in auto exhaust to carbon dioxide and water. (Ch.22)

Catlin, George American painter best known for his depictions of Native Americans from the 1830s. (Ch.4)

Central Park New York City municipal park acquired in 1853, designed in 1858, and developed over the next 40 years. The land that became Central Park on Manhattan Island was unsuitable for building, and had been the site of bogs, shanties, pigpens and slaughterhouses. (Ch.13)

Centrifugal pump Pump invented after World War I, capable of raising hundreds of gallons per minute from aquifers. Use of the centrifugal pump in this century has greatly increased irrigation pressure on groundwater resources. (Ch.21)

Checkerboard pattern A land ownership pattern where alternating square miles are in federal ownership, and the adjacent square miles are in private ownership. This was the pattern of disposal under the railroad land grants of the 19th century. The checkerboard pattern remains with us in many areas today, complicating the task of resource management. (Ch.9)

Chief The title of the head administrator of the U.S. Forest Service. (Ch.4)

Church, Frederic One of the first generation of painters leading the style of the Hudson River School. (CH.4)

Citizen organizations Groups formally organized to represent some specific interests of groups of people. Specific types of citizen organizations include: public interest groups, pressure groups, lobbies, special interests, and voluntary associations. (Ch.14)

Claims Related to mining, claims are the documentation of first right to possession of a mineral deposit and the land above it. (Ch.22)

Classification and Multiple Use Act of 1964 This law endorsed the multiple use mission of the BLM. (Ch.9)

Clean Water Act of 1972 Common name given to the Federal Water Pollution Control Act Amendments of 1972. Federal water quality regulation was first strengthened by the Federal Water Pollution Control Act of 1948, and again by the Water Quality Act of 1965. Federal leadership in battling water pollution, however, was not established until passage of the amendments in 1972. Every Congress since 1972 has added amendments to the Federal Water Pollution Control Act, including the Clean Water Act of 1977, and the Water Quality Act of 1987. (Ch.21)

Clearcutting A silvicultural regeneration (harvest) method used in even-aged timber stand management of tree species that grow well with greater exposure to the sun. Although economical because of maximum timber removal, clearcutting has a bad name because of its aesthetic, soils, and water quality impacts. (Ch.14)

Code of the West Unofficial practice and way of thinking that favored ranching over other uses of western rangelands. (Ch.20)

Cole, Thomas Cole is credited with beginning the Hudson River School style of landscape painting which features wildness and magnitude of nature. (Ch.4)

Collective goods These are the benefits gained by citizen organizations. They are collective because all people can share in them. For example, a non-smoker who dislikes second-hand smoke would benefit from an ordinance banning smoking in public buildings. The ordinance, a result of citizen group pressure, would be considered a collective good, even though it might not sit well with smokers. (Ch.14)

Commerce Clause Article 1, Section 8 of the U.S. Constitution wherein the federal government reserved the right to regulate commerce "among the various states." (Ch.21)

Conservation A philosophy of resource management backing "wise use" of natural resources so that they might supply a continuous flow of products for the long term. Conservation holds that we can manage renewable natural resources in ways that are sustainable, enjoying their use while ensuring their future productivity. This philosophy became the foundation of the managerial missions of the U.S. Forest Service and the Bureau of Land Management. Roughly 80% of federal lands are managed under this general philosophy. (Ch.4)

Consume To use or re-use resources. It is important to note that to consume resources is not necessarily the same as destroying them. Consuming is a process of converting from one form to another. If we consume water for irrigation, we change much of it from fluid form into the water content of plants and into vapor through evaporation. When we consume oil we turn it into such things as energy and petrochemical products. To convert resources through consuming them can be beneficial. However, it can also be problematic when consuming leads to conversions that create pollution or overuse of resources. (Ch.2)

Corporate power The governmental power to levy taxes, collect other revenues, and to spend monies for projects and services. (Ch.13)

Cost-benefit analyses These are comprehensive estimates of the economic value of a program or project. The dollar value of all costs (expenses) is estimated, and compared with the dollar value of all benefits (income). Estimates include both direct and indirect costs and benefits, for both market and non-market goods. Such analyses have been employed since the 1960s in order to pre-determine in the planning process whether a project or program makes good economic sense. (Ch.11)

Council on Environmental Quality (CEQ) Established under the National Environmental Policy Act of 1970 (NEPA), the CEQ was created to interpret and implement regulations under that law. (Ch.5)

Critical environmental concern Areas that contain habitat important to many species. These may be rare environments, such as riparian zones in the arid Great Basin. Protecting the quality of areas of critical environmental concern has become an important management issue for the BLM. (Ch.9)

Cuyahoga River River that became a symbol of the need for water quality regulation in the U.S. after it caught fire where it flows through Cleveland in the 1960s. (Ch.21)

Declaratory judgments A major form of remedy that can be imposed by a court. Often these are findings that an activity will cause damage. Injunctions are frequently attached to declaratory judgments. (Ch.15)

Density In silviculture, density is a measure of the number of trees per acre. (Ch.18)

Desalinized seawater Ocean water that has been purified for drinking and agricultural purposes. The desalinizing process is energy intensive and expensive. (Ch.21)

Desert Land Law of 1877 A land disposal law that granted 640 acres to settlers who would irrigate and plant crops on that area within three years. (Ch.9)

Dingell-Johnson Act of 1950 This statute, also known as the Federal Aid in Sport Fish Restoration Act, is essentially the fishing version of the Pittman-Robertson Act, which had proven successful for 13 years. It places a federal excise tax on the sale of fishing tackle, creating funds for distribution to the states for fish restoration and management projects. (Ch.10)

Disposal The sale or trade of lands from federal government ownership or control, to individual people, corporate entities, or states. (Ch.4)

Division of Forestry, Bureau of Forestry The first small federal offices created for purposes of forest management. Later to become the U.S. Forest Service. (Ch.4)

Division of Grazing A unit established within the Department of the Interior to oversee the grazing districts created under the Taylor Grazing Act of 1934. In 1939 it was renamed the U.S. Grazing Service. (Ch.9)

Doctrine of Limitations A set of four tests of justiciability, including the doctrines of mootness, ripeness, political questions, and standing to sue. (Ch.15)

Doctrine of Official Immunity A doctrine protecting certain government officials such as judges, legislators, and prosecutors from suits for damages because of the nature of their duties. (Ch.15)

Dolan v. City of Tigard Oregon A 1994 Supreme Court decision backing a landowner's claim that a city was trying to "take" property from her in exchange for a permit to expand her store. (Ch.13)

Dominant use The condition where the production of certain natural resources is conducted over and above their use for other purposes. It is the antithesis of the doctrine of multiple use. Though never officially sanctioned because it is a politically untenable position, dominant use has been employed in many areas. Livestock grazing and mining have been the dominant uses of the public lands of the Great Basin region for over a century. Timber has been the dominant use of the forests of the Pacific Northwest, and water management has been the dominant use of every valley flooded by reservoirs. Similarly, it could certainly be said that outdoor recreation and wildlife are the dominant uses of wilderness areas. (Ch.8)

Draining irrigated lands Agricultural runoff from croplands irrigated by flood and furrow methods. Agricultural drainage has been problematic because of the concentration of pesticides, fertilizers, and minerals from soils. (Ch.21)

Ducks Unlimited Citizen organization that acquires and manages lands to provide habitat for waterfowl. (Ch.13)

Due Process From the "due process clause" of the 5th Amendment to the U.S. Constitution, which states: "..nor shall any person ..be deprived of life, liberty, or property, without due process of law; nor shall private property be taken for public use, without just compensation." Though the 5th Amendment protects the right to property, it also recognizes the right of the public to claim private property, provided that due process is followed, and just compensation offered as payment. (Ch.13)

Durand, Asher One of the first generation of Hudson River School landscape painters. (Ch.4)

Earth First! A self-proclaimed "radical" environmental group loosely formed in the early 1980s and following the slogan: "No compromise in defense of Mother Earth!" (Ch.15)

Earth-filled Centuries-old method of constructing dams and levees. Earth-filled dams are constructed of crushed rock, usually with a non-porous clay core. Water seepage into the outer wall of the dam causes a cementing effect, bonding the material into greater strength. (Ch.21)

Echo Park Part of a canyon on the Green River in Dinosaur National Monument that would have been flooded by a Bureau of Reclamation Dam. It was blocked by environmentalists, led by David Brower of the Sierra Club in the 1950s. (Ch.11)

Ecological warfare A method of battling other peoples by destroying the resources on which they subsist. The decimation of the American bison through market hunting was a form of ecological warfare against Great Plains indian tribes whose survival depended on the "buffalo." (Ch.4)

Economic values The value of a benefit or cost, estimated and quantified in dollars. It is relatively straightforward calculating economic values of "market" goods such as timber and minerals. It is much more difficult setting economic values for "non-market" goods such as a day of outdoor recreation, or a bald eagle. (Ch.11)

Economies of scale Saving money by completing large amounts of work with a minimum investment outlay. In timber management, the expense of operating a piece of heavy equipment such as a bulldozer forces a harvesting company to want to move a maximum amount of timber from a given area. It may be uneconomical to haul only a few trees. When the amount of timber to be moved is more valuable than the cost of moving it, then an economy of scale has been reached. (Ch.18)

Ecosystems Management A new term being used to describe the management strategy for lands previously managed under the concept of multiple use. The major difference, beyond just a name change from multiple use, is that through ecosystems management the focus is maintaining the long term health of the ecosystem, rather than a long term flow of natural resource products. Ecosystems management would first determine how to achieve functional ecosystems, and only then to utilize those natural resources that can be harvested without harming the stability of the ecosystem. (Ch.3)

Emerson, Ralph Waldo Famed writer credited with initiating the Transcendentalist movement with his first book *Nature*, published in 1836. (Ch.4)

Endangered Species Act of 1973 An act passed by Congress to protect endangered species of plants and animals, by protecting habitat of species that are designated through a listing process as threatened or endangered Considered by many to be the strongest environmental law in the nation. (Ch.8)

Endangered Species Committee A seven-member board that can provide exemptions to certain protections under the Endangered Species Act, when a specific federal action is considered more important than the potential extinction of a species. (Ch.19)

Energy minerals Minerals, in solid, liquid, and gaseous forms, that are used to produce heat energy. These include oil, natural gas, peat, coal, and uranium. Coal and uranium would also qualify as hard rock minerals. (Ch.9)

Environmental Impact Statement (EIS) The name given to documents drawn up to satisfy the regulatory requirements of NEPA, the National Environmental Policy Act of 1970. (Ch.15)

Environmental movement Title given to a social movement of citizens concerned with the quality of the environment. The U.S. has experienced two major environmental movements. The first took place over 50 years or so straddling the turn of the last century, and the second dates from the 1960s with varying levels of intensity through the present. (Ch.4)

Environmental Protection Agency (EPA) Agency in the Executive Branch established in 1970 as a clearinghouse to oversee the implementation of numerous pollution control and environmental laws. (Ch.5)

Environmental-Utilitarian (E-U) Scale A scale used to measure people's values for natural resources and the environment, ranging from environmentalist-protectionist values to utilitarian-development values. (Ch.14)

Estuarine Resources of estuaries. Estuaries are open to the ocean at one end, and are fed by freshwater streams at the other end, creating a mixture of fresh and salt water. (Ch.21)

Euclid v. Ambler (1926) U.S. Supreme Court decision upholding the village of Euclid's right to enforce its zoning ordinance. (Ch.13)

Executive Order Presidential executive orders are administrative acts which have the effect of law. They must be published in the Federal Register as required under the Administrative Procedures Act of 1946. Usually, executive orders are directed to offices within the Executive Branch, telling them to implement policies in certain ways. (Ch.4)

Exotic species Species that are not native, or indigenous, to a particular area. Also referred to as non-native species. (Ch.9)

Externalities Occurrences that are related to other events, but would be commonly referred to as "side effects." For example, the Bureau of Reclamation builds a dam and a new reservoir is created. Businesses in the nearest town begin to cater to an increase in tourists who come to the reservoir for flatwater recreation. Land prices begin to go up as people start to build vacation homes, and "locals" are forced to move further away to places where they can find affordable housing. This displacement of locals would be considered an externality. (Ch.21)

Federal Aviation Administration (FAA) The agency responsible for regulating air travel, including the designation of flight corridors and the use of airspace. (Ch.7)

Federal Land Policy and Management Act of 1976 The act establishing the permanent management of the public domain lands by the Bureau of Land Management, and mandating multiple use management similar to the direction given the U.S. Forest Service. (Ch.4)

Federal Register The document and official daily publication for federal rules, notices of federal agencies and organizations, and executive orders and other presidential documents. Administered by the National Archives and Records Administration. (Ch.16)

Federal Register Act of 1935 This Congressional statute established the Federal Register as the clearinghouse and repository for all proposed and approved federal rules and regulations. (Ch.16)

Federal Water Pollution Control Act Amendments of 1972 See Clean Water Act of 1972. (Ch.21)

Federal Water Pollution Control Act of 1948 First national law intended specifically to reduce water pollution. (Ch.21)

Fire protection and suppression Forest management practices that include reducing conditions that favor fire (protection), and putting fires out when they occur (suppression). Protection primarily involves reducing and breaking up continuity of grassy and woody fuels, and minimizing human-caused ignition. Suppression involves spotting fires and immediately attacking them before they spread, or in containing fires within boundaries that keep them from spreading further. "Wildfires" can attain huge dimensions, requiring what can best be called armies of firefighters to battle them. (Ch.18)

First English v. Los Angeles Supreme Court decision stating that if a landowner's property has been taken by regulation, that person is entitled to just monetary compensation. (Ch.13)

Fish and Game Commission In California and other states, the Fish and Game Commission is a citizen body appointed by the governor, and given the responsibility for setting policy on wildlife management. (Ch.19)

Fish and Wildlife Coordination Act Amendments of 1958 Law that required consultation with the U.S. Fish and Wildlife Service in considerations over federal permits for water development projects. (Ch.21)

Flatwater recreation Name given to the recreational activities commonly associated with lakes, reservoirs, and their shorelines. (Ch.11)

Flood protection One of the primary resource management benefits of dams, levees, and other water diversion projects designed to reduce floodwater inundation of agricultural lands and areas of human settlement. (Ch.11)

Floodplains Areas adjacent to rivers, creeks and streams at elevations that can be periodically inundated by flooding water. Floodplains are defined by their topographic elevation, and are generally mapped along contour lines. Floodplain areas are also defined by the frequency with which a flood would be expected to cover them. For example, a "five-year floodplain" is expected to be inundated by water every five years on average. A 100-year floodplain is an area that would be expected to flood on average only once in a hundred years. (Ch.21)

Forest and Rangeland Renewable Resources Planning Act of 1974 (RPA) Congressional statute that required the U.S. Forest Service to prepare long-range management plans, and to include the public in a comprehensive planning process. (Ch.8)

Forest Ecosystems Management Assessment Team (FEMAT) A planning team created under the Clinton administration to come up with a regional ecosystems management plan for the federal forestlands of the pacific northwest. (Ch.18)

Forest Management Act of 1897 Considered the Organic Act (organizing act) of the National Forest System. This Act established the initial management methods and purposes for the forest reserves, which were "...to improve and protect the forest within the reservation, or for... securing favorable conditions of water flows, and to furnish a continuous supply of timber for the use and necessities of citizens of the United States." (Ch.4)

Forest Practices Act Many states such as California, Idaho, and Maine have their own comprehensive legislation and regulations governing the management and harvest of timber on public and private lands. Other states have implemented "best practices" to guide the conservation of forest resources.(Ch.18)

Forest Reserve Act of 1891 Actually only a small section of a larger piece of Congressional legislation, the Forest Reserve Act gave the president the power to withdraw and set aside federal lands as forest reserves. The forest reserves eventually became the national forests, administered by the U.S. Forest Service. (Ch.4)

Forest Reserves Lands set aside by the president under the powers of the Forest Reserve Act of 1891 were called Forest Reserves. These later became known as National Forests, and are today managed by the U.S. Forest Service. (Ch.8)

Forest Service culture A term used to describe the internal human culture shared by employees of the U.S. Forest Service. (Ch.8)

Free-rider People who obtain the benefits of a citizen organization, without becoming members. (Ch.14)

Functions The major departments within the U.S. Forest Service, labeled by their area of specialty, such as timber management, engineering, fire management, lands and resources, and outdoor recreation. (Ch.8)

Fund for Animals Citizen organization that collects monies to be used in animal relocation and protection, and for acquisition and maintenance of refuge areas. (Ch.19)

General Land Office (GLO) An office within the Department of the Interior that administered the public lands of the U.S. Primarily, the office was concerned with keeping track of the land transactions of the nation, such as the railroad grants, grants to veterans, and the Homestead Act. The lands remaining in federal hands were referred to as the public domain lands. (Ch.4)

General Mining Law of 1872 Congress passed this law to bring order to the claims on federal lands being made by miners in areas throughout the west. It provided for the processes of filing claim and patent, and made provision to grant ownership to lands occupied by productive mining operations. (Ch.9)

Get the cut out The process of administering the harvest of timber. Effectiveness in carrying out timber production became an important resume builder in a U.S. Forest Service career. Emphasis on this measure of a manager's skills is considered to have helped push the agency toward a dominant use perspective on timber production. (Ch.8)

Giant Sequoia *Sequoia gigantea*. The giant redwood tree of the western Sierra Nevada mountains in California. Considered the largest living organism on earth, though some evidence now indicates massive aspen groves with a single root system may contain more biomass. (Ch.4)

Glen Canyon Dam A massive dam on the Colorado River built in the 1960s and creating 195-mile Lake Powell in Glen Canyon. As part of a compromise to stop Echo Park Dam, environmentalists agreed not to contest the proposal for the dam at Glen Canyon. (Ch.11)

God Squad A name for the Endangered Species Committee, given because of the committee's power to ultimately decide the fate of a species. (Ch.19)

Grand Staircase-Escalante National Monument A 1.3 million acre area of BLM and USFS lands in Southeastern Utah declared as a National Monument by Bill Clinton in 1996. The region is noted for its red rock mesas, canyons, and archaeological resources. (Ch.9)

Grazing The practice of allowing livestock (mostly cattle and sheep) to feed on forage grown on public and private lands. (Ch.3)

Grazing Advisory Boards Citizen committees organized under the Taylor Grazing Act of 1934 to provide expertise and advice on policies regarding grazing permits for the grazing districts. These boards were populated primarily by ranchers who were loathe to limit the number of livestock they were allowed to graze on the public lands. (Ch.9)

Grazing Districts Management units established under the Taylor Grazing Act for purposes of monitoring grazing levels on western rangelands. (Ch.9)

Grazing permits The process by which the BLM and USFS allow private ranchers to graze livestock on public lands. Permits are issued for a quantity of animal unit months (AUMs). (Ch.9)

Great Society The public relations label given to Lyndon Johnson's presidential administration (1963-1969). It was characterized by a strong emphasis on legislation and spending for domestic programs. (Ch.8)

Greenpeace Citizen organization established in the 1970s to protect marine mammals worldwide. Greenpeace became known for its confrontational yet non-violent tactics of protest. (Ch.14:)

Gross Domestic Product (GDP) The value of goods and services produced by a nation in a given year. (Ch.22)

Groundwater Water that accumulates underground, in geologic strata where it fills porous areas in rock and soil. Groundwater is "recharged" by percolation from surface water. (Ch.21)

Habitat The place where wildlife lives, providing the resources needed to survive. Habitat is the most important factor in wildlife conservation. (Ch.10)

Habitat management The process of maintaining or manipulating habitat resources of food, cover, water, space, and arrangement. (Ch.19)

Habituated A change in wildlife behavior patterns where a population adapts to the presence of humans. (Ch.19)

Hard rock minerals Basically those minerals that are contained in solid rock, such as gold, silver, copper, and lead. (Ch.9)

Hardrock Mining Act See General Mining Law of 1872. Hardrock Mining Act is a name commonly used in reference to this law. (Ch.22)

Harm In wildlife management, harm is a form of take that can include injury to a species through habitat degradation. (Ch.19)

Hearing Often referred to as a public hearing. Hearings are opportunities to speak before an agency or representative governmental body. In many cases they are required by law, and in some cases transcribed. There is no requirement for the body holding the hearing to respond. (Ch.17)

Hetch Hetchy A valley in Yosemite National Park just north of the famed Yosemite Valley. It was the site of a major battle in the early 1900s between preservationists and conservationists over the proposal to build a dam and flood the valley for irrigation and the fast-growing city of San Francisco. It is now a reservoir. (Ch.4)

Homestead Act of 1862 The best known of a number of land transfer acts passed by Congress. It essentially said that any citizen or intended citizen over the age of 21 could enter federal land and claim a 160-acre quarter section for cultivation. Free patent, or ownership, to the land would be granted after five years of cultivation and payment of a fee of $26 ($34 on the Pacific coast, an example of early inflated land prices in California!). If a homesteader elected, they could obtain freehold to the land after only six months by paying $1.25 per acre. The Homestead Act was used as a tool to help settle parts of the west by small farmers who would recognize the authority of the U.S. government. It was passed by a Congress absent the southern states, which had seceded and were at war with the states represented in Washington. Southerners opposed the Homestead Act because it supported a small family farming economy, rather than the large slavery-dependent plantation structure. Though homesteading has been heavily romanticized in our culture, it was often a bust because 160 acres was insufficient to support a family on much of the arid western landscape. The grid system of allocating homesteads was made with no regard for topography, soils and water quality. (Ch.4)

Hoover Dam Massive reinforced concrete dam on the Colorado River at the border of Arizona and Nevada. Completed in 1935, and creating at the time, the largest man-made reservoir in the world, Lake Mead. (Ch.21)

Hudson River School A style of uniquely American landscape painting that brought the grandeur of America's wildlands to the public's attention prior to the advent of landscape photography. Famous artists associated with this style include Thomas Cole, Frederic Church, Asher Durand, Albert Bierstadt, and Thomas Moran. (Ch.4)

Humane Society of the United States Citizen organization dedicated to the protection and humane treatment of animals. (Ch.19)

Hydroelectric energy Electricity generated by the movement of water through turbines. (Ch.11)

Industrial Tourism A term used to describe the means by which Americans participate in outdoor recreation, using motorized vehicles, boats, and aircraft. (Ch.3)

Inholdings Privately owned or leased lands that are surrounded by public lands. (Ch.22)

Injunction A court order to stop or change a course of action, such as ordering the U.S. Forest Service to halt a specific timber sale. (Ch.15)

Integrated pest management Systems of dealing with forest "pests" that can decimate stands of trees. Integrated pest management attempts to use ecological relationships to reduce pest infestations. (Ch.18)

Interest group politics Political process dominated by the pressures exerted by various groups with different values and interests. (Ch.14)

Issue Attention Cycle Anthony Downs' theoretical model of the way various issues gain and lose public attention over time. (Ch.14)

Johnstown Flood The 1889 flood of the town of Johnstown, Pennsylvania, that killed 2,200 people. The flood was caused by a privately owned dam that failed. (Ch.4)

Joint Operations Center (JOC) California interagency "command center" that deals with the distribution of surface waters throughout the state. (Ch.21)

Justiciability The determination of whether an issue, case or controversy "qualifies" to be heard in a court of law. (Ch.15)

Kesterson National Wildlife Refuge Wetland created by agricultural drainage from the Westlands Water District in California's Central Valley, and designated a National Wildlife Refuge. Kesterson waters became toxic to waterfowl due to concentrations of selenium washed from agricultural soils. (Ch.21)

Lacey Act of 1900 The Lacey Act prohibited interstate commerce in wild animals and birds killed in violation of state law. Prior to this act, individual states were the sole regulators of wildlife. The Lacey Act brought the federal government into the realm of wildlife management, using the Constitutional power to regulate interstate commerce. The Lacey Act was in response to market hunting and the decimation of species, particularly the passenger pigeon. (Ch.10)

Land and Water Conservation Fund Act of 1965 This law was a direct result of the ORRRC Report. It set up the Land and Water Conservation Fund, a pool of dollars dedicated to the acquisition and development of parklands. (Ch.7)

Land management The management of natural resources, including water resources. Not strictly limited to the physical manipulation of resources, land management is very much a political process involving interaction with many individuals, groups, and institutions. (Ch.5)

Land use regulation Land use regulation can take many forms, and can be enforced on both public and private lands. Government resource managing agencies are charged with the regulatory function. Regulations cover a broad spectrum, from fish and game regulations, to wetland regulations, to regulations on the use of off-road vehicles. Privately owned lands are also subject to regulations that limit the "bundle of rights" an owner possesses. The police power of zoning is a common example of local government regulation of private land use. (Ch.13)

Land-grant Universities The name eventually given to the public universities established on lands disposed to states through the Morrill Act of 1862. (Ch.9)

Lane, Franklin K. Secretary of the Department of the Interior under Woodrow Wilson. (Ch.7)

Leopold, Aldo (1887-1948) Forest ranger, naturalist, ecologist, professor and author, Leopold was instrumental in shaping America's views on natural resource management in the 20th century. Co-founder of the Wilderness Society in 1935. His best known work, and a classic of environmental literature, is *A Sand County Almanac* (1949). (Ch.8)

Letters and testimony Written and spoken versions of people's points of view. Under many laws requiring public involvement, provision of the opportunity to submit letters or give testimony is required. (Ch.17)

Limits of acceptable change A more recent outdoor recreation management model that recognizes natural change and human-caused change over time in natural resource areas. Recreational use is managed to remain within the parameters of change that are appropriate to the type of land, the objectives of the managing agency, and the needs of the visitors. (Ch.3)

Listing process A procedure for identifying species to be protected under the Endangered Species Act, or to be removed (de-listed) from protections under the Act. (Ch.19)

Litigation Legal proceedings. (Ch.17)

Local conditions Because forest resources vary in different regions, as does the human environment, the U.S. Forest Service originally gave considerable autonomy to the District Ranger, the administrator closest to the resource issue in question. (Ch.8)

Local decision-makers In the U.S. Forest Service, this would be the District Ranger, supported by the district staff. The decision-making structure of the agency is hierarchically short: District Ranger, Forest Supervisor, Regional Forester, Chief. (Ch.8)

Local Government Term used to refer to county and municipal governments. It is important to natural resources as most decisions regarding the uses of private lands are made at the local government level. (Ch.13)

Long-term We look at time in a number of ways. Long-term is used to mean a reasonably long period of time, such as several generations of humans. The management of forests is frequently referred to as a long-term process because of the duration of the lifetime of trees, and because the web, or ecology of a forest changes slowly if compared to other types of change that occur in our lifetimes. Short-term, on the other hand, is used to refer to events that take place over relatively short periods of time, like fluctuations in the stock market, or the four-year duration of the President's term of office. Protecting the qualities of resources for the long term is usually considered a noble undertaking. At least it sounds better than using resources for "short-term gains," a phrase often linked with greed, exploitation, and resource depletion. (Ch.1)

Los Angeles Department of Water and Power Agency that provided water to the Los Angeles basin. Today it is known as the Metropolitan Water District of Southern California. (Ch.11)

Louisiana Purchase The U.S.' purchase of France's claim to the Louisiana territory, for $15 million in 1803, including lands west of the Mississippi River to the Rocky Mountains. This area included most of the "great plains" north of Texas. (Ch.4)

Lucas v. South Carolina Coastal Council A 1992 Supreme Court decision backing a beachfront property owner against a South Carolina regulation that would prevent development of property he had bought before the regulation was enacted. The Court told South Carolina either to pay just compensation for the loss of development rights, or change the regulation. (Ch.13)

Mainstream environmental organizations Environmental groups such as the Sierra Club, National Wildlife Federation, Audubon Society, Wilderness Society, Nature Conservancy, and Izaak Walton League. (Ch.15)

Managing surface waters Systems of dams, weirs, levees, dikes, canals, flumes, ditches, pipes, aqueducts, streams and rivers that have been constructed or are manipulated for the many uses of water. (Ch.21)

Manifest Destiny The view held by Americans in the 1840s that it was right and proper that the U.S. should occupy and spread democracy across the continent clear to the Pacific. The phrase is credited to John O'Sullivan, a journalist from New York. (Ch.4)

Marine Mammal Protection Act (1972) A complex law that established a moratorium on the taking of marine mammals, and put regulation of marine mammals in federal hands. (Ch.19)

Market hunting Prior to hunting regulation, virtually any species could be hunted and sold to markets and restaurants as food. The practice led to population decline, extinction, and near extinction of numerous species of birds, fish, and mammals. (Ch.4)

Marketable A good or service is said to be marketable if people are willing to buy it, and in a quantity that produces a rate of return higher than the cost of production. (Ch.22)

Marsh, George Perkins Author of *Man and Nature* (1864), a book that helped awaken America to the dangers of natural resource exploitation. (Ch.4)

Marshall, Robert (1901-1939) Plant physiologist and forester, Marshall was a driving force for the protection of wilderness on lands managed by the Bureau of Indian Affairs and the U.S. Forest Service. Legendary for his hiking and contagious enthusiasm, Marshall was one of the founders of the Wilderness Society in 1935. (Ch.8)

Mather, Stephen First Director of the National Park Service, Mather convinced Congress to create the agency in 1916. (Ch.7)

Meander In hydrology, meander refers to the way streams and rivers cut and fill at their banks over time, gradually winding about on their immediate floodplains. (Ch.20)

Megafauna Large animals. Original target of the Endangered Species Act, including animals such as the bald eagle and grizzly bear. The ESA was eventually interpreted to include smaller organisms and plants as well. (Ch.18)

Megalopolis From the Greek for great city, a megalopolis is a continuous area of urbanization that may include numerous cities. Mexico City's urban area, with over 20 million inhabitants, can be considered a megalopolis. (Ch.2)

Migratory Bird Conservation Act of 1929 This law provided funding for the acquisition and development of a systematic federal program of wildlife refuges. (Ch.10)

Migratory Bird Hunting Stamp Act of 1934 The first major federal statute to establish a special fund for the protection of wildlife. The law requires waterfowl hunters to purchase a federal license known as the "duck stamp." Duck stamp purchases since 1934 have generated more than $750 million for the acquisition and development of wildlife refuges. (Ch.10)

Migratory Bird Treaty Act of 1918 This law established federal authority over the states with regard to migratory birds, using Article 6, the "supremacy clause" of the Constitution. Challenged in the Supreme Court, the law was upheld in Missouri v. Holland 252 U.S. 416 (1920). (Ch.10)

Mineral bearing ores Rock structures that hold accumulations of minerals. The concentration of valuable minerals in these ores, as well as their location, helps determine the economic feasibility of mining them. Ores with high concentrations of minerals are called high grade ores, and those with low concentrations are called low grade ores. (Ch.22)

Mineral Leasing Act of 1920 Law that altered the General Mining Law of 1872 to make energy minerals a possession of the U.S., and to provide that they could only be removed under lease agreements. (Ch.22)

Minerals Substances that can be mined or pumped from at or below the earth's surface. As a broad group, minerals can be solid (such as coal), liquid (such as oil), or gas (such as natural gas). Minerals are often classified into groups such as hard rock minerals, and energy minerals. (Ch.3)

Mining Law of 1866 One of the first federal laws governing mining, the 1866 Act opened most of the western U.S. to minerals exploration. (Ch.22)

Mission The purposes of an agency. Sometimes natural resource agencies are referred to as "mission agencies" and are characterized by their principal activities, such as wildlife, water, park, or forest management. (Ch.5)

Mojave National Preserve California BLM lands moved to the National Park Service under preserve status through legislation pushed by Senator Dianne Feinstein in 1995. (Ch.9)

Monkeywrenching Environmental sabotage. Monkeywrenching is aimed at disabling mechanisms used in commodity development of natural resources. It ranges from symbolic acts, to physical intervention. Tree-spiking is a well known and highly criticized form of monkeywrenching. (Ch.15)

Monongahela Decision, *Izaak Walton League v. Butz* The 1973 federal district court case, affirmed by the 4th Circuit Court of Appeals in 1975, that effectively outlawed clearcutting on U.S. Forest Service lands. A citizen group, the Izaak Walton League sued the agency (named under Agriculture Secretary Butz) for violating the timber harvest provisions of the Forest Service Organic Act of 1897 which said that "mature," "marked and designated" timber was to be "cut and removed" from the forest. The judge ruled that USFS clearcutting practices at times cut immature and unmarked trees, and that they would not always be removed. (Ch.8)

Monumentalism A nationalistic perspective that considered America's frontier and landscapes to be of monumental stature. In many respects monumentalism was a response to America's adolescent status among western nations. Europe could boast the antiquities of ancient civilizations, the castles and cathedrals of the middle ages, and the arts and cityscapes of the renaissance. Lacking the long western history of Europe, Americans turned to their rich landscape as a fountain for national pride. (Ch.4)

Moran, Thomas Hudson River School painter famed for his western landscapes which include many areas now protected as national parks. (Ch.4)

Morrill Act of 1862 A disposal of federal lands given to each state in the amount of 30,000 acres, per senator and congressional representative, to finance public colleges of agriculture and mechanical arts. (Ch.9)

Mountain Lion Foundation Citizen organization created to work for the protection of mountain lions. (Ch.19)

Mountain Lion Initiative, Proposition 117 Citizen initiative passed in 1990 that maintained California's ban on mountain lion hunting. (Ch.19)

Moving livestock The practice of grazing livestock in different areas, moving them before they damage vegetation and soil resources. Rotating livestock through a variety of pastures allows grazed areas to recover before livestock are moved into the area again. (Ch.20)

Muir, John (1838-1914) Traveler, naturalist, author, lecturer, and activist who founded the Sierra Club and became the citizen most often associated with the preservation movement in America. (Ch.4)

Mulholland, William A civil engineer who figured out how to build an aqueduct that would divert water from the Owens River to the Los Angeles basin. He was the head of the L.A. Department of Water and Power. (Ch.11)

Multiple Use A land and resource management strategy that attempts to produce different outputs from an area. Primarily a designation for federal lands, the two principle agencies practicing multiple use management are the U.S. Forest Service and the Bureau of Land Management. Under multiple use, management works toward the sustainable production of timber, water, forage for grazing, minerals, wildlife, and outdoor recreation. Multiple use sounds great conceptually, a little something for everyone. However, it generates conflict because varied groups want different outputs from the managed areas. Timber management and outdoor recreation, or livestock grazing and wildlife management may not be compatible, for example. (Ch.3)

Multiple Use and Sustained Yield Act of 1960 The act mandating that the U.S. Forest Service should manage the "multiple" resources of timber, water, range, minerals, wildlife, and outdoor recreation, and that they should manage to produce a continuous supply of resource benefits for the long term. (Ch.8)

Mustangers Hunters engaged in the roundup of wild horses when this form of hunting was legal. (Ch.19)

National Environmental Policy Act of 1970 (NEPA) NEPA established a planning framework through which federal agencies must consider and document the environmental impacts of proposed agency actions. Documentation of this process is prepared in environmental impact statements (EIS), and made available for review and comment by interested parties. EIS contents include: 1) description of existing environmental conditions, 2) description of the proposed project or activity, 3) unavoidable environmental impacts of the proposal,

4) alternatives to the proposal, 5) mitigation measures (methods to reduce impacts), and 6) justification for the project or activity in light of the unavoidable environmental impacts. NEPA does not require that federal actions have no environmental impact. It simply requires that environmental impacts be considered. The hope is that this planning framework will reduce environmental impacts and avoid costly mistakes by forcing agencies to carefully think through what they intend to do. (Ch.5)

National Forest Management Act of 1976 (NFMA) Congressional statute that modified the two-year-old RPA, and required specific attention to issues such as clear-cutting. With the RPA, it forms the foundation of the U.S. Forest Service's planning process. (Ch.8)

National Forests A managerial designation of units within the U.S. Forest Service (USFS). There are approximately 150 national forests covering an area of 191 million acres, mostly in the western U.S. (Ch.4)

National Marine Fisheries Service (NMFS) Agency within the National Oceanic and Atmospheric Administration (NOAA) with primary responsibility for the regulation of marine fisheries within U.S. territorial waters. (Ch.10)

National Monuments An official designation of units managed by federal agencies, primarily the National Park Service. Monuments can be established by Congress, such as Mount Saint Helens National Monument (U.S. Forest Service), or by the President through the powers granted under the Antiquities Act of 1906. (Ch.4)

National Oceanic and Atmospheric Administration (NOAA) Federal agency within the Commerce Department. Included among its many responsibilities is the management of the National Marine Sanctuaries. (Ch.10)

National Park Service (NPS) The federal agency created in 1916 to manage the national parks and monuments. Today, the agency manages some 83 million acres in more than 380 units of parks, monuments, seashores, preserves, historic sites, memorials, and other designations. (Ch.4)

National Park Service Act of 1916 The act that established an agency to manage America's national parks and monuments. Prior to this time, management was handled by the Army, volunteer caretakers, or there was no management at all. Stephen Mather, a well-to-do California businessman and outdoor enthusiast became the agency's first director. (Ch.4)

National Wilderness Preservation System The system of wilderness areas created under the 1964 Wilderness Act and including those areas that have been designated by Congress since that time. There are roughly 110 million acres in 757 designated wilderness areas in the U.S. Wilderness areas are not managed by a specific agency as are national parks and national forests. The NPS, USFS, USF&WS, and BLM all manage wilderness areas. The USFS manages the most wilderness areas, and the NPS manages the most acres of wilderness. (Ch.18)

Nationwide flood control Flood control throughout the country officially became a U.S. Army Corps of Engineers responsibility in 1936. (Ch.11)

Natural Resources Agency California's version of the Department of Interior. The Resources Agency is the "umbrella agency" under which all of California's natural resources agencies are administered. (Ch.12)

Natural Resources Conservation Service Agency in the Department of Agriculture responsible for identifying, classifying and mapping soils, for enforcing regulations pertaining to soil resources, and to "work with landowners through conservation planning and assistance to benefit the soil, water, plants, and animals for productive lands and healthy ecosystems." Formerly the Soil Conservation Service (Ch.21)

Natural Resources Defense Council Citizen organization that uses the legal system to press for environmental causes. (Ch.20)

Nature Conservancy Citizen organization that acquires and preserves lands that it considers to be ecologically valuable. (Ch.13)

Navigable rivers Rivers and waterways that can be navigated by boat traffic. Maintaining navigable rivers became a major responsibility of the U.S. Army Corps of Engineers. Rivers have been corridors for transportation throughout the nation's history. (Ch.11)

New Deal The name given to the presidential administration of Franklin D. Roosevelt. It was characterized by new federal domestic programs aimed at improving conditions brought on by the Great Depression and years of resource abuse. Well-known natural resource programs of the era included the Work Projects Administration (WPA) and the Civilian Conservation Corps (CCC). (Ch.9)

Nollan v. California Coastal Commission Supreme Court desision blocking the California Coastal Commission from exacting an easement from a homeowner as a condition for allowing them to rebuild their home. (Ch.13)

Northern Spotted Owl A small owl whose habitat is the forests of the Pacific Northwest. Protected under the Endangered Species Act, habitat reservations for the owl have put many forested areas in the region off-limits to timber operations. The owl has become the fulcrum for arguments over the use of old-growth forests. (Ch.9)

Notice and comment A requirement of the Federal Register Act giving public opportunity to review and comment on proposed federal regulations. (Ch.16)

O&C Lands Western Oregon land grants that defaulted and came to be under the management of the BLM. These lands contain a wealth of timber resources. (Ch.9)

Old growth Old growth forests are those that have not been previously logged for timber. Also often referred to as virgin forests. As the amount of old growth forest has dwindled in the U.S., their logging has become more controversial. (Ch.8)

Olmsted, Frederick Law Landscape architect famed for designing Central Park in New York City, and for outlining the purposes for management of Yosemite National Park in California. Olmsted believed in designing landscapes that incorporated nature, provided a mix of open and planted spaces, and offered opportunities for relaxed movement and contemplative recreation. (Ch.13)

On the ground A style of management used by the U.S. Forest Service that would allow for decision-making by people working closely or in direct contact with forest resources. (Ch.8)

Operation Outdoors A 1957 initiative introduced by the U.S. Forest Service to emphasize the development of outdoor recreation facilities on agency lands. It was no coincidence that Operation Outdoors was launched a year after the National Park Service's Mission 66 program. It was partly a move in an old inter-agency rivalry to gain political favor. (Ch.8)

Opinion leaders In communication theory, opinion leaders are people whose opinions are respected by others. Their position and/or ability to express their opinions helps to make them leaders. (Ch.17)

Option 9 Of the many options for forest management presented by FEMAT, the Clinton administration selected Option 9, which was the middle-of-the-road solution between timber interests and environmentalists. Therefore, it was also the most controversial. (Ch.18)

Organic Act of 1897 Another name for the Forest Management Act of 1897. (Ch.8)

Outdoor Recreation Human behavioral activity that depends on an outdoor, or natural resource. For example, fishing depends on a water and wildlife resource base. Whitewater rafting depends on moving rivers and creeks. (Ch.3)

Outdoor Recreation Resources Review Commission, ORRRC Report A commission organized in the early 1960s to study the state of outdoor recreation in America. The commission's report, which became known as the ORRRC Report, called for the development of new parklands and greater opportunities for outdoor recreation. (Ch.7)

Outer Continental Shelf (OCS) Seabed areas at depths of 100 fathoms (600 feet) or less, adjacent to nations' coastlines. (Ch.21)

Overgrazing A condition where forage is not able to recover following grazing, leading to soils loss, erosion, and reduced percolation. Overgrazing can lead to desertification. (Ch.20)

Owens River California river in the Owens Valley, east of the Sierra Nevada mountains. Its waters were diverted 250 miles to the Los Angeles basin in the early 1900s by an engineering feat undertaken by the Los Angeles Department of Water and Power, with help from the fledgling federal Reclamation Service. (Ch.11)

Park concessions The name used for businesses licensed to provide visitor services within government managed parks. (Ch.7)

Partners This term has come into more frequent use as a way of describing the relationship between resource management agencies and their clientele, or stakeholder groups. The idea is to foster cooperation as partners, rather than adversarial relationships. (Ch.17)

Passenger Pigeon *Ectopistes migratorius.* The passenger pigeon, once the most abundant bird in the world, was extinct in the wild by 1900. The last of the species died in captivity in 1914. Several ecological factors are cited for the species' demise, though indiscriminate hunting is considered the principal cause. (Ch.4)

Peak Oil The point where the rate of global petroleum extraction reaches its maximum, followed by permanently declining rates of production. Based on Marion K. Hubbert's "peak theory" developed in the mid 1950s (Ch. 22).

Pelican Island National Wildlife Refuge Considered the first national wildlife refuge, created by Teddy Roosevelt in 1903 on a five-acre island off the Florida coast to prevent indiscriminate hunting that was occurring there. President Harrison had reserved Alaska's Afognak Island in 1892 by proclamation so that salmon, fish, sea animals and land animals would be "protected and preserved unimpaired." (Ch.10)

Peshtigo, Miramichi, Hinckley Enormous forest fires in the 19th century in Wisconsin, New Brunswick, and Minnesota. These fires alerted America to the dangers of poor forest management practices. (Ch.4)

Pinchot, Gifford A charismatic conservationist considered to be the "father of American forestry" and the founder of the U.S. Forest Service. (Ch.4)

Pittman-Robertson Act of 1937 This federal law placed a special tax, known as an excise tax, on the sale of guns and ammunition. Proceeds were placed in a fund earmarked for distribution to states for acquisition of wildlife refuges and habitat restoration projects. Distribution of monies was contingent on a state having its own wildlife conservation laws and management programs, assuring that funds would be used specifically for wildlife protection. (Ch.10)

Plaintiff A person or group complaining in court that they have been aggrieved. (Ch.15)

Planning The sometimes complex process of describing how an agency or organization will change in the future. Planning strives to involve all interested parties in setting goals and objectives, and then outlining methods to complete them. Planning has become a major part of the activities of resource-managing agencies. (Ch.5)

Pluralistic democracy A term long used to describe the American political structure, where pluralism is used to describe multiple interests and democracy to describe relatively equal representation. (Ch.14)

Point source and non-point source pollution Point source pollution can be traced to a specific outflow such as an industrial drainage pipe or sewage outflow. Non-point source pollution is more difficult to trace, and includes pathogens, pesticides, fertilizers and other pollutants carried by runoff from agricultural and urbanized lands. (Ch.21)

Popullution An intentionally misspelled word combining population and pollution, inferring that overpopulation is a form of pollution. (Ch.2)

Potable Drinkable. (Ch.21)

Preservation mandate The portion of the National Park Service Act that requires that the agency shall "...conserve the scenery and the natural and historic objects and the wildlife therein...and leave them unimpaired..." (Ch.7)

Primitive Area A designation of U.S. Forest Service lands that was the forerunner of the wilderness classification. Originally, primitive areas would not have roads built in them, and would be primarily managed for wildlife, watershed, and recreational values. The first primitive area designated in 1924 was the Gila Roadless Area, a 500,000-acre tract in New Mexico first proposed by Aldo Leopold. (Ch.8)

Prior Appropriation Doctrine In water law, the prior appropriation doctrine provides for the ownership of water by private parties or business entities. (Ch.21)

Private non-profit organizations A classification of citizen organization that is not taxed in the manner of other business entities. (Ch.13)

Progressive Movement A middle-class social movement at the turn of the century that advocated reform on many fronts, including women's rights, labor reform, anti-discrimination, prohibition, urban poverty, and managerial efficiency in government. The nation's natural resources also became a subject for the progressive movement, and greater governmental control was viewed as the means to better protect resources for the future. (Ch.4)

Protective measures The specific protections for endangered species, including prohibitions against taking or harming individuals of the species. (Ch.19)

Prudent person test A "common sense" determination of whether a mineral deposit is valuable, or able to provide an economic return. (Ch.22)

Public education A wildife management tool considered essential to building public awareness of wildlife management methods. (Ch.19)

Public good A project or activity which is determined to promote the welfare of the public. Managing National Parks, for example, is considered a public good. "The public good" is also referred to as a condition of improved well-being of the people. (Ch.13)

Public interest groups, pressure groups, lobbies, special interests, voluntary associations These are all terms used to describe various types of citizen organizations. (Ch.14)

Public Rangelands Improvement Act of 1978 Congressional law that further required the BLM to obtain public input in the agency's planning process. PRIA, as the law is known, also relaxed some of the requirements of the Wild Free Roaming Horses and Burros Act, allowing the BLM greater discretion in managing feral horses and burros. (Ch.9)

Qualified Immunity A doctrine that partially protects executive officials from prosecution. This form of immunity does not protect executive officials if they have possibly violated a legal right of which they should have been aware. (Ch.15)

Rangers The name in common use to refer to the government employees who patrol and manage public parks and natural areas. Originally, rangers were agents of the King of England, appointed to walk the forests, watch deer, and prevent trespasses. In the U.S. Forest Service, Ranger is the specific position title of the head administrator (line officer) of a Ranger District, a geographic division of a National Forest. (Ch.8)

RARE II A second attempt to finalize the question of which areas of USFS lands would be declared as wilderness. Conducted during the Carter administration from 1977 to 1980, RARE II eventually fizzled when Reagan became president. He pushed wilderness designation proposals onto the states' congressional delegations. (Ch.18)

Recharged The processes of percolation and infiltration, by which groundwater in aquifers is replenished by surface water. (Ch.21)

Reclamation Act of 1902, or the Newlands Act Federal law authorizing the Department of Interior to withdraw dam, reservoir sites, and their adjacent lands, for development of irrigation projects. Withdrawn lands and their associated irrigation water were to be sold to homesteaders in parcels between 40 and 160 acres. (Ch.11)

Reclamation Service Created in the Department of Interior under the 1902 Newlands Act, the Reclamation Service was responsible for identifying and assisting water development projects, and for acquiring and distributing lands "reclaimed" by irrigation. The Reclamation Service became the Bureau of Reclamation (as it is known today) in 1923. (Ch.11)

Recreational carrying capacity A management concept borrowed from biological carrying capacity. Recreational carrying capacity is a hypothetical point at which the number of recreationists in a given area, coupled with the types of activities in which they are engaged, can be sustained without irrevocable harm to the environment or the experiences of the recreationists themselves. (Ch.3)

Recycled The systems by which waste is turned into raw material useable for re-processing. Common examples are the recycling of cardboard, newspaper, glass containers and aluminum cans. (Ch.22)

Redwood National Park A federal park in northwestern California established amid considerable controversy to protect the tallest living trees on Earth. (Ch.7)

Regeneration methods In silviculture, regeneration methods are the means by which trees are harvested. The method of harvest determines the way trees will be re-grown on the site. Tree species respond differently to varying methods of regeneration, some favoring sunny sites, and others favoring shaded settings. Regeneration methods, particularly clearcutting, can be controversial because of their immediate visual impacts, and because of the potential for soils erosion, reduction in water quality, and changes to wildlife habitat. (Ch.8)

Regulated monopoly A method to provide services to park visitors by allowing a single company to run the lodging, restaurants and stores in parks. This would reduce competition for tourist dollars among businesses, and thus minimize the impacts of these businesses on park resources. Because the single selected company would have a monopoly, their pricing and other operations would be regulated by the park managing agency. (Ch.7)

Regulatory authority The legal foundation and responsibility of an agency. For example, many state departments of game and fish have regulatory authority over what can and cannot be done with wildlife in the state. Many of us know these rules as the state's game and fish regulations, and we consult them before hunting, fishing, collecting, or trapping. (Ch.5)

Reinforced concrete A construction method improved by the invention of Portland Cement in the 1920s. Employed in dam construction from the 1930s. Concrete is poured and cured over a framework of steel reinforcing rods, called "re-bar," adding immensely to its structural strength. (Ch.21)

Remedy In legal terms, a remedy is whatever improvement might be gained by a plaintiff if a court decides in their favor. (Ch.15)

Representation In the context of public involvement, representation is a problem as various stakeholder groups are not equally represented. (Ch.17)

Resource Mobilization Theory A theory describing the formation of citizen organizations. When social movements well up, entrepreneurs tap the available resources of people within the social movement, and pull the resources together to form an organization that will represent their interests. For example, Mothers Against Drunk Drivers (MADD) was started by a woman who lost her daughter in a drunk-driving accident. Recognizing many people are concerned about drunks on the road, she was able to gather members and to use those resources to successfully lobby many states into stiffening penalties for driving under the influence. (Ch.14)

Resources-Needs Matrix The resources-needs matrix was developed in order to simplify our relationships with natural resources to a most basic model. On earth we have air, water, land, and energy. To live, we use these resources to meet our needs for air, water, food, shelter, and self-actualization. It is possible to group all of our resource uses within this matrix. (Ch.1)

Retorts Heating mechanisms, or "ovens" used to melt oil out of coal, oil-shale, tar sands, and sandstone. (Ch.22)

Rip-rapped A technique of stabilizing streambanks against erosion. Rip-rapping usually involves grading the bank to a slope, and then covering the slope with large rocks. (Ch.21)

Riparian areas Terrestrial environments adjacent to and including waters such as springs, streams, creeks, rivers, ponds and lakeshores. Proximity to water enhances plant growth in riparian areas, and forms the base for the flourishing of diverse species of plant and animal life. (Ch.7)

Riparian Doctrine In water law, the riparian doctrine essentially upholds usufructuary rights, the right to use water without degrading it for downstream users. (Ch.21)

Rivers and Harbors Act of 1899 Law that gave the U.S. Army Corps of Engineers the power to rule on permit applications that sought to alter tidelands, estuaries and navigable waterways for varying purposes such as landfill, flood control, or harbor construction. (Ch.21)

Roadless Area Review and Evaluation (RARE) A USFS study conducted in the early 1970s to settle the question of which lands should be designated as wilderness and which lands should be managed for multiple use. The process failed when the Sierra Club filed suit citing USFS non-compliance with NEPA. (Ch.18)

Roadless Areas Federal lands that have no maintained roads. Roadless areas are potential wilderness areas, and have been inventoried for possible inclusion in the wilderness system. When a roadless area is slated for possible wilderness status it is usually designated a "wilderness study area." (Ch.18)

Roosevelt, Theodore A conservation-minded president who served shortly after the turn of the last century. Roosevelt was responsible for setting aside many of the areas now managed by the National Park Service and the U.S. Forest Service, and he is credited with establishing the first of many national wildlife refuges. He is considered by many to have been one of America's great presidents. (Ch.4)

Sagebrush Rebellion A grassroots drive by citizens of several western states to transfer federal lands to state, local, or even private control. The "rebellion" gained notoriety in the early 1980s under President Reagan and his Interior Secretary, James Watt. (Ch.20)

Saint Francis Dam Dam engineered by William Mulholland to store Owens River water for delivery to the San Fernando Valley. The dam failed in 1928, killing an estimated 450 people. (Ch.11)

Salinity The salt content of water. Water salinity can be a problem when salts are leached from soils and bedrock into aquifers or surface waters, or when ocean water moves into freshwater areas through tidal action, storms, or displacement of fresh water. (Ch.21)

Seaward resources Oceanic resources extending seaward from the mean low water line. Varying national and international laws regulate uses of seaward resources including seabed, surface, territorial sea, and fisheries. (Ch.21)

Second growth A term used to refer to stands of trees that have regrown in areas previously harvested. (Ch.18)

Section 7 (ESA) The section of the Endangered Species Act that forces agencies to protect endangered and threatened species. (Ch.19)

Seed tree Silvicultural regeneration practice where 10 - 20 trees per acre are left standing on a harvested site to provide a seed source for reforestation. (Ch.18)

Selection Silvicultural method where certain trees are "selected" for removal, leaving most of the stand intact. (Ch.18)

Shade intolerant Term used in silviculture to refer to tree species that do not grow well in shade, but prefer open, sunny locations. (Ch.18)

Shipping lanes Oceanic areas internationally designated as corridors for shipping traffic. (Ch.21)

Sierra Club A citizen organization formed in 1892 with John Muir as its first president. The Sierra Club was established to protect and share the wonders of the Sierra Nevada Mountains of California. It has evolved into a major player in the political struggles for resource protection and preservation. (Ch.4)

Sierra Club v. Morton (1972) The famed "Mineral King" case where the Sierra Club was denied standing to represent the environment of the Mineral King Valley in the Sierra Nevada mountains. (Ch.15)

Silvicultural From silviculture, the management of tree production essentially as an agricultural commodity. (Ch.8)

Smokestack scrubbers Systems using combinations of water vapor and crushed limestone (wet scrubber), or a slurry of fine particles and fabric filters (dry scrubbers) to remove toxic gasses and particulates. (Ch.22)

Smokey Bear The mascot of the U.S. Forest Service, a bear who wears pants and a hat, and carries a shovel. The real Smokey was a black bear orphaned as a cub by a forest fire. He lived out his life in the National Zoo in Washington D.C. Smokey was an instant public relations success for the U.S. Forest Service, carrying his message: "Only you can prevent forest fires." (Ch.8)

Snail darter A small fish that became the first symbol of the Endangered Species Act when the Act was invoked to protect it from the environmental impacts of the Tellico Dam in Tennessee. Dam proponents ridiculed environmentalists' desire to protect the snail darter, saying that such an insignificant species was less important than all the benefits that would come from another dam. (Ch.11)

Special Districts As the name implies, these are governmental units organized to provide special services that may not be well provided by state, county, or municipal organizations. Often associated with school districts, irrigation districts, and park and recreation districts. District boundaries are geographically described, and the residents within the district have the right to vote for representatives to the district's governing body. Special districts have the right to tax district residents to produce revenue necessary to provide services. (Ch.13)

Staff officers The heads of functions (or departments) noted above. Staff officers direct the activities of their respective functions and provide technical and advisory support to administrative decision-makers, who are referred to as "line officers." (Ch.8)

Standing One of several qualifications necessary to bring a case to court. In short, standing is used to determine whether a potential plaintiff is truly aggrieved. (Ch.15)

State's Rights The 10th Amendment of the U.S. Constitution is called the "state's rights amendment." It proclaims that powers not delegated to the federal government by the Constitution are therefore reserved to the states and the people. The 10th Amendment forms the basis for state management of natural resources. (Ch.12)

State Water Project In California, the State Water Project is a state-managed water diversion project that moves water from northern to southern parts of the State. The dams, reservoirs and aqueducts are on a scale usually only associated with federal water projects. (Ch.12)

Statutes at Large The document where all Congressional statutes are published. (Ch.16)

Steering committees, stewardship committees, stakeholder groups All are forms of citizen groups created to provide public opinion in the resources planning process. Generally these groups are comprised of people with varied interests, chosen to represent a point of view. It is hoped that these groups will be able to engage in two-way and convergence communication. (Ch.17)

Stocking Placing wildlife into areas with sufficient habitat to support their population. (Ch.18)

Storage Holding water, usually behind a dam, for future release and distribution. (Ch.11)

Subsidized A term used to describe forms of assistance given by the government to private parties, supposedly for the public good. Farmers of agricultural commodities such as corn, cotton, soybeans, wheat, tobacco, dairy, rice, and peanuts are subsidized to the tune of about $20 billion annually to stabilize farm income. Critics of federal lands timber and grazing management claim these industries are subsidized. Even public radio and television are subsidized, both targets of congressional budget slashers. (Ch.9)

Suits for damages A court remedy used after damage has occurred. If a plaintiff wins a suit for damages, the guilty party is often required to pay them monetary restitution. (Ch.15)

Superfund A special billion-dollar fund established in the Environmental Protection Agency (EPA) under the Comprehensive Response, Compensation, and Liability Act of 1980 (CERCLA) to begin to pay for the clean up of toxic waste sites identified for inclusion on the National Priorities List. (Ch.14)

Surface Mining Control and Reclamation Act of 1977 Congressional legislation aimed at ensuring the rehabilitation of surface mined lands. The law was particularly concerned with surface mining of coal. Established the Office of Surface Mining. (Ch.22)

Surface water Streams, rivers, lakes, ponds, marshes, reservoirs atop terrestrial (land) areas. (Ch.21)

Sustainable Sustainable is the idea that something can be done for an extended period of time. This term is often used in relation to levels of use, or consumption. For example, we are concerned that our extraction of timber from a forest should be sustainable. For the timber harvest level to be sustainable the forest must grow at least as much timber as we extract. Sustainable levels of resource use are our goals. To use resources at rates that cannot be sustained is to invite scarcity and potential collapse of the resource base. Sustainability is the objective of maintaining long term biological, social, and economic well being of the human and earth environments. (Ch.2)

Synfuels Synthetic fuels. Synfuels resemble those produced from oil and natural gas, but they are created by melting oil out of coal, oil-shale, or tar sands. (Ch.22)

Tailings The material cast off in the mining process. Tailings are the overburden and remnants of ore left after mineral extraction. Tailings piles can be the source of air and water pollution. (Ch.22)

Take In wildlife management, the killing or removal of an animal by hunting, fishing, trapping, or collecting. (Ch.19)

Taking An unlawful removal of property or property rights from a private owner for public uses. The "right to property" is conditionally protected by the Constitution's 5th Amendment. (Ch.13)

Taylor Grazing Act of 1934 A law passed to halt damage to the public grazing lands which until this time had been essentially unmanaged by the General Land Office. (Ch.9)

Technologies From the Greek terms for art and words, technologies are practical applications of science and art. The technologies that bring these words to the reader include applications of science and art such as the development of language, writing, the printing press, and computerized word-processing. (Ch.2)

Tellico Dam A dam built on the Little Tennessee River in the 1970s and early 1980s. It became the site of an important controversy over the Endangered Species Act, when the new law was used to protect the snail darter. The dam was opposed for a number of other reasons as well, but the strength of the ESA became the most powerful tool that dam opponents could use. Eventually, snail darters were discovered elsewhere, and the dam was completed. (Ch.11)

Terracing Together with clearcutting, cut-over slopes on the Bitterroot National Forest were terraced to provide vehicular access and reduce soil erosion. The striped mountainside appearance left by these methods helped prompt the debate over timber management practices on the forest. (Ch.14)

Teton Dam An earth-filled dam constructed by the Bureau of Reclamation on the Teton River in Idaho in the 1970s. It collapsed as it was being filled in 1977. (Ch.11)

Thoreau, Henry David Writer and essayist famed for his views on nature and his philosophy of transcendentalism. His best known works include the books *Walden*, and *The Maine Woods*, and the essay *Civil Disobedience*. (Ch.4)

Threatened The first level of designation under the Endangered Species Act, invoking certain habitat management and other protective measures under the act. (Ch.18)

Timber Trees that can be harvested to form the raw material of the wood products industries. (Ch.3)

Timber Culture Law of 1873 A land disposal law somewhat similar to the Homestead Act. Under the Timber Culture Law a settler could gain title to a second homestead if they planted and maintained 40 acres of trees on each for 10 years. An extension of five more years could be requested, providing more time for the homesteader to offer "proof" of planting and cultivation. In 1873 it was a common belief that trees would bring rain to arid areas. Recall the legend of Johnny Appleseed. (Ch.9)

Timber mining A phrase coined to describe the uneconomical practices of timber management conducted by the U.S. Forest Service on the Bitterroot National Forest in Montana in the early 1970s. (Ch.8)

Toxic wastes Name given to describe a wide variety of toxic chemicals dumped on land and in waterways over the years. Places where these wastes have been dumped are called toxic waste sites, and they can pose considerable danger to human health. (Ch.14)

Tragedy of the Commons A theory that common resources must eventually be depleted or ruined because there is no individual incentive to invest in their care. Common resources are effectively free to use. In an economic input-output model, if the inputs are free, greater value can be gained from the outputs. Therefore, to reap the greatest short-term benefit, people are unwilling to pay for the long-term upkeep of the common resources. The tragedy, thus, is that the common resources must inevitably go into decline from over-use. (Ch.3)

Transfer Act of 1905 The federal statute that transferred management of the forest reserves from the Interior Department to the Department of Agriculture. (Ch.4)

U.S. Grazing Service A federal agency created from the Division of Grazing in 1939. The Grazing Service was the forerunner that became the Bureau of Land Management in 1946. (Ch.9)

Unlawful Inclosures Act of 1885 Congressional statute that made it illegal for ranchers to fence off lands they did not own. It was an unsuccessful attempt to bolster the Homestead Act and keep lands open for farming settlement. (Ch.20)

Unpatented mining claim A status giving a miner exclusive use of a 20 acre piece of land for purposes "reasonably incident to mining." From the General Mining Law of 1872. (Ch.22)

Urban sprawl The spread of urbanized areas over the landscape. (Ch.2)

Usufructuary right The rights of a landowner adjacent to a stream or river to use water without hindering the ability of others to also use that source of water. (Ch.21)

U.S. v. Students Challenging Regulatory Agency Procedures (1973) A Supreme Court case that liberalized the Doctrine of Standing to Sue, widening the opportunities to bring environmental cases to the judiciary. (Ch.15)

Visible reduction The loss of visibility over distance, resulting from air pollution. The most easily observed effect of smog. (Ch.22)

Water cycle The progression of water from liquid form to vapor through transpiration and evaporation, and back to liquid through condensation and precipitation. (Ch.21)

Water quality The condition of water for various purposes. Drinking water requires the highest levels of quality. Water quality is based on clarity, pH, turbidity, dissolved solids, dissolved oxygen, pathogens content, and temperature. (Ch.21)

Water Quality Act of 1965 Congressional legislation aimed at strengthening pollution controls. Established the Federal Water Pollution Control Administration, which was transferred to the new Environmental Protection Agency in 1970. (Ch.21)

Watershed The land area from which water drains to a point on a creek or river. The watershed is the area upstream from that point, including all the tributaries, springs, and catchment areas that supply water into that specific system. (Ch.4)

Watt, James Highly controversial Secretary of the Interior appointed by Ronald Reagan in his first term of office. Watt advocated reduced federal control and regulation of the public lands, making him the nemesis of environmental groups nationwide. (Ch.20)

Weeks Act of 1911 Permitted the federal government to buy private lands to protect headwaters of rivers and watersheds in the Eastern U.S. Much of the land had been cut over and was in bad shape. Weeks Act lands became the "Eastern National Forests," adding about 20 million acres to the national forest system. Their restoration is one of the great successes of national forest management. (Ch.8)

Welfare of the community Often called "the common good." It is in the name of the welfare of the community that we limit individual rights, and protect natural resources needed by all. Upholding the community welfare also includes protecting individual rights, and allowing circumstances where natural resources can be developed to meet human needs. (Ch.1)

Wetlands Areas with soils that are constantly or seasonally saturated with water. May be partially or completely flooded, and supporting vegetation adapted for life in saturated soils. Swamps, marshes, bogs, tidal areas and estuaries are considered wetlands. (Ch.21)

Wild and Free Roaming Horses and Burros Act of 1971 Law passed by Congress to protect feral horses and burros on public lands. Lands managed by the National Park Service were exempt from this law because the agency is required to reduce the presence of exotic species. (Ch.9)

Wild Horse Annie Velma Johnson, nicknamed Wild Horse Annie for her crusade to protect wild horses. (Ch.19)

Wild Horse Organized Assistance (WHOA) One of several citizen organizations established to work for protection of wild horses. (Ch.19)

Wilderness Act of 1964 Congressional legislation creating the National Wilderness Preservation System on federal lands. Areas designated under the law are called wilderness areas, and are places of historic, natural, or scenic quality where "man is a visitor who does not remain." Wilderness areas are a minimum of 5,000 acres, without roads, where there is no form of mechanized transport. (Ch.18)

Wilderness Areas Federal lands designated under the Wilderness Act of 1964 and part of the National Wilderness Preservation System. Wilderness Areas are established by Congress and are managed under strict preservation guidelines. The U.S. Forest Service manages the most wilderness areas among federal resource agencies. (Ch.7)

Wilderness Society Founded in 1935 and including charter members Aldo Leopold, Robert Marshall, and Robert Sterling Yard, this citizen organization has fought for the preservation and management of wilderness. (Ch.8)

Wildlife Animals that are not domesticated. Wildlife managers frequently refer to wildlife as game, and non-game species. Game species are those that can be legally hunted, trapped, or fished. Non-game species are those that cannot be taken. (Ch.3)

Withdrawal The term used to describe "withdrawal from entry," which essentially meant that federal control of land was implied. A withdrawal of federal land meant that the area was no longer open and available for disposal through land grants or other tools such as the Homestead Act. The setting aside of Yellowstone National Park in 1872 was a withdrawal. (Ch.4)

Worthless lands argument This was an argument presented to defend the establishment of new national parks. Because of the political strength of utilitarian interests, park proponents pointed out that areas being considered for national parks were "worthless" for resources such as minerals, timber, and grazing. They said that the only real value of these lands was their scenery, and opportunities for tourism. (Ch.4)

Yellowstone National park in northwestern Wyoming and small parts of Montana and Idaho, famed for its geothermal features. Established by Congress in 1872, it was the first national park in the world. (Ch.4)

Yosemite National park in the central Sierra Nevada mountains of California, famed for its cliffs, waterfalls, and "big trees." Originally granted to the State of California by Congress and Abraham Lincoln in 1864, Yosemite later became a 1500 square mile federal "forest reservation" in 1890, soon to be known as Yosemite National Park. Yosemite was reduced in size by roughly 500 square miles in 1904, and in 1905 California officially returned the Yosemite Valley and Mariposa Grove to federal control. (Ch.4)

Zoning Zoning is a method used to define the bundle of rights for various types of lands. In the U.S. we have adopted zoning as a means to organize our lands so that uses across different ownerships are relatively compatible. We speak of residential zones and commercial zones, agricultural zones and open space zones. Within these zones, land uses are to be fairly consistent. For example, houses, condos, or apartments are the principle development in residential zones. Downtown shops and WalMarts usually occupy commercial zones. Farms and ranches are in agricultural zones, and parks, preserves, and refuges often occupy open-space zones. (Ch.1, Ch.13)

Index

A

Abbey, Bob, 202
Abbott Laboratories v. Gardner, 151
Abundance, Era of, 28–29
acid mine drainage (AMD), 250
acid precipitation, 221
activism
    See also citizen involvement
    vehemence in citizen groups, 145–148
administrative agencies
    and federal regulatory process, 57–59
    rise of, 59–61
administrative bureaucracy, 61
administrative law, 149
Administrative Procedures Act of 1946, 150, 151
advocacy statements, 168–169
aesthetic values, 7
agencies
    See also specific agency
    government agency Web sites, 268–269
    rise of administrative, 59–61
agricultural use of water, 229–235
air
    Clean Air Act, 53
    common resource, 5
Alaska National Interest Lands Conservation Act, 71
Alaska Native Claims Settlement Act of 1971, 70
Albright, Horace, 64, 65
AMD (acid mine drainage), 250
American Bison, 31–33, 99
American Forestry Association, 43
Amory, Cleveland, 201
Andrus, Cecil, 70
Angel Island deer, 198–199
animal rights, 147–148
Antiquities Act, 41–42
APA 1946, PL 79-404, 158–159
appropriation, 44
aquifers, water, 222
Arctic National Wildlife Refuge, 191
Association of Data Processors v. Camp, 152
Auburn Dam, 111
Audubon, John James, 37, 38
automation, industrialization, and technology, 12

B

Babbitt, Bruce, 73, 94, 254
Bald Eagle Protection Act (1940), 195
bald eagles, 206

"Bambi Syndrome," 102–103
Bean, Michael, 206
Bierstadt, Albert, 35
biodiversity, 6, 176
Birds of North America (Audubon), 37
birth rate and mortality rate, 11
bison, slaughter of, 31–33, 99
Bitterroot controversy, 132–135, 156
Bivens v. Six Unknown Federal Narcotics Agents, 150
Bob Marshall Wilderness, 81
Bolle Report on forestry practices, 134
"boom and bust" cycles, 178
Boone and Crockett Club, 100
Boston Common, 29, 123
bounty hunting, 195
boycotting, 170
BP Deepwater Horizon oil spill (2010), 137, 248
Brandis, Dietrich, 43
bundle-of-rights concept, 4–6
Bureau of Biological Survey, 101
Bureau of Indian Affairs (BIA), 52–53
Bureau of Land Management (BLM), 48, 52, 97, 202
    issues and controversies, 92–96, 213
    overview of, 89–92
    planning and public involvement, 160
Bureau of Reclamation (BR), 52, 105–107
burros on public lands, 199–202
Bush, Pres. George W., 63–64, 255

C

Calaveras Grove of Big Trees, 34
California
    Angel Island deer, 198–199
    Forest Practices Act, 187
    Joint Operations Center (JOC), 241
    lands management, regulation, 116–119
    Proposition 209, 170
    wildlife management in, 195, 202–204
California Department of Conservation (DC), 117–118
California Department of Resources Recycling and Recovery (CalRecycle), 118
California Desert Conservation Area, 95
California Redwood State Park, 116
carrying capacity, 21, 192, 198–199
Carson, Rachel, 47
Carter, Pres. Jimmy, 70, 111, 139
Catlin, George, 35, 36, 37

cattle grazing, 16, 209–218
Central Park, New York City, 123
Chandler, Harry, 106
Church, Frederic, 35
cities, organization of, 128
citizen initiatives, 169–170
citizen involvement
    capture concept, 135–136
    citizen organizations, 139–143
    effective avenues for public participation,
        163–170
    environmental movement, 131
    "issue-attention" cycle, 137–139
    legal avenues for environmental issues,
        149–154
    legal requirements for public involvement,
        158–161
    methods and strategies, 165–170
    paths to, 155–158
    profiling an informed citizen, 257–263
    publics, and controversy, 132–135
    vehemence in citizen groups, 145–148
    Web sites for, 267–271
Civics 1A
    quiz and answers, 57–59
    rise of administrative agencies, regulations,
        59–61
Civilian Conservation Corps (CCC), 69, 70
Clean Air Act, 53
Clean Water Act of 1972, 53, 229
clearcutting, 132–135, 178–180
Cleveland, Pres. Grover, 43, 78
Clinton, Pres. Bill, 95, 255
coal resources, 245–247
Cole, Thomas, 35, 37
Coleman, Alfred, 253
colonial period of natural resource
    management, 28–32
Columbus, 27
commodity values, 6–7
common lands, 15–21
commons, tragedy of the, 21–22
community welfare, 5–6
Comprehensive Environmental Response,
    Compensation, and Liability Act of 1980,
    228
concessions, park, 66
congressional committees on natural resource
    issues, 54, 55
conservation
    in colonial period, 28–29
    movement vs. preservation movement,
        44–46
    philosophy, 42–44
Constitution
    10th Amendment (state's rights), 115
    Commerce Clause, 238
    judicial access for environmental issues,
        149–154
    and regulatory agencies, 59–61

controversies
    See also specific issue
    Angel Island deer, 198–199
    Bureau of Land Management (BLM), 92–96
    forestland and timber management, 173–189
    National Park Service (NPS), 69–75
    Tennessee Valley Authority (TVA), 111–112
    U.S. Forest Service (USFS), 86–87
    water management, 227–236
    wildlife management, 195–205
convergence communication, 157
cooperative programs, 167–168
corporate power, 124–128
cost-benefit analyses, 108
cougars, 202–204
Council on Environmental Quality (CEQ), 54
counties, organization of, 128
cover, and habitat, 192
Cowan, John, 193
Crater Lake, 41–42
Crosby, A.W., 27
Culhane, Paul, 135
culture, and natural resources, 14
Cumberland Dam, 108
Cuyahoga River, 228–229

D
dams, federal authority over, 106–112
de Tocqueville, Alexis, 139–140
Declaratory Judgments Act of 1934, 149
Deepwater Horizon oil spill of 2010, 137, 248
demonstrations, protests, 168
Dennis, Steve, xii
Department of Defense, 53
Department of Energy (DOE), 53
desalinized seawater, 229
diffusion of innovations theory, 157–158
Dingell-Johnson Act of 1950, 101
directories, Web sites for citizen involvement,
    267–271
disease, and conquest of New World, 27
Division of Forestry, 44
Doctrine of Limitations, 150–151
Doctrine of Official Immunity, 150
Doctrine of Ripeness, 151
Doctrine of Standing to Sue, 151
Dolan v. City of Tigard, 128
"dolphin safe" tuna, 170
Dombeck, Mike, 255
dominant use doctrine, 82
Downs, Anthony, 137
drinking water, 223–224
DuBois, Mark, 148
Ducks Unlimited, 129, 142
due process, equal protection, 125, 149–150
Duke, David, 169
Durand, Asher, 35

E
Earth First!, 146–147, 148, 168, 169
Earth Liberation Front, 201

Eaton, Fred, 106
Echo Park dam project, 112
ecological warfare, 31
economies of scale, 186–187
ecosystems management, 15, 48
Ecosystems Management Era, 47–48
education
    of informed citizens, 257–263
    and natural resources, 14
    wildlife management, 198
electrical energy, 8
Emerson, Ralph Waldo, 36
Endangered Species Act of 1973 (ESA), 53, 84,
    101, 103, 110, 111, 176–177, 204–207, 213
environment
    areas of critical environmental concern, 94
    legal avenues for environmental issues,
    149–154
    citizen involvement. See citizen involvement
environmental disasters
    See also controversies
    and exploitative resource practices, 33–35
environmental impact statements, 152–153
environmental movement, 47, 131
Environmental Protection Agency (EPA), 53, 153
Environmental Quality Act (California), 115
environmental-utilitarian (E-U) scale, 136
EPA (Environmental Protection Agency), 53, 153
estuarine, wetlands, 238–239
Euclid v. Ambler Realty Co., 125, 127
Everglades National Park, 73
Evolution of National Wildlife Law, The (Bean),
    206
Ex Parte Young, 150
executive orders, 42
exotic species, 93, 197
Exploitation, Era of, 29–32
externalities, 231
extirpation of pests, 197
Exxon Valdez oil spill, 139

F
federal
    agencies. *See specific agency*
    land classifications, 51–53
    regulators, 53–55
Federal Aviation Administration (FAA), 73–74
Federal Land Policy and Management Act of
    1976, 48
Federal Lands Recreation Act of 2004, 74
Federal Register Act (1935), 158
Federal Tort Claims Act of 1946, 150
Federal Water Pollution Control Act Amendments,
    239
Feinstein, Sen. Dianne, 95
feral horses, burros, 199–202
fire protection and suppression, 182–183
First English v. Los Angeles, 127
Fish and Wildlife Coordination Act Amendments
    of 1958, 239
fish hatcheries, 196

Flast v. Cohen, 151–152
"flatwater recreation," 105
flood control, 108–109, 110, 127, 223, 226–227,
    260–261
Flood Control Act (1944), 108
flood protection, 105
floodplains, 233–234
FOIA (Freedom of Information Act), 161
Foreman, Dave, 147, 148
Forest and Rangeland Renewable Resources
    Planning Act (RPA), 160
Forest Ecosystems Management Assessment
    Team (FEMAT), 177
Forest Management Act of 1897, 43, 44
forest practices, 178–189
Forest Practices Act (California), 187
Forest Reserve Act of 1891, 43, 44, 77
forest reserves, 77
Forest Service rangers, 79
forestland
    forest practices, 178–188
    wilderness preservation, roadless area
    management, 174–177
Forsman, Eric, 176
Francis, St., of Assisi, 25–26
Freedom of Information Act (FOIA), 161
Frothingham v. Mellon, 151
Fund for Animals, The, 201

G
General Land Office, 43–44, 59, 93
General Mining Law of 1872, 92, 94, 251,
    252–256
Gibbs, Lois, 139
Gila National Forest, 80
Glacier National Park, 42
Glen Canyon, 6, 7, 72
Glen Canyon Dam, 112, 147
glossary, 273–298
gold mining, 248, 249
government agency Web sites, 268–269
Grand Canyon National Park, 5, 6, 72, 73–74
Grand Staircase-Escalante National Movement,
    95
grazing lands
    See also range management
    during Era of Exploitation, 31
    and tragedy of commons, 21
grazing permits, 94
Great Chicago Fire, 33–34
Great Ponds Act (Massachusetts), 115
Greenpeace, 139, 145–146, 168
grizzly bears, 205
gross domestic product (GDP), 244
groundwater, 222, 227–228, 232

H
habitat, 102, 191–194, 197, 204
Hardin, Garrett, 21
Hardrock Mining Act, 251
Harrison, Pres. Benjamin, 43, 78

harvesting wildlife, 198
hearings, agency, 163–164
Hetch Hetchy Valley, Yosemite, 45–46, 64
Hicks, Edward, 27
Hinckley forest fire, 33
Historic Sites Act of 1935, 68, 69
Hodel, Donald, 254
Homestead Act of 1862, 30, 211
Hoover Dam, 232–233
horses on public lands, 93–94, 199–202
Hot Springs, Arkansas, 41
Hudson River School of painters, 35
Human Management, Era of, 39–46
Humane Society of the United States, 200
Hurwitz, Charles, 147
hydroelectric energy, 105, 107, 235

I
Ice Harbor Dam, 109
income and increased resource consumption, 14
industrial tourism, 20
industrialization, automation, and technology, 12
information dissemination, communications, 166
injunctions, 149
interest group politics, 140
Interstate Commerce Act of 1887, 60
Interstate Commerce Commission (ICC), 59–60, 152
Isaak Walton League, 100
Izaak Walton League v. Butz, 85
"issue-attention" cycle, 137–139

J
Jefferson, Thomas, 29, 30
Johnston, Velma, 93, 200
Johnstown Flood, 33–34
Judeo-Christian tradition, and land ethic, 25
judiciary, access to for environmental issues, 149–154
Judiciary Act of 1875, 150
justiciability, and legal standing, 149

K
Kelo v. City of New London, 125–128
Kempthorne, Dirk, 213
Kenna, Iris, 204
Kennecott Copper Mine, 246
Kesterson National Wildlife Refuge, 234–235

L
Lacey, John F., 42
Lacey Act of 1900, 100–101
Lake Oroville, 16
Lake Powell, 6, 112
land
    common. See common lands
    federal classifications, 51–53
    ownership. *See* ownership
Land and Water Conservation Fund Act of 1965, 70
land use regulation, 126

lands management
    federal agency authority, 54
    private lands managers, 129
    special districts, county, city involvement, 121–122
    by states, 116–119
Lane, Franklin K., 64
lawn care, 261–262
laws
    See also specific law or legislation
    water management, 239–240
    wildlife management, 194–195
legal
    avenues for environmental issues, 149–154
    laws. *See specific law or legislation*
    litigation, 168
    requirements for public involvement, 158–161
leisure time, and work, 13–14
Leopold, Aldo, 80, 81
Lewis and Clark, 30, 199
Limbaugh, Rush, 203–204
limits of acceptable change, 21
Lippincott, Joseph, 106
litigation, 168
livestock. *See* range management
lobbying, 166
local government
    corporate and police power, 124–128
    county and city involvement in natural resources, 123–124
    zoning powers, 124–128
Los Angeles Dept. of Water & Power, 106
Louisiana Purchase, 29
Love Canal controversy, 138–139
Lowi, Theodore, 135, 136
Lucas v. South Carolina Coastal Commission, 127–128
Lucretius, 24
Lujan, Manuel, 254

M
Man and Nature (Marsh), 37–38
Manifest Destiny, 29
Maramichi Fire, 33
Marine Mammal Protection Act (1972), 195
Mariposa Redwood Grove (Yosemite), 41
market hunting, 31, 99
Marsh, George Perkins, 37–38
Marshall, John, 251
Marshall, Robert, 81, 86
Massachusetts v. EPA, 153
Mather, Stephen, 64, 65–66, 82
McCain, John, 169
McNerney, Jerry, 169
Mead, Elwood C., 232–233
megafauna, 176
megalopolis, 12
Metcalf, Sen. Lee, 134
Migratory Bird Conservation Act of 1929, 101
Migratory Bird Hunting Stamp Act of 1934, 101
Migratory Bird Treaty Act, 101

migratory fish, and dams, 110–112
"Mineral King" case, 152
Mineral Leasing Act of 1920, 252
mineral resources
    environmental issues, 249–251
    mineral classification, supply, 244–245
    mining methods, processing, 246–248
    overview of, 243–244
    policies and laws, 251–256
mining, 246–256
Mining Law of 1866, 251
Minuteman National Historic Monument, 70
Mission 66, NPS program, 69
missions, 51
mobility and natural resources, 12–13
Mojave National Preserve, 95
"monkeywrenching," 147
Monongahela decision, 85
monumentalism, 40
moral values, 7
Moran, Thomas, 35, 36
mortality rate, and birth rate, 11
Mountain Lion Foundation, 202, 204
Mubarak, Pres. Hosni, 168
Muir, John, 40–41, 45–46
Mulholland, William, 106, 111
Multiple Use and Sustained Yield Act of 1960, 84,
    173
multiple use doctrine, 15, 16–17
Multiple Use Era, 47–48

N
national battlefields, 68
national cemeteries, 68
National Environmental Policy Act of 1970
    (NEPA), 55, 84, 150, 152, 158–159, 239
National Forest Management Act of 1976 (NFMA),
    84, 160–161
national forests, 42, 78
national historical parks, 68
national historical sites, 67
national lakeshores and seashores, 68
National Marine Fisheries Service, 101
national memorials, 68
national monuments, 42, 67
National Oceanic and Atmospheric Administration
    (NOAA), 53, 101
National Park Service Act of 1916, 42, 63, 69
National Park Service (NPS), 52
    building forest management program, 79
    early development of, 64–66
    establishment of, 46
    growth, and controversies, 69–75
    historical areas, recreation areas, 68–69
    management and natural areas, 66–67
    mission of, 63–64
national parks, 67
National Parks Service, 19
national parkways, 68
national preserves, 67
national recreation areas, 68

National Rifle Association (NRA), 169
national rivers, trails, 68
National Trails Act of 1968, 68
National Wilderness Preservation System, 174
national wildlife refuges, 101–102
Native Americans
    and colonials, 28
    and conquest of New World, 26–27
    and ecological warfare, 31
    reservation roadless areas, 81
Natural Resource Conservation Service, 239–
    240
natural resource management eras
    Era of Abundance: colonial period, 28–29
    Era of Exploitation, 29–32
    Era of Human management, 39–46
    Era of Preservation: changing views, 32–39
    Eras of Multiple Use, Ecosystems
        Management, 47–48
    road to the Americas, 23–27
natural resources
    See also specific resource
    California's management of lands, 116–119
    citizen involvement. See citizen involvement
    contradictory, conflicting uses, 20–21
    county and city involvement in, 123–124
    demands on, 9–14
    federal resource managing agencies,
        authority, 51–55
    legacy, 265–266
    ownership, 4–6
    private lands managers, 129
    special districts, 121–122
    terminology. See glossary
    values of, 1–8
    water. See water management
Natural Resources Agency (California), 116–118
Nature Conservancy, 129, 142
navigable rivers, federal authority over, 108–
    109, 239–240
NEPA (National Environmental Policy Act of
    1970), 152, 158–159
New Melones Dam, 148
Newlands, Francis, 105
NOAA (National Oceanic and Atmospheric
    Administration), 53, 101
Nollan v. California Coastal Commission, 127
nonrenewable natural resources, 1
Northern Spotted Owl, 86, 93, 176–177
Norton, Gale, 213, 255
"notice and comment" requirements of Federal
    Register Act, 158

O
O&C lands controversy, 92–93
Obama, Pres. Barack, 169, 205
oil drilling, offshore, 137–138
oil resources, 245
Olmsted, Frederick Law, 123
Olson, Mancur, 140
Operation Outdoors (USFS), 82–83

opinion leaders, 164
Ordinance of May 20,1785, 29
Organic Act of 1897, 43, 78, 85
ORRRC Report, 70
Otis, Harrison Gray, 106
outdoor recreation
    and multiple use doctrine, 15–21
    and tragedy of commons, 21–22
Outdoor Recreation Resources Review
    Commission, 70
overgrazing, 214–216
oversight monitoring, 170
Owens River, and L.A. Aqueduct, 105–106, 229
ownership
    alodial, disposal, 29
    of natural resources, 4–6, 8
    of U.S. lands, 123–124

P
Palin, Sarah, 138
Pan, panic, 24
passenger pigeon, 33, 99
Pelican Island National Wildlife Refuge, 101
Peshtigo Fire, 33
pest management, 182
philosophy, and natural resources, 14
Pinchot, Gifford, 43, 44, 45, 78, 82, 86, 178
Pittman-Robertson Act of 1937, 101
pluralistic democracy, 140
pollution, water, 228–229
Polo, Marco, 26
Pombo, Richard, 169
population, population, 10–11, 21–22
pork, federal authority over, 109
"pork barrel," 109
position statements, 168–169
predator control, 195
preservation
    movement vs. conservation movement, 44–46
    philosophy, growth of, 39–42
Preservation, Era, 32–39
pressure groups, 140
primitive areas (USFS), 80
prior appropriation (of water) doctrine, 236
profiling an informed citizen, 257–263
progressive movement, 39
pronghorn antelope, 16
property
    ownership. See ownership
    rights Web sites, 269
    'taking,' 'eminent domain,' 125–128
protests, demonstrations, 168
"public good," 125–126
public involvement. See citizen involvement
Public Lands Politics (Culhane), 135–136
public meetings, 169
public participation
    See also citizen involvement
    effective avenues for, 163–170
Public Rangelands Improvement Act of 1978, 94,
    161, 201

public relations, 156
Public Relations and Communications for Natural
    Resource Managers (Fazio & Gilbert),
    132–133
publics, 132

Q
'qualified immunity,' 150
quarrying, 247

R
railroads, as lands managers, 129
Rainbow Warrior (Greenpeace), 146
Rainer National Park, 41
ranching. See range management
range management
    grazing issues, 214–218
    overview and history, 209–212
    regulations, 212–214
Rangeland Renewable Resources Planning Act of
    1974 (RPA), 84
RARE II, 175
Reagan, Pres. Ronald, 175, 213
Reclamation Act of 1902, 105
Reclamation Service, 105–106
recreation, "flatwater," 105
recreational carrying capacity, 21
recycled minerals, 243
Redwood National Park, 70
referendums, 169–170
refuges, wildlife, 196
regeneration methods, 81
regulations
    See also specific law or legislation
    California's natural resource, 118–119
    land use, 126–127
    range management, 212–214
    rise of administrative agencies and, 59–61
    state land management, 116–119
Renaissance, land ethic during, 26
renewable natural resources, 1
representation, citizen, 165
Resource Conservation and Recovery Act (1976),
    228
resource consumption, 11
resource mobilization theory, 141
Resources-Needs Matrix (fig.), 2
rights
    animal, 147–148
    ownership, 4–6
    state's, 115
    usufructuary, 236
riparian areas, 72
rip-rapped river, 234
Rivers and Harbors Act of 1899, 238
Roadless Area Review and Evaluation (RARE)
    study, 175
roadless areas, 174–175
Roe v. Wade, 151
Roman empire, 25

Roosevelt, Pres. Theodore, 41, 42, 43, 44, 79, 100, 105, 107, 110
Roselle, Mike, 147

S
Safe Drinking Water Act (1974), 228
Sagebrush Rebellion, 213
Saint Francis Dam, 107, 111
salinity, soil, 234
San Francisco Bay resource managing districts, 122
Sand County Almanac, A (Leopold), 80
scarcity
    and natural resources, 3
    outdoor recreation and, 15–22
    overused resources, 9
    and regulated resources, 5
Schlesinger v. Reservists Committee to Stop the War, 151
Schoener, Barbara, 203
Sea Shepherds Conservation Society, 146
seaward resources, 237–238
seed tree regeneration, 180
selection, timber regeneration, 180–182
Sequoia National Park, 41
shade intolerant trees, 180
Shasta Dam, 106
shipping lanes, 237
Sierra Club, 40, 45, 112, 148, 152, 175
Sierra Club v. Morton, 152
silviculture management, 81, 133–134, 173, 178–189
slant drilling, 75
Smokey Bear campaign, 83–84, 134
snail darter, endangered species, 110–111
social media campaigns, 166–167
soil salinity, 234
special districts, 121–122
Spotted Owl, 86, 93
St. Francis of Assisi, 25–26
stakeholder groups, 164
standing, legal, 149
State Water Project (California), 117
states
    See also specific state
    10th Amendment (state's rights), 115
    lands management, regulation, 116–119
steering committees, 164
stewards of natural resources, 4
Stewart, Sen. William, 251
stewardship committees, 164
stocking wildlife, 196
Stone, Christopher, 152
strategic values, 6
suits for damages, 149
Superfund Act, 228
superfund legislation, 140
Surface Mining Control and Reclamation Act of 1977, 254
surface water, 228–229, 232
sustainable consumption, 11

T
Taft, Pres. William Howard, 79, 125
tailings, mine, 249–250, 255
taxation, 121, 124
Taylor Grazing Act of 1934, 92, 212, 216
technologies, industrialization, and automation, 12
Tellico Dam, 110–111
Tennessee Electric Power Company v. TVA, 152
Tennessee Valley Authority (TVA), 110–112
terminology, glossary, 273–298
Teton Dam, 107, 111
Thoreau, Henry David, 36–37
threatened species, 177
Tidwell, Tom, 85
timber
    mining, 85, 134
    and multiple use doctrine, 15
time, leisure and work, 13–14
tourism, industrial, 20
toxic wastes, 138
transcendentalism, 36–37
Transfer Act of 1905, 44
Tree Stamp Act, 28–29

U
United States
    common lands of, 15–22
    federal resource managing agencies, authority, 51–55
Unlawful Enclosures Act of 1885, 212
urban sprawl, urbanization, 12
U.S. Army Corps of Engineers (COE), 52, 108–109, 224
U.S. Fish and Wildlife Service (USFWS), 52
    federal wildlife regulation, 100–101
    National Wildlife Refuge system, 101–102
    origins of, 99–100
    Wildlife management, 102–103
U.S. Forest Service (USFS), 52
    beginnings of, 77–79
    Bitterroot controversy, 132–135, 156
    ecology and wilderness, 80–81
    forestry methods, 81–85
    Northern Spotted Owl controversy, 176–177
    planning and public involvement, 160
    and roadless areas, 175
    structure of, 85–86
U.S. v. Students Challenging Regulatory Agency Procedures, 152–153
USFS. See U.S. Forest Service (USFS)
usufructuary rights, 236

V
values and definition of natural resources, 6
Vanderbilt, George, 43

W
Washington, George, 108
water cycle, 221
water management
    concepts, 221–223

issues and controversies, 227–236
lawn care, 261–262
overview of, 225–227, 240–241
politics of water, 236–240
water uses, 223–225
water quality, 224, 227–228, 238–239
Water Quality Act of 1965, 238–239
watersheds, and deforestation, 34
waterways, federal authority over, 108–109
Watson, Pau, 146
Watt, James, 213, 254
Web sites for citizen involvement, 267–271
Weeks Act of 1911, 79
wetlands, 238–239
Wild and Free-Roaming Horses and Burros Act
    of 1971, 93–94, 200–201, 213
Wild Horse Organized Assistance (WHOA), 200
Wild and Scenic Rivers Act (1968), 68
wilderness
    areas (USFS), 75
    in Judeo-Christian tradition, 25
Wilderness Act of 1964, 81, 84, 174
wildlife management
    basic concepts, 191–194
    cougars, 202–204
    habitat management, public education, 198–
    199

laws, 194–195
market hunting and, 31
and multiple use doctrine, 15
predator control, refuges, stocking, 195–196
USFWS. See U.S. Fish and Wildlife Service
water uses, 235–236
wildlife refuges, 196
withdrawal (from disposal), 39
Wolke, Howie, 147
wood products companies, as lands managers,
    129
work, and leisure time, 13–14
Work Projects Administration (WPA), 69, 107
World Trade Organization protests, 168
worthless lands argument, 41
WTO protests, 168

Y
Yard, Robert Sterling, 81
Yellowstone National Park, 18, 19, 35, 36, 38,
    41, 74–75
Yosemite National Park, 19, 41, 45, 71–72, 123

Z
zoning
    local power to, 124–128
    regulation affecting ownership, 5–6